THE SHOW MU!
POPULAR SONG IN BI
THE FIRST WOI

For Marie-Lise

The Show Must Go On!
Popular Song in Britain During the First World War

JOHN MULLEN
University of Paris East, Créteil, France

ASHGATE

Originally published in France under the title *La Chanson populaire en Grande-Bretagne pendant la Grande Guerre 1914–1918*. Copyright © L'Harmattan, 2012. www.harmattan.fr

Published by
Ashgate Publishing Limited
Wey Court East
Union Road
Farnham
Surrey, GU9 7PT
England

Ashgate Publishing Company
110 Cherry Street
Suite 3-1
Burlington, VT 05401-3818
USA

www.ashgate.com

British Library Cataloguing in Publication Data
A catalogue record for this book is available from the British Library

The Library of Congress has cataloged the printed edition as follows:
Mullen, John, 1960– author.
   The show must go on! : popular song in Britain during the First World War / by John Mullen.
      pages cm. – (Ashgate popular and folk music series)
   Includes bibliographical references and index.
   ISBN 978-1-4724-4158-4 (hardcover) – ISBN 978-1-4724-4159-1 (pbk.) –
ISBN 978-1-4724-4160-7 (ebook) – ISBN 978-1-4724-4161-4 (epub) 1. Popular music
– Great Britain – 1911–1920 – History and criticism. 2. Popular music – Social aspects
– Great Britain. 3. Music-halls (Variety-theaters, cabarets, etc.) – Great Britain – History
– 20th century. 4. World War, 1914–1918 – Great Britain – Music and the war. 5. Great
Britain – Social life and customs – 20th century. I. Title.
   ML3650.5.M86 2015
   782.421640941'09041—dc23

2015005580

ISBN: 9781472441584 (hbk)
ISBN: 9781472441591 (pbk)
ISBN: 9781472441607 (ebk – PDF)
ISBN: 9781472441614 (ebk – ePUB)

MIX
Paper from
responsible sources
FSC
www.fsc.org   FSC® C013985

Printed in the United Kingdom by Henry Ling Limited,
at the Dorset Press, Dorchester, DT1 1HD

Contents

A Note on the Author

John Mullen is senior lecturer at the University of Paris-East Créteil. He has published widely on the history of British popular music. Articles include a reflection on 'ethnic' music festivals and immigrant identity (1960–2000), and a piece on racial stereotyping in music-hall songs from 1880 to 1920. His website is www.johncmullen.net.

General Editors' Preface

Popular musicology embraces the field of musicological study that engages with popular forms of music, especially music associated with commerce, entertainment and leisure activities. The *Ashgate Popular and Folk Music Series* aims to present the best research in this field. Authors are concerned with criticism and analysis of the music itself, as well as locating musical practices, values and meanings in cultural context. The focus of the series is on popular music of the twentieth and twenty-first centuries, with a remit to encompass the entirety of the world's popular music.

Critical and analytical tools employed in the study of popular music are being continually developed and refined in the twenty-first century. Perspectives on the transcultural and intercultural uses of popular music have enriched understanding of social context, reception and subject position. Popular genres as distinct as reggae, township, bhangra, and flamenco are features of a shrinking, transnational world. The series recognizes and addresses the emergence of mixed genres and new global fusions, and utilizes a wide range of theoretical models drawn from anthropology, sociology, psychoanalysis, media studies, semiotics, postcolonial studies, feminism, gender studies and queer studies.

Stan Hawkins, Professor of Popular Musicology, University of Oslo and
Derek B. Scott, Professor of Critical Musicology, University of Leeds

Preface and Acknowledgements

This book was first published in French in 2012 as *La Chanson populaire en Grande-Bretagne pendant la Grande Guerre 1914–1918* by L'Harmattan, Paris. For the English edition I have silently corrected a small number of minor errors. I have also added in a dozen or so places explanatory paragraphs to take the analysis further, in particular where new knowledge has come to light in the last couple of years.

Thanks are due to numerous colleagues who asked questions at seminars which made me think, and to Michel Prum, Goulven Guilcher, Renée Dickason, Claude Chastagner, Derek Scott and Susan Finding, who gave useful feedback after the publication of the French edition. Thanks also to library staff, especially in London and in Paris, and to my family, who have been promised that, now the English edition is ready, I will no longer work on Sundays.

Introduction
Battles, Society and Entertainment

What were British people like when they went out on a Saturday night to have a good time during the Great War? The ordinary people of the time loved above all the music hall: they knew nothing of exotic holidays, and radio and television were still a long way off. The British music hall was quite different from the more sophisticated Parisian version: it was more knockabout, with no room for tragic love themes and often taking inspiration from circus acts. The aim of this book is to give a taste of the atmosphere and a glimpse at the meaning of British entertainment during the First World War. It is a period very distant from us in two senses. First, so much has changed in technology, ideology and psychology over the last hundred years, and secondly, very few of us have lived the traumatic, extreme experience of total war.

I hope to be able to put across a little of the magic of the Saturday night out, as well as explaining the themes of the songs and why they were important to our ancestors. In order to do this, I have collected over a thousand songs and tried to analyse the reasons for their success. Their context: the life of British people during the war, in the trenches or in Britain, will also be presented. So as not to base my study only on a small number of emblematic hit songs, I will be quoting hundreds of songs in the coming chapters. The reader will be able to hear original recordings of several dozen of the most popular ones – almost all forgotten today – by following the internet links provided.

Our journey will begin (Chapter 1) with a portrait of the entertainment industry in Britain in 1914. We will meet the entrepreneurs who made and lost fortunes, the would-be singing stars, semi-employed lyricists, overworked musicians and honest or dishonest showbiz agents. We will see how these groups reacted to the trauma of war.

Next (Chapter 2) I will be introducing each of the types of show that existed in the business: music-hall, revue, pantomime, 'blackface minstrelsy' and several others. We will also look at the thousands of touring shows entertaining the British troops in France, and at the amateur show troupes set up by each regiment to amuse and occupy the soldiers during a long and often immobile war.

Chapters 3 to 5 will discuss the favourite themes of the songs, and what they can teach us about the life and the fantasies of the ordinary people in the audience. We will look at dreams of a lost rural paradise, novelty songs and xenophobic songs, songs protesting against a new law or a mean mother-in-law, almost all including a sing-along chorus. Chapter 4 will look at how women were shown in the songs, and how the image of women changed somewhat in parallel with the transformed roles played by women in wartime. Chapter 5 will deal with the hundreds of songs about the war and about life in wartime Britain.

Finally, Chapter 6 will look at non-commercial songs of different sorts: hymns and folk songs, for example. But most of the chapter will be dedicated to soldier songs, invented in their hundreds on the front line to express Tommy's particular view of the war, of the omnipresence of death, and of little-loved superior officers. Between chapters, the reader will find short portraits of popular music stars of the time, since sometimes a close-up view of one individual can give more depth to an analysis of a mass phenomenon such as popular entertainment.

Yet another book on the First World War!

The number of books published on the subject of the Great War is huge: there are tens of thousands of them. Every month, at the time of writing, three dozen new works are published in English on the subject. Military and diplomatic history account for many of them. Books of 'military history from below', which describe the life of soldiers on the front line, are the most popular, and a good number of collections of letters, diaries or interviews have sold very well. The arrival of the centenary has seen a rapid rise in sales for new and old books attempting to pin down the causes of the war.

In university history departments, military history is less dominant: social history, and, even more than that, cultural history, occupies a good number of scholars. The types of source studied grow constantly, as historians work on postcards or medical records, cinema or readers' letters to the press, battlefield archaeology or war monuments. The questions asked of the sources are also more and more varied. Recent books have dealt with the history of nurses, of conscientious objectors, of NCOs, of priests and of executions. Others have looked at the war in Africa, the soldiers from India and the youngest soldiers (some were only 13 years old). Much work has been done on memory, commemoration and cultural representations of war, both in high art and popular art. New thinking about gender has given rise to histories of masculinity and femininity in wartime.

Historians do not agree on many aspects of this war. In France, where I work, debate goes on about different ways that people 'refused' the war, and about the meaning of the mutinies, unofficial ceasefires, and other ways of avoiding fighting. In Britain, a series of historians, some of whom name themselves 'revisionists', criticize what they see as an anti-militarist consensus in history books, school textbooks and television series about the Great War. In particular, they defend the thesis that British First World War generals were much more talented and praiseworthy than has generally been thought, and that, far from being a criminal waste, the Great War was tragic, but necessary and useful. The political positions of these writers and their critics are obviously very significant in understanding these debates. With the beginning of the centenary some politicians have chosen to intervene directly in these debates. But the commemoration of the First World

War has always included clearly political content. In Britain, the Poppy Day campaign, organized by the Royal British Legion, has succeeded in building up a wide consensus around this symbol of commemoration. Millions of people wear poppies in the weeks leading up to the 11th of November, and public figures who do not wish to wear a poppy are subject to real media pressure. The campaign in recent years included billboard posters in the London Underground praising British soldiers then in Afghanistan, while the poppies themselves were often sold by serving soldiers detailed to do so by the Army.[1]

In France, the government announced in 2011 that the day of commemoration of the 1918 armistice, the 11th of November, should henceforth be used to pay homage not only to those who died in the Great War but to all soldiers killed on the French side in any war since. The political use of commemoration, it seems, is unavoidable.

History from below

For any historian, the choice of an object of study and of the questions they wish to highlight cannot be neutral. I have chosen to study popular songs in the hope of better understanding the ordinary people of the time. Although, over the last fifty years, the idea of 'history from below' has gained much ground, popular history books, films and TV documentaries still tend to concentrate on kings, queens and elites.

The difficulty of writing the history of ordinary people has often been underlined. Working-class families from the beginning of the twentieth century leave far fewer written traces of their existence than do families of the elite. The majority of memoirs published are those written by the elite. What they have to say is important, but partial in every sense. In addition, there is an ever-present danger of considering the working class of a given period as a homogeneous bloc with one culture and one set of opinion, whereas in reality, 'the ideologies of any period are diverse and contested'.[2]

One British historian, Gareth Stedman Jones, sums up the pitfalls of writing the history of working-class people: the frequent lack of archival material, the danger of being anecdotal or making abusive generalizations, and, in the case of the history of leisure, the danger of looking at leisure activities out of their context.[3] These are real difficulties, yet the project is an important one. Another historian of leisure activities underlines the fact that 'To achieve a full understanding of twentieth century British history, it is as necessary to examine the impact of the

---

[1]   Their website – http://www.poppy.org.uk/ – makes clear their priorities.

[2]   Alexandra Carter, *Dance and Dancers in the Victorian and Edwardian Music Hall Ballet* (Aldershot: Ashgate, 2005), 4.

[3]   Gareth Stedman Jones, *Languages of Class: Studies in English Working-class History 1832 to 1982* (Cambridge: Cambridge University Press, 1983), 80–88.

everyday cultural experiences of the "majority" as it is to study specific political events'.[4] Entertainment must not be studied in isolation. The First World War was a trauma which marked every aspect of life. And yet the population of all social classes wanted and needed to maintain some continuity with life before the war. Leisure activities helped with this.

It is true that music-hall audiences changed during the war. There were far more uniforms in the house, since military men on leave had money to spend. The percentage of higher-class people in the hall rose (officers had five times as much leave as rank-and-file soldiers did, and barriers stopping elite groups from going to popular musical shows loosened up during the war). But much stayed the same too, as we shall see throughout the present study.

Popular song

The definition of 'popular song' has given rise to a certain amount of debate.[5] In this study, I have retained a very basic definition: simply the songs which were the most well-known and the most frequently sung at the time. In a highly urbanized country, the majority of these songs were communicated by commercial bodies: the variety theatres and the music publishers were the key actors.

Over the last few decades, popular music has become a subject of study for social scientists and historians, and even for musicologists, who had long limited their attention to art music. Previously, university researchers had considered popular music too 'trivial' for serious study, and even today such prejudices have not completely vanished. The present study is based on the assumption that these songs and musical activities can give a unique insight into popular attitudes during the Great War, provided naturally they are not considered as the unmediated voice of a homogeneous working class, but as documents of which one can analyse the content, the reception and the social meaning. Peter Bailey, the most influential expert on the history of music hall, insists that the genre was constantly developing, but warns against a simplistic vision of music hall presenting a gradual and seamless move from some 'authentic' and gritty people's culture to a commercialized and respectable mass culture. He calls for music hall to be examined in its social context, and in relation with other contemporary leisure activities. He regrets, moreover that many studies of music hall have been based on small numbers of songs, and that the period after 1914 has been generally neglected.[6] Peter Bailey's reflections were part of what made me decide to write

---

[4]   James Nott, *Music for the People: Popular Music and Dance in Interwar Britain* (Oxford: Oxford University Press, 2002), 9.

[5]   Richard Middleton (Ed.), *Studying Popular Music* (Milton Keynes: Open University Press, 1990), 3–11.

[6]   Peter Bailey (Ed.), *Music-hall: The Business of Pleasure* (Milton Keynes: Open University Press, 1986), xii–xiii.

the present book, in the hope of filling some of the gaps in our knowledge of musical entertainment of the time.

Sources

Many different kinds of sources were used for this book: historical studies, published collections of letters and diaries, posters and photos. The reader will find them in the footnotes. The majority of the songs are kept in sheet-music form at the British Library in London, though I have been able to listen to some 300 or so recordings of songs from the time. Published collections of songs, and a catalogue put together by a gentleman who had spent his whole career in music hall, contributed the rest of my corpus.[7] The trade press of the period was an indispensable source of information. *The Encore* published news from the music hall every week and served as a link between artistes and theatre managers. Another weekly paper, *The Era*, dealt more generally with stage news – 'legitimate' theatre and music hall alike. *The Performer*, official magazine of the Variety Artistes Federation – the trade union of music-hall performers – showed the entertainment world from the artistes' point of view, often that of the poorer ones. *Phono Record* gave monthly news of newly released records and advances in technology for the fans of the new leisure activity, the gramophone. And of course daily newspapers such as *The Times, The Guardian* and *The Scotsman* were helpful, as was *The Herald*, the main regular publication opposed to the war.

Studies on music hall have tended to concentrate on the capital city, even if some books on provincial towns do exist. In order to help integrate information about smaller towns, I have studied in some detail one small textile town in Lancashire, Burnley, through its local newspapers. Frequent references to this town help to confirm whether or not general analyses also apply to this locality which we consider to be representative. At the end of the book, the reader will find a chronology of key events. This is a very personal selection, and follows my general intention to look at the war from the point of view of ordinary people, to the extent to which it is possible to do so.

Historians aim at writing truths about the past, not just opinions, and yet a completely neutral book on the First World War is quite inconceivable. The choice of sources and of key questions to investigate reveals in every case a positioning by the author. It would be unfair to readers, then, not to indicate from the start that my own sympathies lie with those who feel that the end of the British Empire was something to celebrate, and that the First World War was a tragedy in which the interests and the lives of ordinary people were sacrificed for the sake of the projects and objectives of a wealthy elite.

---

[7]   Michael Kilgarriff, *Sing Us One of the Old Songs: A Guide to Popular Song 1860– 1920* (Oxford: Oxford University Press, 1999).

Chapter 1
Portrait of an Industry: Producing Popular Music, 1914–1918

A number of authors have recounted the history of the Victorian music hall and the gradual emergence of a true entertainment industry;[1] there has been far less work done on early twentieth-century music hall.[2] After sketching out the context of entertainment and leisure in this period, this chapter will describe the industry as it was at the beginning of the Great War. The different actors – companies, showmen, workers and others – will each be examined. In the following chapter we will look at the different genres of musical show of the time, along with their contents, their market shares and their audiences.

First let us look at the range of musical entertainment available in 1914 to the various social classes. Dancing was not yet a mass activity for urban workers – that would come at the end of the 1920s. But already on bank holidays, dance halls in seaside resorts were becoming popular. The new dances, such as the foxtrot, which was introduced in 1914, were easier to learn and thought of as more sensual than the formal dances of previous decades, and the waltz was now danced more slowly and intimately.[3] For middle-class young people, more and more tea dances were available at the Lyons Tea Houses or elsewhere. There they could try out the latest crazes (the tango or the Boston, the Turkey Trot, the Camel Walk, the Bunny Hug or the Grizzly Bear). Dances were ever bigger – in 1911, 4,000 people came to a ball in honour of William Shakespeare.[4]

Amateur singing was widespread. Elite families, with a little help from their servants, organized musical evenings at their homes, in which classical singing around the piano was often mixed in with the singing of a few music-hall numbers of which they had bought the scores, even though they might feel themselves too 'respectable' to frequent the halls themselves. They would also sing numbers from the latest musical comedies. In working-class homes too, at family parties, each

---

[1]   Notably Peter Bailey (Ed.), *Music-hall: The Business of Pleasure* (Milton Keynes: Open University Press, 1986); Peter Bailey, *Popular Culture and Performance in the Victorian City* (Cambridge: Cambridge University Press, 1998); J. S. Bratton (Ed.), *Music Hall: Performance and Style* (Milton Keynes: Open University Press, 1986).

[2]   But see Ronald Pearsall, *Edwardian Popular Music* (London: David & Charles, 1975).

[3]   Ibid., 183.

[4]   Ibid.

person had to know one or two 'party piece' songs to sing[5] (as late as the 1920s, in the army, the tradition continued that everyone present at an evening should 'sing, say, pay or show your arse').[6]

Singing was sometime accompanied on the banjo or the accordion, but group singing was generally centred around a piano, both a precious entertainment tool and a symbol of social ambition or at least respectability. In 1914 there were between two and four million pianos in Britain – around one for every fifteen inhabitants.[7] Robert Roberts tells us how his parents, in the slums of Salford, bought a – rather rickety – family piano for two pounds.[8] During the war, the buying of pianos by men and women workers in the munitions industry, who were enjoying better wages than they were used to, was much commented upon.[9] And those new social layers – office workers, minor civil servants, or sales representatives, earning between three and six pounds a week – bought pianos in large numbers. The automatic piano, or Pianola, which played by itself using perforated rolls which encoded the music, sold well, and could be bought on credit for 65 pounds in all. The Pianola would never become as popular as it did in the United States in this period, however.

Working-class people enjoyed singing and dancing in the streets. Many accounts of the beginning of the war tell of group singing of patriotic songs at recruitment centres, or to accompany soldiers to the train station.[10] At pub doors, singers would try to earn a few pennies, and sheet music was also sold. Many of the performers were more desperate than they were talented, but several major stars such as George Lashwood or Harry Champion, began their career as street singers.[11]

More formal organizations of musical leisure – choirs and brass bands – involved very large numbers of people. Any town with more than 20,000 inhabitants would have at least one mass choir with 100 to 300 singers, often subsidized by local employers. Since the 1880s regular competitions were organized. The pieces sung became technically more challenging,[12] and the repertoire included classical

---

[5]   Robert Roberts, *A Ragged Schooling: Growing Up in the Classic Slum* (London: Fontana, 1978), 29.

[6]   Roy Palmer, *'What a Lovely War!' British Soldiers' Songs from the Boer War to the Present Day* (London: Michael Joseph, 1990), 13.

[7]   Ibid., p. 71.

[8]   Roberts, *A Ragged Schooling*, 53.

[9]   Cyril Ehrlich, *The Music Profession in Britain since the Eighteenth Century: A Social History* (Oxford: Clarendon, 1985), 186.

[10]   Ilana Bet-El, *Conscripts: Forgotten Men of the Great War* (Stroud: The History Press, 2009), 66.

[11]   Andrew Horrall, *Popular Culture in London c.1890–1918: The Transformation of Entertainment* (Manchester: Manchester University Press, 2001), 13–15.

[12]   Dave Russell, 'Varieties of life: the making of the Edwardian Music Hall', in M. R. Booth and J. H. Kaplan (Eds) *The Edwardian Theatre: Essays on Performance and the Stage* (Cambridge: Cambridge University Press, 1996), 201.

song and opera, but also some music-hall hits.[13] The brass bands, organized by groups of workers from the same mine or factory, by the Salvation Army, or by secular organizations, had hundreds of thousands of members: there were more than 30,000 brass bands in the country in 1900.[14] The town of Bradford alone had twenty brass bands and thirteen choirs, as well as its two major music halls.

Far more people went to see shows even than joined choirs or bands, and musical shows will be at the centre of this study. The gramophone was still a rare luxury: many soldiers saw one for the first time during the war. Music hall, musical comedy, and other shows were big business where millions were won and lost gambling on mass taste. Sheet music based on the songs heard on stage sold in millions to those who wanted to sing them at home or on the streets. A fully fledged entertainment industry had emerged after 1880. It hoped to make profit from mass demand, but had to deal with elite fears of seeing large numbers of workers gathered to listen to working-class singers. The result was an industry which was ever more dominated by big companies, and truly obsessed with the principles of 'respectability', an ideology which it hope would ward off the two principal demons of the 'dangerous classes': vulgarity and political radicalism.

In Victorian times, elite campaigns for 'rational leisure' for workers had often condemned music hall out of hand, but by 1914, music hall was considered to be far more acceptable. Even the King attended occasionally, in particular since the first music-hall evening organized specially in his honour, the Royal Variety performance of 1912. Nevertheless, working-class music shows were still looked upon with suspicion. When theatres needed their licence renewed, managers had to demonstrate to magistrates that they were not allowing vulgar songs to be performed, that the women on stage were not too scantily dressed, and that the establishment's foyer or promenade was not being used by prostitutes to pick up clients.

The two key dynamics which explain the entertainment industry in this period are then the economic drive to the concentration of capital and the ideological drive to building respectability. Economic concentration was limited, however, by the nature of the shows. Once the record industry had taken off, US domination would gradually arise, as it would in film production. A mechanically reproduced product – a record or a film – allows a far more centralized industry than does a live show: music-hall evenings, presented in hundreds of towns across Britain every night, could not be dominated by US artistes. They would have been more expensive, and would have had more difficulty building the rapport with local audiences which was still important for a turn to be a success. Thus, if the entertainment industry was becoming national, it was not fully transnational.

---

13   Russell, 'Varieties', 218–220.

14   Dave Russell, *Popular Music in England, 1840–1914: A Social History* (Manchester: Manchester University Press, 1988); Trevor Herbert, 'Volunteers, Salvationists and Committees: Consensus versus Regulation in Amateur Victorian Brass Bands', *Cahiers victoriens et édouardiens* 50 (1999).

Variety theatres and theatre chains

We shall be looking in turn at the main active components of the industry. The first is the entrepreneur, theatre owner or even owner of a chain of theatres. Considerable expansion led to there being, in 1910, 63 halls in London and 254 in the rest of the country.[15] So, for example in Glasgow, in 1914, there were 18 music halls and six 'legitimate theatres',[16] while in 1888 there had been only three music halls.[17] In Newcastle at the start of the war there were three music halls and three 'legitimate theatres'.[18] A larger hall could sell 70,000 tickets a week, and more than a million tickets were sold in London each week.[19] In Burnley, the two main music halls could seat 7,000 people a night – that is, more than 5 per cent of the town's population![20]

The industry was ever more professional, and theatres were tightly run businesses. Every year, they were bigger and involved more and more capital investment, partly to match new fire regulations, but mainly to allow them to attract a socially mixed audience in a highly competitive market. The appearance of luxury was essential, and this characteristic is suggested by the very names of the theatres: The Empire, the Palace, the Coliseum or the Alhambra. At the Oxford theatre in London one moved among 'Corinthian columns and bars smothered in flowers and glittering with mirrors'.[21] At the Palace, a 'grand staircase columned with green marble and gilt capitals' led up to the royal box.[22] The Nottingham Empire boasted smiling idols representing Krishna on either side of the stage, and four giant gilt elephant heads in the four corners of the auditorium.[23] The new theatres in Glasgow (the Empire, opened in 1897 and the Pavilion, opened in 1904) were lit by electric light and featured huge sliding roofs which could open in fine weather (few of the audience would have had electricity at home).[24] Behind the curtains, stages and facilities were ever grander, meaning quicker scene changes. Machines allowing performers to appear to fly were to be found, along with enormous glass water tanks for synchronized swimming turns, film projectors and equipment to perform spectacular 'scientific experiments'. Theatres which did not

---

[15]   Bailey, *Music-hall*, xxi; but these figures no doubt omit many smaller halls.

[16]   At the time, the term 'legitimate theatre' referred to those halls which presented plays, perhaps by Shakespeare, George Bernard Shaw or J. M. Barrie. Seats were far more expensive than in the music hall.

[17]   Paul Maloney, *Scotland and the Music Hall, 1850–1914* (Manchester: Manchester University Press, 2003), 57.

[18]   *The Performer*, 4 February 1915.

[19]   Felix Barker, *The House that Stoll Built* (London: Frederick Muller, 1957), 27.

[20]   The town possessed 126 pubs and bars.

[21]   James Harding, *George Robey and the Music Hall* (London: Hodder & Stoughton, 1990), 16.

[22]   Ibid., 70.

[23]   Russell, *Popular Music*, 83.

[24]   Maloney, *Scotland and the Music Hall*, 76.

have the capital to keep up fell by the wayside – like the London Tivoli, identified with old-style music hall rather than modern extravaganza, which had to close down and was demolished in 1914 to the great regret of the traditionalists. [25]

The domination of theatre chains was constantly reinforced; many independent halls felt compelled under the economic pressure to join one. This process was, however, slow and it is estimated that in 1914 only around half of all tickets sold in the country were sold by the big theatre chains. In 1901, theatre-chain owner and impresario, Edward Moss, paid out high dividends of 12½ per cent.[26] Others were paying out between 9 per cent and 12 per cent. The artistes' trade union claimed that Oswald Stoll, another theatre-chain owner personally made £35,000 a year from his theatres in 1907.[27] Profits in wartime were healthy. In 1915, the London Coliseum paid out 25 per cent, the Leicester Palace 10 per cent and the Hackney Empire 6 per cent. By far the highest profits were made in the West End music halls around Leicester Square, which were profiting from the rapid development of public transport.[28]

At the beginning of the war, four theatre chains were very powerful: two in London, London Theatres of Variety (LTV) and London Syndicate Halls, and two outside the capital: Moss Empires and the Variety Theatres Controlling Company (VTCC). In addition to economies of scale, they had other advantages: they could sign up top stars for an entire season, thus preventing competitors from using the best-known names in their advertising; they could by-pass theatrical agents and negotiate directly with the stars; and they could buy from foreign networks a monopoly of touring artistes from those networks. Thus in 1910, the VTCC chain signed an exclusive contract with one of the main vaudeville chains in the United States.[29]

Between the theatre chains, fierce rivalry alternated with mutual interest agreements. They might organize jointly tours of particular stars or revues, or agree on maximum salaries for artistes, but every time a new theatre was opened by one or another chain, no punches were pulled and harsh competition was the order of the day. In 1915, for example, the owners of the Alhambra theatre in London, a large music hall which had been proudly independent for decades, announced that for financial reasons, they were obliged to join one of the major chains. LTV and VTCC were both very keen, and it was the former which won out after long negotiations;[30] two years later, the VTCC got its revenge by incorporating another London venue, the Empire.

---

[25]   *The Times*, 31 January 1914.
[26]   Other, more precise, measures of profitability are difficult to find for this period. The dividends paid out may serve as a rough and ready indicator.
[27]   *The Performer*, 31 January 1907.
[28]   Barker, *The House Stoll Built*, 12.
[29]   Andrew Crowhurst, 'The Music Hall 1885–1922' (PhD thesis, Cambridge University, 1991), 298.
[30]   Ibid., 374.

The theatre chains were in the vanguard of the rationalization of work processes and of capital investment. It was Edward Moss who first introduced the four-shows-a-day schedule, in London in 1904, and who pioneered an advance seat-reservation service. Meanwhile, inside the companies, the division of labour was changing, with the invention of a series of new roles such as that of stage manager.

In parallel with the grander music halls, there also existed more modest, independent venues, often sited in the suburbs, and exhibiting a more working-class atmosphere (though these halls were not immune to the campaign for respectability). Paul Maloney remarks on the clear difference between a town-centre music hall in Glasgow and a hall, such as the Panopticon, in a poor part of town. This latter, seating 1,500 spectators, was reputed to give artistes a rough time if they did not please. It scheduled four shows a day, the first one in the morning to cater for workers leaving the night shift.[31]

Right at the bottom of the scale was a patchwork of multi-use venues such as working men's clubs and assembly halls of different sorts (religious or otherwise). These alternated evenings of entertainment along music-hall lines with other events such as lectures or theatre plays. The working men's club movement had been founded in 1862 by an Anglican vicar who aimed at promoting temperance and encouraging religion, but had developed into a network of autonomous associations with wider interests. Music-hall evenings might be held in these clubs alongside productions of Shakespeare or Socialist lectures and sing-songs.[32] In Burnley, at least five cooperative halls had a licence to produce musical entertainment, including the Weavers' Institute Cooperative Hall. Even small villages which did not boast a permanent hall, would host touring shows of a music-hall type, generally composed of three or four artistes and a pianist.

Respectable leisure

Heavy investment in new theatres accelerated the tendency of the theatre chains to be searching for a better-off audience to occupy the more expensive seats. The frantic campaign to eliminate 'vulgarity' should be seen in this context.

> it seems likely that [managers were attempting] to install middle-class values or notions of respectability ... in the music hall, so that upwardly mobile sections of the lower classes would feel they could attend music hall without compromising their social aspirations ... for their part, managers did not care if middle-class patrons' appreciation was often 'ironic' in the sophisticated modern sense.[33]

---

[31]   Ibid., 16.

[32]   John Taylor, *From Self-Help to Glamour: The Working Man's Club 1860–1972* (Oxford: History Workshop, 1972).

[33]   Maloney, *Scotland and the Music Hall*, 86–87.

Within the buildings themselves, great pains were taken to cater to the social needs of more privileged classes: there were separate entrances for different parts of the theatre, and no access to the stalls from the circle or gallery. Pricing too ensured segregation: remember that the spectators would have paid anything from four pence to two shillings (six times as much) to attend in 1916.

The move towards ever more respectability was not only a marketing reflex, but also very much the effect of the social ambition of theatre owners and managers. By 1914, these people could finally see themselves as fully integrated into local elites, be invited to society events, and even organize birthday parties to which everybody 'who was anybody' locally would turn up.[34]

Emphasis on respectability, finally, reflected the fear of owners and managers of losing their entertainments licence under the pressure of moralist organizations aiming at 'cleaning up' the entertainment industry. Although such organizations were in a minority and were frequently the butt of mockery, they had real power, as local magistrates and police chiefs listened to them when considering the renewal of licences.

The coming of war saw owners move to defend their interests. At the same time as they supported the imperial cause, they worked to defend their market sector against the encroachments of the war economy and to ensure continued profitability. In 1914, in the expectation of falling income, a wage reduction agreement was made with the trade unions. In 1917, when the government announced it wanted to cut down on the number of shows allowed per week in music halls, the industry mobilized to oppose the plan.[35] A meeting between Neville Chamberlain, representing the government, and industry leaders led to an agreement not to limit the number of shows, but to encourage simpler productions without expensive special effects, with the aim of freeing labour power for the war drive. At the same time, other rationing measures were introduced: advertising posters could henceforth be no bigger than 600 square inches. In some towns, including Burnley, halls had to close at 10.30 pm, despite tenacious lobbying by theatre managers,[36] and this measure was applied nationally in 1918.[37]

The implication of music halls in war charities should be seen in the context of charitable activity before the war. The halls, especially those in working-class areas, had a long tradition of being involved in such activity, at a time when the role of charitable organizations was much more central to the survival of the poorer parts of society than it is today. Music halls organized annual days out for children, and soup kitchens in hard times, in addition to a large number of concerts to raise money for different causes. This social role was easily transformed into an active role in the war, which was presented as one more humanitarian cause.[38]

---

[34] Ibid., 151.
[35] *The Encore*, 4 January 1917.
[36] *Burnley Express*, 3 March 1917.
[37] *Hansard, House of Commons Debates, 20 March 1918, vol. 104, c1090.*
[38] Horrall, *Popular Culture*, 25.

Now the characteristics and priorities of theatre owners and managers have been sketched out, let us look at the people who worked inside the theatres.

Stage hands, musicians and dancers

Stage hands were employed by each theatre, paid by the (57-hour) week, or by the hour; there were ever more of them as stage productions became more spectacular. They took part in the great music-hall strike in London in 1907, along with their trade union, the National Association of Theatrical Employees, which had been set up after a strike in 1890. Most of the vast newspaper coverage of this strike concentrated on the well-known stars involved, but the strike also managed to establish a minimum wage for each job in the industry (30 shillings a week for an electrician, for example, or 10½ pence an hour for a decorator's assistant).[39]

In September 1917, the stage hands' union threatened strike action over a wage claim. The editorialist of the main trade paper, *The Encore*, called for calm and negotiations, insisting that 'Nobody wants strikes in war time'. According to the trade union, wage rises were urgent: there were foremen in London earning only 9½ pence an hour, 'less than building labourers',[40] while the women who sold programmes earned only 12 shillings a week.[41] Government intervention resolved the conflict, and granted a substantial wage rise to the stage crews. Stage managers and chief electricians got 10 shillings a week more, and a minimum wage of 55 shillings a week was agreed for these grades. Male head cashiers would henceforth receive 37½ shillings a week (but only 30 shillings if the head cashier was a woman). Cleaning women would receive a minimum of 15 shillings a week. [42]

What of musicians? Between 1870 and 1930, the number of professional musicians was multiplied by seven, while the population of the country only doubled.[43] Every music hall, cinema or opera house employed a house orchestra. During the war, the departure of many to the front raised demand considerably, and in *The Era* each week, one could see fifty or more adverts asking for musicians, as well as many from musicians offering their services. Wages were not high. In 1915, the non-unionized musicians at the Coventry opera house earned 20 shillings a week (3 shillings more than an agricultural labourer at this time).[44] In one Cheltenham orchestra the rate was 25 shillings, whereas in one of the biggest

---

[39]   See John Mullen,'Velours rouge et piquets de grève – la grève du music hall à Londres en 1907', *Cahiers victoriens et édouardiens* 67 (2008).

[40]   *The Encore*, 6 September 1917. At the time there were 240 pennies, or 20 shillings, in a pound.

[41]   *The Era*, 5 September 1917.

[42]   *The Era*, 16 January 1918.

[43]   Ehrlich, *The Music Profession*, 55.

[44]   Department of Employment and Productivity, *British Labour Statistics: Historical Abstracts, 1886–1968* (London, HMSO, 1971).

music halls in Birmingham, the soloist received 36 shillings. Even players in the prestigious Halle Orchestra only earned 80 shillings a week in 1917.[45] Working conditions could be hard for musicians playing up to four shows a day in addition to rehearsals for upcoming programmes, in a smoky auditorium. Damp in the halls contributed to tuberculosis, a frequent cause of death. Even if the figure given by the trade union – 40 per cent of musicians dying from tuberculosis – is on the high side, it was clearly a major cause of early death.[46]

The very first musicians' unions in Britain appeared in the 1870s, with the foundation of the Manchester Musical Artistes' Protective Association, which soon opened a London branch.[47] These organizations only survived for a few years. Others followed, hybrids between friendly associations and trade unions, and often criticized by some musicians who refused to look at their position as artists from the point of view of the defence of working conditions. The latter philosophy lay behind the founding of non-union professional associations such as The Incorporated Society of Musicians, whose patron was the Duke of Edinburgh.

In the 1890s, a more stable trade union was established, the Amalgamated Musicians Union. The cost of joining was lowered, from seven and a half shillings a year in 1890 to two and a half in 1898, a sign of the desire to recruit all grades of musician. In 1894, the AMU affiliated to the Trades Union Congress. One of the most important debates in the union at this time was the question of whether part-time musicians, who had other jobs too, should be allowed to join. The union grew (it would reach 20,000 members in 1921) and was involved in strike action in 1893 and in 1898, in addition to the big 1907 strike. Sources are not readily available for the many smaller local strikes by musicians, but there are some known examples during the war years. In Leicester in 1914, musicians working for the Stoll music-hall chain went on strike: union leaflets encouraged local people to boycott the halls and the manager was obliged to make concessions.[48] In Burnley the same year, orchestras from two halls went on strike for over a month after four union members had been dismissed. The Independent Labour Party held a public meeting in support of the strike, which was addressed by Fenner Brockway, a socialist activist who would later be imprisoned for opposing the war.[49] In November 1917, a dispute arose concerning the numerous charity shows which were played in all the halls. The musicians refused to continue playing at these shows without pay, and were denounced by the editor of *The Encore* for their position on this question.

---

[45]   Ehrlich, *The Music Profession*, 189.

[46]   See www.musiciansunion.org.uk (accessed 15 January 2010).

[47]   This short summary of the history of musicians' trade unionism is based on the seminar paper of Angèle David-Guillou 'Premiers syndicats d'artistes musiciens, sociabilités musicales et art en France et en Angleterre', given at Paris 13 University in 2005.

[48]   Jeremy Crump, 'Provincial music hall: promoters and public in Leicester, 1863–1929' in *Music-hall: The Business of Pleasure*, ed. Peter Bailey (Milton Keynes: Open University Press, 1986), 67

[49]   *Burnley Gazette*, 16 September, 19 September, 17 October 1914.

All of these strikes show that the musicians' union was part of the British trade union movement of the time, and also that, just like other sections of the workforce, their general acceptance of the need to win the war did not prevent them from resorting to strike action in order to defend pay and conditions. Indeed, Britain saw far more strikes during the war years than did France or Germany: between 1915 and 1918 there were 3,227 strikes, making a total of almost 18 million strike days. The most serious conflicts were the dockers' strike of 1915 and the three major engineering strikes (1916, 1917, and 1918). Numbers of trade union members rose from 4.1 million in 1913 to 6.5 million in 1918, and this despite the fact that millions of men had joined the army, and so were not entitled to join a trade union.[50]

Like many other groups of workers, musicians who managed to avoid the massacres saw their standard of living rise during the war years. There was full employment, and opportunities for women musicians which had not existed previously, as well as vacant jobs due to the eviction of many German and Austrian immigrants who worked in the orchestras. Ehrlich explains:

> Shortages of goods left more cash to be spent on pleasure, and audiences were augmented by soldiers on leave. Native musicians at every level found it easier to get jobs ... Even the humblest piano teachers acquired new pupils among children whose parents were buying the 'munitions workers' pianos' which symbolized a new working-class prosperity.[51]

The recruitment of Belgian or French refugees as musicians was sometimes opposed for protectionist motives, and at least one union branch (in Burnley in 1916) demanded that no foreign musician be employed.[52] Others complained about the recruitment of women, and wrote long pieces in the union journal about the supposed poor quality of their work. One editorial attack in the union journal deplored that women lacked 'vim, particularly in the climaxes and anti-climaxes necessary to a proper performance'.[53]

Let us turn now to another group of workers in the industry, the dancers. The rise of the musical comedy after 1890, and of the revue after 1910, produced a new group of employees: the chorus girls, a 'numerous, interchangeable and readily replaceable category of semi-skilled workers employed in long production runs in

---

[50]   Ian Beckett, *Home Front 1914 to 1918: How Britain Survived the Great War* (London: National Archives, 2006), 50; Crowhurst, 'The Music Hall', 172.

[51]   Ehrlich, *The Music Profession*, 186.

[52]   Ibid., 188.

[53]   Ibid. Such prejudices were not rare. For the case of the tax clerks' union see A. J. Brown, *The Taxmen's Tale – the History of the Inland Revenue Staff Federation* (London: IRSF, 1983), 18.

a large scale culture industry'.[54] The Tiller Girls, established in Manchester in the last years of the nineteenth century, were the most famous example.

Dancers, and their employers, worked hard to ensure that their eroticized stage persona did not spill over into their private lives. They had to be respectable young ladies outside the theatre, and elocution lessons were even provided to help them be so.[55] One editorial in *The Encore* protested against what would today be called sexual harassment of dancers by some stars during shows or rehearsals, complaining that some young women were regularly 'mauled'.[56] Since they were easy to replace, the chorus girls worked in difficult conditions, and wages could be very low. In 1918, *The Era* reported an extreme case in which dancers for a musical comedy in an army training centre were paid only one pound a week (whereas since 1907 the minimum wage for musicians, for example was a pound and ten shillings).

Music publishers

Half a dozen large publishing companies such as Star, Feldman or Francis, Day & Hunter, employed popular music composers and lyricists, published scores and owned the rights to the songs, which they sold to the singers. They also bought songs from freelance authors, and organized competitions in the hope of finding the next smash hit. The Performing Rights Society, launched in 1914, gradually managed to stop artistes performing songs on stage without paying royalties. The Copyright Act of 1911 had introduced protection for publishers, and for the first time both recording companies and theatres had to pay out royalties, the latter paying a global fee on a sliding scale according to the size of their resident orchestra.[57]

The publishing houses took out regular advertisements in the trade press ('Feldman's new songs by the world's greatest writers')[58] and issued warnings about pirating their pieces. A full-page advertisement in 1916 intoned 'The Feldman song "A Little Bit of Heaven" MUST NOT BE PARODIED. Artistes and theatres who use this song will be prosecuted.'[59] Firms were always on the look-out for new ways to sell songs: for example, Lawrence Wright sold slide shows, illustrating their hit songs, to cinema managers.[60]

---

[54] Peter Bailey, 'Naughty but Nice: Musical Comedy and the Rhetoric of the Girl' in *The Edwardian Theatre: Essays on Performance and the Stage*, ed. M. R. Booth and J. H. Kaplan (Cambridge: Cambridge University Press, 1996), 39.
[55] Bailey, 'Naughty but Nice,' 41.
[56] *The Encore*, 18 January, 1917.
[57] Cyril Ehrlich, *Harmonious Alliance: A History of the Performing Rights Society* (Oxford, Oxford University Press, 1989), 22.
[58] *The Encore*, 11 February 1915.
[59] *The Encore*, 20 January 1916.
[60] *The Encore*, 25 February 1915.

Once a year, at the beginning of the pantomime season, publishers sold temporary 'pantomime rights' to their songs, valid for the two or three months of the pantomime season. This was a crucial moment in the industry year: a pantomime hit might be sung in dozens of shows and sell hundreds of thousands of copies in sheet music, as well as a few thousand records. During the winter of 1916–1917, for example, Star publishers launched two major hits: 'Take Me Back to Dear Old Blighty' and 'Some Night, Some Waltz, Some Girl!'. Each was performed by around fifty different artistes in pantos around the country.[61] The following year, the song 'Down Texas Way' was sung by at least 62 performers.[62] For the remainder of the year, only one artiste had the right to perform a given song. If, in 1916, you wanted to hear the song 'Now You've Got Yer Khaki On' performed on stage, your only option was to wait until Marie Lloyd was topping the bill at your local hall.

Music publishing was big money. Between 1900 and 1910, one of the main companies, Francis, Day & Hunter, released forty to fifty songs every month.[63] Print runs were rarely under 25,000, and a hit song could sell hundreds of thousands of copies at sixpence apiece. In 1919, the number of people who bought the sheet music of the hit 'That Old-fashioned Mother of Mine' was greater than the combined membership of the Church of England and the Church of Scotland.[64]

The companies were proud of their reactivity. In 1875, when Captain Webb became the first man to swim the Channel, 'a commemorative song was written, printed, and on sale, within 24 hours'.[65] From the hour war was declared in 1914, a feverish search for new hits broke out. Francis & Day organized a competition for a wartime song, and first prize was taken by 'Pack Up Your Troubles in Your Old Kit Bag'.[66] Abbott, who worked in the industry, describes his pride and pleasure in his work: 'bringing into being some catchy tune or song and watching its growth until it was being sung or whistled by half the adult population in the country'.[67]

Lyricists and composers

Lyricists and composers generally worked freelance, and only a few were full-time employees. These last worked mostly in London: Maloney writes that in

---

[61]   *The Encore*, 4 January 1917.

[62]   *The Era*, 2 January 1918.

[63]   James Nott, *Music for the People: Popular Music and Dance in Interwar Britain* (Oxford: Oxford University Press, 2002), 104.

[64]   Ibid., 1.

[65]   John Abbott, *The Story of Francis, Day & Hunter* (London: William Chappell, 1952), 15.

[66]   Online at http://www.firstworldwar.com/audio/packupyourtroubles.htm (accessed 20 July 2014).

[67]   Abbott, *Francis, Day & Hunter*, 11.

Scotland, for example, only a handful of people made a living from writing songs. But there was a large network of semi-professionals who sold their songs directly to the artistes, often in pubs.[68] Singing star George Robey said he bought four or five songs a week during the whole of his career;[69] while Vesta Tilley claimed to have bought 'thousands of songs', generally paying two pounds a song;[70] and Marie Lloyd explained that you had to buy at least ten songs to find one good one.[71]

One of the most prolific lyricists, Joe Tabrar, claimed to have written 10,000 songs in all, among which there were a number of hits including 'Daddy Wouldn't Buy Me a Bow-Wow'.[72] Harry Hunter[73] wrote many hundreds, Fred Godfrey 800, and many were highly successful.[74] However, as can be seen in Kilgarriff's music-hall song catalogue, very many lyricists had only one or two well-known songs to their name.[75] It is to be noted that, although women were fairly well-represented on the stage, lyricists and composers were almost all men.

Freelancers ran small ads in the trade press. For a shilling, one could buy the (non-exclusive) rights to the song 'If I were King for a Day', described as a 'comic topical song, for tramp make-up or any eccentric character, with extra war verse'.[76] Other adverts declared: 'Songs to order: words only seven shillings and sixpence, words and music ten shillings and sixpence. Extra verses written to any songs for ninepence each.'[77] Would-be lyricists could even sign up for a course at the songwriters' school set up by Joe Tabrar.[78] Herbert Darnley, a lyricist who had written hits for the great Dan Leno, gave this advice in a column in *The Era*:

> except as a hobby, I advise no one to go in for comic song writing. There is no money in it. ... Even if [an agent] buys the song, what do you get? Perhaps five pounds with a chance of making another ten or twenty if the song is published![79]

And indeed, it was not rare for top lyricists to die in poverty.[80] The fact that Fred Godfrey, whose songs sold tens of millions, never became rich, is an illustration

---

[68] Maloney, *Scotland and the Music Hall*, 112.

[69] Harding, *George Robey*, 38.

[70] Matilda De Frece, *Recollections of Vesta Tilley* (London: Hutchinson, 1934), 124.

[71] Quoted in *The Age*, 28 December, 1935.

[72] Original recording on Youtube: www.youtube.com/watch?v=dJnj7RlP9-A (accessed 20 July 2014).

[73] Michael Pickering, '"A Happy Instinct for Sentiment": a profile of Harry Hunter', *Cahiers victoriens et édouardiens* 50 (1999).

[74] See www.fredgodfreysongs.ca.

[75] Michael Kilgarriff, *Sing Us One of the Old Song: A Guide to Popular Song 1860–1920* (Oxford: Oxford University Press, 1999).

[76] *The Encore*, 11 February 1915.

[77] Ibid.

[78] Abbott, *Francis, Day & Hunter*, 17.

[79] *The Era*, 28 February 1917.

[80] Ehrlich, *Harmonious Alliance*, 4.

of their situation. The only lyricists who made a fortune were those few who, like Lawrence Wright, were able to found their own publishing house. In the 1920s, the rise of the record industry, particularly the American one, transformed the situation for successful lyricists. Ivor Novello or Noel Coward, for example, enjoyed a celebrity lifestyle that Joe Tabrar or Fred Godfrey could never have dreamed of.

Singers and other artistes

Who were the artistes and how did they work? We have a large amount of information about the most successful stars, but here we want to look at the run-of-the-mill music-hall artistes, whose life and work can be glimpsed in the pages of the trade press and the union journal. Around 10,000 to 15,000 artistes appeared in shows regularly in 1914, and half of them were singers. It is not easy to distinguish them in the census categories of 1911, but we see that the category 'Musicians, music masters and singers' included 47,116 individuals, 10,000 more than in 1901. In addition, 28,194 men and 4,021 women worked in support occupations within the entertainment industry, and this category included some music-hall artistes as well as cinema employees, race course attendants and so on. Most of the singers were men, even though over the last fifty years since the first woman music-hall singer, the number of female artistes had risen considerably. During the war, a third of songs were sung by women.

From an economic point of view, the artistes were in a contradictory position. On the one hand, one might classify them as independent artisans, since they negotiated individually with their customers (theatres or record companies), and were in direct competition with others to get bookings or top billing. Some, heads of acrobat teams or magicians, were even small employers. Some aspects of this social position, in addition to the specific nature of artistic work, meant that the artistes were, according to their union historian, 'Staunch individualists for whom a "red nose" was infinitely preferable to the red flag'.[81]

And yet, the economic power of theatre managers (and chains of theatres) tended to reduce the entertainers to the status of wage workers, dependent on their employer, and artistes made use of collectivist tactics to improve their situation. Mutual aid associations were founded in the 1870s, in particular the Music Hall Artistes Railway Association (MHARA), which negotiated special tariffs for music-hall entertainers on trains, and gradually took on other union roles, not without vigorous polemics between pro- and anti- trade union artistes. By 1897, there were 5,000 members of the MHARA. In 1906, its leaders joined up with other organizations to found a true trade union, the Variety Artistes Federation, which had 4,500 members a year later. Its weekly journal, *The Performer*, carried

---

[81]   Peter Honri, *Music Hall Warriors: The History of the Variety Artists Federation 1906 to 1967* (London: Greenwich Exchange, 1997), v.

the slogan on every issue: 'the greatest enemy to freedom is not the tyrant, but the contented slave'.

During the great music-hall strike in London in 1907, allied with the stage hands' and musicians' unions, and supported by the whole of the British trade union movement, the artistes were able to force a government arbitration which introduced important improvements in standard contracts. In particular, the right of theatres to ban artistes from playing in other venues in the same town was limited, and additional shows such as matinees had from then on to be remunerated. The top stars had little need for these reforms, but many joined the strike out of solidarity with rank and file entertainers. The strike was active and dynamic and lasted 22 days. On both sides, the conflict was experienced as a standard, and bitter, industrial dispute, and all the habitual union and management tactics were implemented. Some theatre managers doubled the salaries of non-strikers for the duration of the conflict, and others put pressure on artistes to sign a written promise not to join the union. On the strikers' side, rallies and picket lines were organized in front of the theatres, and over a million leaflets were given out. Strike-breakers were expelled from the union, and alternative evenings of entertainment were held with big name stars to raise money for the strikers. Only the London theatres were on strike, but union members in the rest of the country gave 5 per cent of their salary every week to the strike fund.[82]

The agreement signed at the end of the strike was regularly revised in following years by the government arbitrator. Nevertheless, local disputes broke out from time to time. Just before the outbreak of the war, in July 1914, for example, a rally was organized in front of the Pavilion theatre in East London, in support of a strike by the Union of Anglo-Jewish Artistes.[83]

In the middle of the Great War, the Variety Artistes' Federation (VAF) had 3,600 members. [84] They paid a £1 entrance fee on joining, in addition to monthly subs, but the one pound could be paid in up to eight instalments if required: care was taken to attract poorer artistes.[85] Members accepted union discipline and refused to sign contracts which paid less than the agreed union rate. In 1915, the union position was to refuse contracts which involved less than a week's work, and not to work on Sundays (even for charities, with the exception of war charities): several members were subject to disciplinary procedures for not having respected the majority decision.[86]

---

[82]   Ibid., 12.

[83]   *The Encore*, 16 July 1914.

[84]   Exact information about the percentage of trade unionists in the industry is not available, but this figure can be compared with that of the 310 or so variety theatres in the country.

[85]   *The Performer*, 21 January 1915.

[86]   *The Performer*, 7 January 1915.

A proposal to demand a closed shop in theatres was rejected by members.[87] However, the union felt a need for a voice in parliament: in 1917, union financial support was given to sponsor a parliamentary candidate.[88] The union was conscious of its links with the national and international workers' movement: when, in 1917, the vaudeville artistes in the USA were on strike, members of the VAF were asked to send 5 per cent of their salary every week to the Americans' strike fund.[89]

Let us examine the professional life of these artistes. If they were working in London, they would often play at three or four theatres during any given day; but they were often on tour, staying in specialized lodging houses, often run by retired artistes or artistes' widows. These offered 'three to a room, [and] cost thirty five pence, and that included a morning cup of tea and fish and chips at night'.[90]

Artistes began working on the stage very young (sometimes at the age of six or seven), and normally came from working-class backgrounds or poorer groups still. The trade was passed from father to son or father to daughter. Performers often began by singing in the streets. One could get oneself a name locally by taking part in 'open evenings' in the smaller music halls, even if the audiences were often rather aggressive. Competitions were also organized, the prize being a week's contract in one of the halls.[91] Those who were to succeed needed to be single-minded: 'Of course there is no open sesame to fame. An artiste may succeed because of a good voice or a telling personality or an adorable (or even mobile) face.'[92]

Many many artistes earned only just enough to scrape by, and were frequently unemployed. The comic singer Billy Merson was not untypical. He began his career working in a lace factory while giving shows in the evening, and recounts that, once he took up show business full-time: 'for something like six years I struggled along on a salary that barely kept body and soul together.'[93]

The average artiste was often most concerned with earning enough to live on, in a job no doubt more attractive than the other trades available to working-class people at the time,[94] and with that tiny but real chance of making it to stardom. In 1905, the customary minimum wage for an artiste was four or five pounds a week.[95] After the 1907 strike, many aspects of working conditions were negotiated between unions and employers in the presence of government mediator Lord

---

[87]   *The Encore*, 6 August 1914.
[88]   *The Era*, 28 March 1917.
[89]   *The Era*, 14 February 1917.
[90]   Harding, *George Robey*, 27.
[91]   For example, *The Encore* 6 August 1914.
[92]   Julia James, 'The Secret of Success', *The Era*, 3 January 1917.
[93]   *The Era*, 3 January 1917.
[94]   In the 1911 census, the four most common professions were domestic servants (1.3 million), agricultural labourers (1.2 million), miners (971,000) and textile workers (624,000).
[95]   Crowhurst, 'The Music Hall', 317.

Askwith, who had played this role in industrial disputes in many other sectors of the economy.[96]

Having a booking cancelled at the last moment, or not being paid by bankrupt or unscrupulous theatre managers, were considered as normal occupational hazards.[97] Artistes often went to court to defend their rights, or were taken to court by theatre managers. Professional solidarity was strong: benefit concerts were commonly organized to help ill or aged artistes, and relief funds as well as rest homes were established by the profession, in 1895 in Scotland and in 1911 in England.[98] In 1917, a boxing competition between artistes was held in aid of the music-hall artistes' rest home.[99] During the war, the Music Hall Ladies Guild organized aid for wives of artistes who had joined up or been conscripted, and delivered free coal to sick artistes in the winter.

Every performer dreamed of 'making it', and in the meantime was satisfied with getting regular bookings. 'Tour of Africa six to fourteen weeks; tour of Australia twenty weeks; tour of India four weeks!': adverts in the trade press offered the chance to get one's name known elsewhere in the empire. Artistes in this period, as in others, were characterized by a grim determination not far from obsession. The artiste had to please. 'You're just a fill up until you create YOUR OWN PUBLIC' advised one expert in his column in *The Era*.[100] Among other things, the music hall represented for the poor the dream of escape into the luxury and recognition of stardom; the salaries which the top artistes made were the subject of excited speculation and discussion among audiences.

Recording companies

The gramophone and record industry was only embryonic in 1914. Later, it would transform popular music by making available to anybody a wider variety of musical works than that which a music-hall goer would have heard in their entire life. The rise of the record would allow the development of specialist audiences, fan clubs and connoisseur circles of each kind of music. It was to make possible the cover version, the live version, the unplugged version and the studio remix, and many other innovations, but all this was a long way off.

During the war years, Columbia, Coliseum or Regal records did all they could to persuade music-hall stars to record their best-known songs. Many distrusted this new technology, sure that people would no longer buy tickets for their shows if they could listen to the music at home, but others accepted, sometimes persuaded by the argument that soldiers at the front needed musical entertainment from home.

---

[96]   Lord Askwith, *Industrial Problems and Disputes* (London, John Murray, 1920).
[97]   Crowhurst, 'The Music Hall', 108.
[98]   Maloney, *Scotland and the Music Hall*, 153.
[99]   *The Encore*, 17 May 1917.
[100]   *The Era*, 10 January 1917.

Before the war, the European gramophone industry had been dominated by German companies, which ran factories in England and elsewhere. The closing or confiscation of these firms when war broke out, combined with heavy customs tariffs on 'luxury products' such as gramophones, allowed a British industry to take off, even if it was handicapped by the shortage of raw materials.[101] The total value of production in Britain soared from £74,000 in 1907 to £2.3 million in 1924.[102] In 1914, 90 per cent of gramophones were imported; by 1924, only a quarter were. British industry continued to depend, however, on American capital investment and technological innovation.[103]

In 1914, the gramophone, invented some twenty years earlier, was out of the reach of most ordinary citizens. For the price of one record containing two songs, one could buy six tickets for a music-hall show, and for the price of the cheapest gramophone, 220 tickets. Many soldiers had never seen such a machine; others would have listened to hit songs on one on a day out to the seaside, in specialist shops, wearing a sort of stethoscope. Or they might have heard classical music on a gramophone in a public park concert (despite poor amplification) organized by one of London's borough councils.

The better-off recruits might have read the adverts in *The Times* praising the latest models of gramophone, like this one:

> So accurately is this sound reproduced … that even scientific analysis shows practically no variation from the original … more than a mere gramophone – it is a musical instrument constructed by the largest and most eminent firm of musical instrument builders in the world: its designers are – men who have given their whole lives to the study of sound in its relation to musical instruments. Its tone is richer, of greater depth and roundness than has ever before been obtained in a tone-reproducing instrument, and it is the only gramophone that is provided with a completely practical and musically satisfactory means of tone control – the Graduola device. [104]

The Pathé company sold its machines for prices from £5 to £63. In 1914, a portable model was produced which allowed officers, or even rank–and-file soldiers, to listen to music in the trenches. Lockwood Gramophones, moved by patriotism or the desire to corner the market, decided to produce only the portable models for the duration of the war, and to sell them only to military hospitals.[105]

The gramophone companies also produced the records, featuring top hits of pantomimes, musical comedies and music hall as well as classical music, opera, sketches, lectures and language classes. At this time, artistes were not linked by

---

[101]   *The Times*, 25 September 1914.
[102]   Nott, *Music for the People*, 13.
[103]   Ibid., 19–20.
[104]   *The Times*, 3 November 1916.
[105]   *Phono Record*, March 1917.

exclusive contracts to specific record companies and it was not unusual to record the same song for four or five different studios. We must remember though that records remained very much less important than live shows. The hit song 'Take Me Back to Dear Old Blighty' sold 38,000 copies in 1916; but during that one pantomime season, 60,000 people must have heard it *every evening* on stage.

Governmental bodies, and pressure groups

The government fixed the statutory framework for the industry. There were rare instances of censorship even in peacetime, but informal pressure was almost always sufficient. In 1912, an MP protested in the House of Commons debate about a musical comedy which was alleged to be insulting to the Indian princes allied to the British Empire. The song in question was rapidly changed.[106] The government also acted as a mediator in industrial disputes in the entertainment industry, as we have seen, and, during the war, frequently intervened in connection with the rationing of precious resources.

Local authorities involved themselves in various ways in the economy of the musical show. They organized cheap classical concerts, often aiming at popularizing English composers, which attracted audiences from all social classes. 'Penny concerts' by choral societies were also very successful. These events were hosted in dozens of municipal concert halls such as Saint George's Hall in Liverpool, which had been established in the 1850s, with the declared aim of entertaining and elevating the masses. Such initiatives were part of a much wider trend towards the 'elevation' of working-class people, including the advent of universal primary education from 1870, and the building of town libraries: there were 295 of these across the country by 1900.

It was also local authorities which accorded permits to music halls: permits for musical entertainment and/or permits to sell alcoholic beverages. Losing a licence was a real danger for music-hall managers, even those belonging to the major chains. In London, in 1917, five halls lost their alcohol licence, and one was refused an entertainment licence, while another, belonging to the Stoll circuit, regained its licence on the promise by Mr Stoll himself that 'nothing to which the least objection could be taken should be presented'.[107]

The music industry was surrounded by organizations which criticized the entertainment provided, and occasionally tried to supply alternatives. Among the most influential were the temperance leagues, who campaigned against the consumption of alcohol, often encouraging individuals to 'sign the pledge' to no longer drink alcohol. The current had a long history: even within Chartism, the great campaign for democracy of the 1840s, 'temperance Chartism' had been influential. The National Temperance Federation, an organization with links to

---

[106] Hansard, *House of Commons Debates, February 1912, vol. 34, cc1543–1544.*
[107] *The Times*, 2 November 1917.

the Liberal Party, had been set up in 1884. These campaigns had real influence: by 1900, the 'gin palaces' where only hard liquor was sold, had practically disappeared.[108] The coming of the war was seen by temperance leagues as an opportunity to put forward their ideas. One such body organized factory-gate meetings at the textile mills in Burnley throughout the war years. The leagues contributed to the government decision to reduce the alcohol content in ale, and to limit pub opening hours, a reform which was to mark British culture for the whole of the twentieth century. Meanwhile, political and military leaders denounced the dangers of drink: Lord Kitchener asked civilians not to treat soldiers to drinks, Lloyd George declared that alcohol was a greater threat to the war effort than were German U boats, and the King himself swore off alcohol 'for the duration' from April 1915.

The leagues also wished to demonstrate that one could amuse oneself without recourse to alcohol. In Glasgow, the Glasgow Abstainers' Union organized very popular concerts every Saturday evening in the town hall. These were produced continuously from 1854 to 1914.[109] A number of music-hall managers in the town rallied to temperance values and no longer served alcohol in their venues, as well as staging, among other attractions, singers of temperance songs such as 'My Drink is Water Bright' or 'Dare to Be a Daniel':

> Standing by a purpose true,
> Heeding God's command,
> Honour them, the faithful few!
> All hail to Daniel's band!
>
> Dare to be a Daniel,
> Dare to stand alone!
> Dare to have a purpose firm!
> Dare to make it known.

The dominance of the Presbyterian religion among Scottish elites was a strong encouraging factor in moves towards temperance. In London and elsewhere there were quite a number of 'temperance music halls' which enjoyed real success, though neighbouring bars might do good business in the interval. After 1883, in London, for example, there was the Royal Victoria Hall and Coffee Tavern, and in 1890 the King's Temperance Music Hall opened in Stepney. Many other venues did not have a licence to serve alcohol, without being temperance venues as such. In 1909, of Oswald Stoll's twenty-nine halls, only eight sold alcohol, while in Burnley only one venue had a drinks licence.

---

[108]   Small organizations still exist today: for example, the one at http://www.sonsoftemperance.abelgratis.co.uk.

[109]   Maloney, *Scotland and the Music Hall*, 7.

Temperance organizations were not the only ones criticizing and intervening around the entertainment industry. Edwardian socialist organizations did so too, in particular the Fabian Society, the Independent Labour Party and the Social Democratic Federation.[110] The debates in these organizations showed tensions between those who accepted the superiority of the whole of 'high culture' and so limited their demands to that of increased access to high culture for workers, and those who believed an 'authentic' working-class popular culture, could be encouraged, created or rediscovered. Many socialist leaders in Britain subscribed to the ideas of 'rational leisure' put forward over the previous fifty years by sections of the elite. This current supported the right of working-class people to leisure activity (and aided the foundation of libraries, parks, lecture theatres and choral societies, for example), but it also aimed at 'improving' the workers, drawing them away from 'vulgar' pursuits, and often hoped in addition to help neutralize social unrest. The rational leisure movement represented 'both a series of activities the middle classes urged workers to adopt and a way of talking about leisure'. In particular it was opposed to 'frivolity or unmeaning mirth'.[111]

The rise of mass leisure gave rise to debates among socialists. Increasing commercialization and domination by larger firms was denounced by many, but others replied that these changes had improved the quality of the entertainment enjoyed by workers. The socialist magazine *The Clarion* rejoiced that music hall had tempted working-class people away from more vulgar and alcoholic activities. The centre of the debate became the perceived need to raise the cultural level of ordinary people, rather than challenge any ideological content in the music hall show.

Like the temperance organizations, socialist groups did not content themselves with commenting on the entertainment industry. They also proposed alternatives, albeit on a small scale. The Fabian Society, a grouping of socialist intellectuals aiming at a gradual transformation of society, demanded the municipalization of the entertainment industry, feeling it was an essential part of social life and so should be organized by a public, accountable body. They believed that the commercial supply of entertainment was bound to reveal itself to be 'cheap tawdry and demoralizing'.[112]

Other socialist activists founded their own institutions. The 'Socialist Sunday Schools', of which there were 200 around the country by 1912, aimed at countering the influence of religious catechism schools, but also at encouraging rational leisure and raising the demand for culture among the workers.[113] Another important initiative was the creation of a network of socialist choirs, the Clarion Vocal Union, which was also a way of recruiting, through leisure activities, new activists to the socialist movement (a network of Clarion cycling clubs followed

---

[110] Which became the British Socialist Party after 1911.

[111] Chris Waters, *British Socialists and the Politics of Popular Culture 1884–1914* (Manchester: Manchester University Press, 1990), 22.

[112] Ibid., p. 41.

[113] See *The Socialist Sunday Schools Song Book* (Glasgow, S.L. Press, 1919).

a similar objective).[114] The Vocal Union's objective was both to encourage wider participation in singing, and to popularize 'non-commercial' forms of song. From 1897 on, for thirty years, an annual competition of socialist choirs was organized (though it was suspended from 1915 to 1922 due to transport difficulties).

Socialist choral societies were not without their contradictions. All too often, the choice of 'good music' to sing simply corresponded to the taste of the middle-class socialist leaders. As Waters comments in his study, 'voluntarism often smacked of elitism'.[115] The book *Songs for Socialists*, published in 1888 (and again in 1890, 1912, 1916 and 1922)[116] was the songbook most commonly used by the choirs. Almost half the songs were written by socialists for the movement, the rest being made up of old Chartist hymns or poems by Percy Shelley or William Morris set to music for the purpose. Waters undertakes a detailed study over time of music used by one choral society in Bradford. He notes that, in particular with the rise of choral society competitions, the music used becomes much more technically demanding, and the presence of 'non-socialist' music (generally canonical choral pieces) more common. It becomes clear that it is one thing to desire the creation of a great cultural space for the socialist movement, independent of commercial or outside cultural influence ; it is quite another to succeed in this quest. The socialists had some small-scale success in showing alternative possibilities for cultural activities, but these had little weight compared with that of the entertainment industry.

The deluge

The most important actors of the entertainment industry have now been introduced. Like the whole of European society, this industry, this community, this entertainment, were thoroughly shaken up and reshaped by the arrival of total war on the stage of history. It is difficult for us who have not lived through total war to imagine the cataclysm: 10 million soldiers were to die, 23 million would be wounded, and every aspect of life in society – economic, social, psychological and cultural – would be changed forever.

The popular music industry was actively involved in the war drive from the first day, its constituents generally identifying the interests of the British Empire with the interests of humanity as a whole, of freedom and of decency. If popular enthusiasm in 1914 has often been overstated,[117] it is clear that the minority which opposed the war was very much marginalized in Britain. Music halls immediately staged short patriotic war plays, and allowed Army recruitment speakers to intervene at the beginning or the end of shows, with the keen support of several

---

[114]   Waters, *British Socialists*, 126.

[115]   Ibid., 49.

[116]   *Songs for Socialists* (No place: Fabian Society, 1912).

[117]   Adrian Gregory deals with this question in depth in *The Last Great War: British Society and the First World War* (Cambridge: Cambridge University Press, 2008), 9–40.

favourite stars, who sometimes worked along the lines of 'two shillings for the first man to join the Army here tonight !'[118] After a few months of war, halls refused to employ men of military age.[119]

The government was aware of the importance of places of entertainment. In September 1914, a letter was addressed to London theatre managers requesting them to put up recruitment posters and stage patriotic songs. In most cases, the variety theatres, used to reacting to current events, had already planned a large amount of 'patriotic' content. Indeed, the halls were to be be important for recruitment, and would also host innumerable benefit shows to raise money for all manner of 'war charities' in order to help the wounded, the widows, the blind or the orphans, or to send gloves, cigarettes or bibles to the troops out in France and elsewhere.

At the very beginning of the war, the entertainment industry lost a great deal of money; the London Theatres of Variety chain alone lost more than £10,000 in the first three weeks.[120] An emergency agreement was negotiated with the variety artistes' trade union for the reduction of wages in theatres where attendance had dropped sharply. A pro-rata system of remuneration was worked out to share out the losses. Artistes and managers were extremely worried about the effects of the war on the industry, but a few months later when it became clear that attendance was back to normal, if not higher, the unions withdrew from the agreement.[121]

Music publishers produced large numbers of war songs, and sent free scores to soldiers who requested them, to be used in amateur shows near the front line or in training camps.[122] Lyricists wrote songs to keep up morale, gramophone companies sent free records, and artistes put on free entertainment in hospitals and on the Western Front.[123] Trade unions of the various professions worked together to ensure that all German immigrants were excluded from the industry. Above all, many men from the sector volunteered to join the army, under heavy pressure from practically the whole of the leadership of civil society (and no doubt encouraged too by the frequent unemployment they endured in their chosen career). Politicians, intellectuals, feminists and trade unionists called on men to join up, and family pressure could also be an important factor. Further, after the first few months, men of military age might be booed as they went up on stage, a sure-fire way of curtailing their chances of getting further contracts in theatres. They might even receive a white feather, the symbol of cowardice distributed to civilian men of military age after a campaign initiated by Mrs Humphrey Ward, the anti-suffragist,

---

[118]   Horrall, *Popular Culture*, 192.
[119]   *The Encore*, 3 February 1916.
[120]   Crowhurst, 'The Music Hall', 178.
[121]   *The Encore*, 21 January 1915.
[122]   *The Encore*, 11 February 1915.
[123]   A short silent film on this entertainment is available at www.britishpathe.com/video/grand-fete-leyton-hetty-king-and-george-mozart-ent/.

was taken up by feminist leaders Emmeline and Christabel Pankhurst.[124] Even in parliament, concern was expressed about the bad example shown by young men who continued to appear on stage during the war; a report was commissioned on the subject.[125] In the columns of *The Performer* in 1915, a proposal was made for a battalion recruited exclusively from music-hall workers, along the same lines as the 'Pals battalions' which the government had set up early on in the war, to allow men recruited from the same town to be part of the same military unit.

The nature and depth of popular enthusiasm in the early months of the war has been the subject of considerable polemic. Motivations for joining up would be varied and even contradictory, for men of the entertainment industry as for others.[126] The perspective of escaping from poverty, patriotic conviction and social pressure all contributed to enlistment. Yet it should not be forgotten that only half of fit men between the ages of 19 and 25 volunteered.[127]

The enthusiasm of 1914 faded fast in the face of the horrors of war, but the pro-war consensus maintained itself in most sections of the population. In 1915, only seven of the delegates at the Trades Union Congress voted against the war. The music-hall milieu, ever anxious to appear respectable, may have been more permeable than most to war propaganda. Nevertheless, while mobilizing for the war drive, industry leaders and other actors worked hard to defend their own economic interests. The attempts by theatres to avoid suffering from rationing and curfew policies have already been mentioned. But the war provided new opportunities to make money while remaining patriotic. A 1915 advertisement urging theatre managers to hire a refugee singer, gives a glimpse of the commercial instrumentalization involved:

> Joseph Henry is the possessor of a magnificent baritone voice, and he is introduced by J. E. Cooke, who relates Joseph Henry's experiences while escaping from the terrible onslaughts of the German armies. Let your audience hear the truth about the German atrocities! Without doubt the cheapest top bill act touring at present.[128]

Music publishers, lyricists, theatre chains and gramophone companies had similar opportunistic attitudes. In this they were perhaps no different from thousands of other companies who hoped to make money from the war, like the 'bullet-proof

---

[124]   Will Ellsworth-Jones, *We Will Not Fight...: The Untold Story of World War One's Conscientious Objectors* (London: Aurum, 2008), *passim*.

[125]   Hansard, *House of Commons Debates, 13 May 1915, vol. 71, c1803.*

[126]   Gregory's contribution was mentioned above. David Silbey, *The British Working Class and Enthusiasm for War, 1914–1916* (London: Frank Cass, 2005), attempts a psychological analysis.

[127]   Bernard Waites, *A Class Society at War: England 1914–18* (Leamington Spa: Berg, 1987), 190.

[128]   *The Performer*, 7 January 1915.

vest' manufacturers who advertised in local newspapers ('a shield worn like a bulletproof jacket: deflects revolver bullets and shrapnel. We pack and post to any front. Single 35 shillings, double 70 shillings. Recommended by a major general.').[129]

This chapter has aimed at describing and perhaps bringing to life the actors in British show business as it was a century ago. In the following chapter, the different types of show will be examined, for the most part commercial initiatives, but also non-commercial ones such as free shows to entertain the troops far from home.

---

[129]   *Burnley Express*, 27 January 1917.

A Star in Focus 1
Harry Lauder – 'Scottish ambassador'?

'Men don't cry here when they die, they smile.'[1]

Allegedly described by Winston Churchill as 'Scotland's greatest ever ambassador',[2] Harry Lauder was thought to be King Edward VII's favourite artiste.[3]

Lauder was born in 1870 and began working in a factory at the age of 12. His working-class origins were an important element in his success. He would become the first British artiste to sell a million gramophone records, and was one of the rare stars of the time to write his own songs.

On stage, Lauder appeared in character as a stereotypical down-to-earth, canny and miserly Scotsman, wearing a kilt and carrying an improbable walking stick. He sang of love for his betrothed ('My Bonny Bonny Jean', 1916) and of nostalgia for the lovely landscape of the highlands ('Back Back to where the Heather Grows', 1917), but also performed comic songs ('Stop Your Tickling, Jock', 1905, or 'The Reason Now I Wear a Kilt',1906) and Scottish traditional pieces (such as 'A Wee Deoch an Doris',[4] or 'Loch Lomond'). This extract from 'Stop Your Tickling, Jock' gives something of the flavour:

> Oh I'm courting a farmer's dochter, she's one of the nicest ever seen
> Her cheeks they are rosy red, and her age is just sweet seventeen

Being from a strict Presbyterian background, he avoided all suggestive content and any reference to 'immoral' activities. His pieces often contain a part which is recited, and another part sung, and are characterized by a larger than life bonhomie, often interrupted by a loud laugh which sounds false to modern ears.[5]

In the course of his career Lauder sang over a hundred songs, and became a roaring success on his 22 tours of the United States, as well as in South Africa,

---

[1]   From a 1918 monologue 'Granny's Laddie', which can be heard on YouTube at https://www.youtube.com/watch?v=lnKVkzfIunM (accessed 16 July 2014).

[2]   Ian Peddle, 'Playing at Poverty: the Music Hall and the Staging of the Working Class' in *The Working-Class Intellectual in Eighteenth- and Nineteenth-Century Britain*, ed. Aruna Krishnamurthy (Aldershot: Ashgate, 2009).

[3]   A number of photographs are available at http://parlorsongs.com/issues/2004-12/thismonth/feature.php (accessed 22 January 2015).

[4]   Original recording at https://www.youtube.com/watch?v=Q6XBOw73kno (accessed 29 July 2014).

[5]   A number of original recordings can be found at http://www.archive.org/details/HarryLauder (accessed 16 July 2014).

Australia and New Zealand. On his arrival in the USA in 1907, he was welcomed by a crowd of Scottish expatriates who festooned his car with tartan. 'However much he consorted with millionaires and presidents ... he retained a down-to-earth demeanour and a classless inclusive appeal that suited the New World.'[6] Already in 1911, he could pocket up to a thousand dollars a show, the equivalent of over twenty thousand dollars today.

During the war years he threw himself heart and soul into the war drive: he formed a military band which toured the country appealing for recruits. Lauder himself spoke out often and loudly at rallies urging people to do their patriotic duty. As one observer remarked, he 'made a speech which had in it nothing to laugh at. It was a speech from the real Lauder, divested of paint and trappings. Stern and straight, it was a challenge to every free young man to get into khaki.'[7] Lauder's autobiography is filled with anecdotes about men who later thanked him for having talked them into volunteering for the army, and he emphasizes the personal links he retained with many men who had gone to the front.

In 1916, he went on a singing tour of the Western Front, and gave hundreds of – sometimes impromptu – concerts very close to the front line (see Chapter 2). Back home, he launched a collection aiming at raising a million pounds for the care of wounded soldiers, who received at the time little government aid.

His patriotic songs were often hits – 'While the British Bulldog's Watching at the Door'', 1915; 'The Laddies Who Fought and Won', 1916. After his own son was killed in the war, he sang 'Keep Right On to the End of the Road'[8] in an attempt to boost flagging enthusiasm for the war amongst the British people. On tour in America in 1918, Lauder bitterly denounced the fact that the German language was still taught in US schools, and that German-language newspapers could be published and sold.[9] After the war, he was knighted for his services to the country and celebrated the armistice with a new song, 'Don't Let Us Sing about War Any More, Just Let Us Sing of Love!'

His stage character, which seems just as present in his three autobiographies as in his act,[10] was that of a romantic and conservative, hail-fellow-well-met Scotsman, who defended 'common sense' and 'good old values' and communicated in a very mild form of Scots dialect, in order to be easily understood by English and Commonwealth audiences. Music-hall specialist W. Titterton described how his fans experienced his act:

---

[6]   Paul Maloney, *Scotland and the Music Hall, 1850–1914* (Manchester: Manchester University Press, 2003), 176.

[7]   Private J. Quigley, *The Slogan – Sidelights on Recruiting with Harry Lauder's Band* (London: Simpkin, 1916), 14.

[8]   A 1920s recording of Lauder singing this can found at https://www.youtube.com/watch?v=vbM86eiczAg (accessed 29 July 2014).

[9]   *The Performer*, 23 May 1918.

[10]   Harry Lauder, *A Minstrel in France* (New York, Hearsts, 1918); *Between You and Me* (New York: James A McCann, 1919); *Roamin' in the Gloamin'* (London: Hutchinson, 1928).

The lilt of the music runs through his body … you feel happy and comfortable and you don't know why … you see the slow deliberate thoughts puckering his brow, you mark the deliberate gesture and the halting speech … and yet one longs for the exuberance. And when the exuberance comes it carries us away, and leaves us with a pleasant taste in the mouth and a sense of the Sun having shone upon us.[11]

Lauder and other 'stage Scotsmen' have been criticized by some Scottish writers, in particular those connected with a Scottish nationalist tradition, since such acts were seen as aiming at amusing the English with stereotypes of Scottish people. Nationalist and poet Hugh MacDiarmid (1892–1978) went as far as to say that he had 'never met a single intelligent Scott who would be seen at a Lauder performance'.[12] But it is clear that opinion was divided. Lauder was popular in Scotland, too, and among the Scottish diaspora in the USA and in Australia. According to some, his staging of Scottishness allowed an expression of pride in Scottish identity, in a period which was difficult for the nation.

He carried on performing until as late as 1935, and came out of retirement to entertain troops during the Second World War. He died, at the age of 79, in 1950.

---

[11] David Cheshire, *Music Hall in Britain* (Newton Abbot: David & Charles, 1974), 77.
[12] Maloney, *Scotland*, 2.

Chapter 2
A Patchwork of Genres

In the first chapter, we met the hundreds of businesses and theatres, the thousands of singers and the tens of thousands of other actors in the entertainment industry. The coming together of their diverse economic, ideological and artistic objectives and the wartime audiences was to give rise to over a million shows of all kinds, put on during the war years. How can such a deluge of entertainment, such a multitude of ephemeral evenings out, be understood? How can these phenomena be put into the context of a society at war and of the history of popular music? The issue will now be approached from two viewing perspectives: firstly that of genre, and then that of the songs themselves. Each genre has its specific artistic content, but also its own social rules and values, since, in wartime as at any other time, the musical show can define the person who attends it almost as much as it entertains them.

By the start of the twentieth century, the variety of shows available was immense. As Peter Bailey, the most influential of the specialists in music hall, reminds us: 'when a man walked out of the factory gates in the big industrial city, he was in a sense freer than in any previous age'.[1] And during the war, the shows were not simply a matter of individual enjoyment: the authorities understood the crucial importance of morale, and therefore of leisure activities, whether for civilians or soldiers. Lord Derby, Minister of War from 1916 on, declared:

> The people's amusements ... should go on ... Let those who come home be met with cheerful faces. Let them feel that their leave from the trenches should be marked by amusements that will abstract them from all the anxieties and dangers.[2]

The fact that the minister felt the need to make this declaration shows that it remained a little controversial, and some occasional dissenting voices could be heard, like the gentleman who wrote to the local newspaper in Burnley complaining of those who, he claimed, wasted their money on tickets for the music hall instead of feeding their families.[3] Such opinions were isolated: Neville Chamberlain himself, head of national service, had insisted that 'the amusement of the people is

---

[1] Peter Bailey, *Leisure and Class in Victorian England: Rational Recreation and the Contest for Control, 1830–1885* (London: Routledge & Kegan Paul, 1978), 4.

[2] *The Era*, 31 January 1917.

[3] *Burnley Gazette*, 17 October 1914.

an essential part of national work'.[4] In the following pages, we shall present each of the major genres of musical entertainment from the war years.

The era of the music hall

Musical entertainment shows came in many forms, but the first and most important was music hall. Novelist, inventor of Jeeves, and keen observer of contemporary mores, P. G. Wodehouse wrote in 1909:

> Historians, when they come to deal with the opening years of the twentieth century, will probably call this the Music-Hall Age. At the time of the great invasion the music-halls dominated England. Every town and every suburb had its Hall, most of them more than one. The public appetite for sight-seeing had to be satisfied somehow, and the music-hall provided the easiest way of doing it. The Halls formed a common place on which the celebrity and the ordinary man could meet.[5]

Indeed music hall was in its Golden Age: serious or comic singers performed – alongside short plays, acrobats, classical music interludes, ventriloquists, magicians and many more – to mass audiences. The front page of local newspapers around the country carried adverts for the halls; in the small industrial town of Burnley there were three music halls and one cinema in 1914. Gramophone companies did all they could to persuade music-hall stars to record for them, while the biggest stars were regularly interviewed by the press and sought out lucrative sponsorship deals.

The music-hall genre had changed considerably since the 1860s. There was no more eating and drinking in the auditorium, and an entrance fee was charged rather than the owner relying on the sale of drinks for profitability. The newer halls were grand 'variety theatres', with thousands of seats. The show had also become somewhat more tranquil, one now rarely had to complain 'on a bank holiday' that 'the audience was traditionally drunk and riotous'.[6] The nineteenth-century habits of throwing nuts – or steel rivets[7] – from the balcony if the singer was not up to par, and hiring a bouncer to drag unsatisfactory artistes from the stage, had disappeared.[8] During the war, additional restrictions on alcohol, and the

---

[4]   *The Era*, 7 March 1917.

[5]   P. G. Wodehouse, *The Swoop! Or How Clarence saved England* (London: Alston Rivers, 1909), chap. 2. Online at http://www.gutenberg.org/ebooks/7050 (accessed 22 July 2014).

[6]   James Harding, *George Robey and the Music-Hall* (London: Hodder & Stoughton, 1990), 19.

[7]   Judith Bowers, *Stan Laurel and other Stars of the Panopticon* (Edinburgh: Birlinn, 2007), 106.

[8]   Harding, *George Robey*, 28.

absence of millions of young men away at the war, calmed the atmosphere further. 'There is very little of the old fashioned chucking out these days,' one reads in the trade press in the middle of the war. 'Certain halls have at certain times become notorious for disturbances by groups of young people ... fortunately there is less beer being drunk and so less drunkenness now.'[9]

The carefully-timed music-hall show played from two to six times a day. The industry was becoming evermore professional, more and more artistes hired agents, and the stars commanded big salaries. Fierce competition prevailed between acts and between theatres; each artiste worked freelance, negotiating his or her salary according to popularity. The present study is to concentrate on musical entertainment, but let us first look at the turns which came before or after the songs on the music-hall stage, and which established the atmosphere which influenced the choice and content of songs performed.

Many acts aimed to impress by their novelty, such as Fred Dyer, billed as 'the celebrated Welsh singing boxer',[10] the cyclists from the Far West,[11] the handcuffed violinist[12] or Frou Frou, 'the French dog that understands the English language'.[13] Lockhart's elephant act might be followed on stage by a spiritualist. Faith healers such as Mr Bodie, who decorated the theatre doorways with the crutches his patients no longer needed, were very much in demand. Or one might see Rex Fox, 'the ventriloquist on the high swinging wire'.[14] Lightning cartoon artists, hat jugglers and sharpshooters waited in the wings.

The culture of the time still finds it acceptable to exhibit disabled people as 'human freaks' for entertainment, and a number of acts are based on this desire. At the Panopticon in Glasgow, bearded women, dwarves and people born without arms and legs are part of the show. The owner of this music hall even opened, a few doors down from the theatre a museum of 'human freaks' including 'the ugliest woman in the world'. This last, whose name was Mary Anne Bevan, would go on to win an ugliness contest against fifty rivals, in London in 1918.[15] At the Bristol Empire, one could see in 1904 'the fat boy from Peckham'. If one believed the billing, he was five and a half years old, weighed 72 kilograms and was putting on three-quarters of a kilogram every day.[16] The same year, Siamese twins played the violin on stage, and, in 1916, 'Frederick the Great, the giant' was part of the bill.[17]

---

[9]   *The Encore*, 29 March 1917.
[10] *The Encore*, 16 July 1914.
[11] *The Performer*, 21 January 1915.
[12] Ibid.
[13] *Burnley Express*, 1 January 1916.
[14] *Burnley Gazette*, 26 September 1914.
[15] Bowers, *Stan Laurel*, 135.
[16] Terry Hallett, *Bristol's Forgotten Empire: The History of the Empire Theatre* (Westbury: The Badger Press, 2000), 45.
[17] Ibid., p. 65.

From the 1880s on, music halls began to include more prestigious art forms in the mix. In Burnley in September 1914, extracts of Verdi's opera *Il Trovatore* were presented, whereas the Coliseum in London presented songs from Wagner's operas just before the outbreak of war,[18] and in 1917, one could hear classical music played on a 'gigantic eight-ton cathedral organ built at a cost of two thousand pounds', which needed, the advertising pointed out, nine railway wagons to transport it on its tour around the country.[19] In May of that year, another touring show presented extracts from different operas, and violinists or cellists playing classical music would often figure on an evening bill.[20] In the Hippodrome, a famed Russian pianist was performing.[21] In the continuous attempt to attract audiences, the Coliseum decided to present non-canonical examples of high culture: in 1914, twelve performances of *The Awakening of a City* and *The Meeting of Automobiles and Aeroplanes*, by the Futurist leaders Marinetti and Russolo were programmed. According to *The Times* on 16 June:

> [The piece's] weird funnel-shaped instruments resembled the sounds heard in the rigging of a channel-steamer during a bad crossing, and it was, perhaps, unwise of the players – or should we call them 'noisicians'? – to proceed with their second piece after the pathetic cries of 'no more' which greeted them from all the excited quarters of the auditorium. The audience seemed to be of the opinion that Futurist music had better be kept for the Future. At all events, they show an earnest desire not to have it at present.[22]

Ballet, which had been replaced by opera in late Victorian times as the favourite entertainment of the elite (being then considered too sensual to be respectable), survived in Britain because of its presence in the music hall.[23] Between 1884 and 1915, two of the most important halls in London, the Alhambra and the Empire, produced no fewer than 141 original ballets. Although sandwiched between other acts, they were the main attraction on the programme.[24] In 1918, Diaghilev produced his *Ballets Russes* at the Coliseum.

Short plays, sometimes by established playwrights, were included in the evening's entertainment, in particular after the 1912 law which formalized the authorization for music halls to present plays, provided they last no longer than 40 minutes. The same year, J. M. Barrie, author of *Peter Pan*, agreed after much hesitation to have his plays grace the stage of the Coliseum. The same Coliseum

---

[18]   *The Encore*, 23 July 1914.
[19]   *Burnley Express*, 27 January 1917.
[20]   *Burnley Express*, 9 May 1917.
[21]   *The Encore*, 24 May 1917.
[22]   *The Times*, 16 June 1914.
[23]   For an excellent full-length study, see Alexandra Carter, *Dance and Dancers in the Victorian and Edwardian Music Hall Ballet* (Aldershot: Ashgate, 2005).
[24]   Ibid., p. 1.

presented the following year extracts from Shakespeare, concentrating on some of the more dramatic scenes, such as the battle scene in *Richard III*, with a hundred soldiers fighting on stage. Even *The Times* was impressed.[25] During the war years, extracts from Shakespeare became commonplace in halls around the country.[26]

George Bernard Shaw also wrote short plays for the Coliseum. In his preface to *Annajanska, the Bolshevik Empress*, in 1918, he stressed that he did not want to approach the music-hall audience in a condescending manner: '[Let it not be said that] we would set down the art of the variety theatre as something to be condescended to, or our own art as elephantine. We should rather crave indulgence as three novices fresh from the awful legitimacy of the highbrow theatre.[27]

Top actors and actresses might also be staged in the halls. Sarah Bernhardt, by far the most famous of French actresses at this time, played the Coliseum on a number of occasions, the last in 1916, and provoked the anger of some who were shocked to see a great actress abase herself by appearing at a music hall.[28] Oswald Stoll, the Coliseum's owner, had agreed to pay her £1,000 a week for her contribution, which had the additional merit of keeping his theatre on the front page of the newspapers. Lena Ashwell, the great British Shakespearian actress, played in patriotic melodramas at the Coliseum: the war atmosphere allowed her to accept performing on stages which previously would not have seemed sufficiently respectable for her work. [29]

Naturally, the vast majority of the hundreds of short plays[30] performed were written and acted by far less well-known people. During the war the patriotic melodrama was a frequent part of the bill. In September 1914, a short play was touring in which a German soldier offers money to a young British man who needs it in order to save the life of his dying mother; the British man hesitates at first, but, walking by a music hall and hearing the patriotic choruses from within, he understands his duty, refuses the money and strangles the enemy soldier. Another play, *Pro Patria*, shows a French governess raped by a German officer, while in a third piece a German soldier is killed in cold blood because he dares to start a conversation with the fiancée of a British infantryman.[31] Later in the war, in 1917, one could see the short play *A Daring Exploit*, which showed, with sumptuous

---

[25]   Felix Barker, *The House that Stoll Built* (London: Frederick Muller, 1957), 99.

[26]   Raymond Mander and Joe Mitchenson, *British Music Hall: A Story in Pictures* (London: Studio Vista, 1965), 30; Hallett, *Forgotten Empire.* 65.

[27]   George Bernard Shaw, *Annajanska, the Bolshevik Empress* (London: Kessinger, 2004; first published 1918), preface. Available on line at http://www.gutenberg.org (accessed 30 July 2014).

[28]   Barker, *House that Stoll Built*, 107.

[29]   Margaret Leask, 'Lena Ashwell: Actress, Patriot, Pioneer' (PhD thesis, University of Sydney, 2000), 158.

[30]   At the time they were often referred to as 'sketches', though they were frequently around half an hour long.

[31]   Barker, *House that Stoll built*, 118.

special effects, a German warship attacked by a British submarine.[32] The same year, *For Those in Peril on the Sea*[33] recounted the dangerous lives of the sailors at war, while the following year[34] *In the Trenches* was a success across the country.[35] Other pieces such as *The Wartime Philanthropist*[36] presented a moralist message about the efforts required of civilians in wartime.

Plays could cover other social and moral questions. The editorial of *The Encore* in 1917 complains:

> The threatened tide of sketches dealing with syphilis and its attendant horrors appear to be commencing. We are very sorry to see it is so. We are no advocates for hiding the truth ... however, the music halls are not places for ventilation of public questions and controversies.[37]

By this time, cinema was also a regular feature on a music-hall programme, having first been included in 1896.[38] Cinema represented competition to music hall and its sister genres, since it offered a cheap evening's entertainment, but while it remained silent, the danger was contained. To reduce the effect of the competition, almost all variety theatres now included short cinema films at the end of the evening. In the war years, these were often short films about the activities of the army and the navy; *The Times*, in December 1916 for example advertised a tour of war films from around the world.[39] Audiences keen to understand what their loved ones were going through so far away, flooded in;[40] the popularity of war films was even greater due to the fact that in the first years of the war there was little censorship, the government having not yet understood the importance of the medium.[41]

Despite this tremendously rich commercial and artistic mix in the music halls, singers remained at the centre: love songs, comic songs suggestive or parodic, moving ballads or patriotic refrains, including more often than not a sing-along chorus (sometimes the songs were simply referred to as 'chorus songs'). Among the singers, there were representatives of art music – opera sopranos or baritones, whose virtuosity, along with the prestigious glow of high culture, may have constituted their primary appeal. Other turns were hybrid: Odette Myrtil 'sings

---

[32]   *The Encore*, 7 January 1915.
[33]   This is also the title of a very well-known hymn.
[34]   *The Encore*, 4 January 1917.
[35]   *Burnley Express*, 26 January 1918.
[36]   *The Encore*, 4 January 1917.
[37]   *The Encore*, 5 July 1917.
[38]   Mander and Mitchenson, *British Music Hall*, 28.
[39]   *The Times*, 26 December 1916.
[40]   *Burnley Express*, 2 February 1916.
[41]   For a comprehensive analysis, see Michael Williams, Michael Hammond and Angela Williams (Eds) ,*British Silent Cinema and the Great War* (London: Palgrave, 2011).

a French song and plays the violin whilst dancing'.[42] For the most part, though, singers were distant from high culture. Far more common were such artistes as 'the Dublin street singer',[43] and, especially, singers of comic songs, either playful ditties or pieces imbued with ironic social comment.

Andrew Horrall underlines the fact that music hall aimed to be always up to date;[44] we shall see that the songs reflect the latest events of the war. Music-hall singers will sing about the popularity of ragtime, about rationing, conscription or the new tanks of 1916, just as before the war they had sung about suffragettes, automobiles and the introduction of National Insurance.

Who was filling the halls? If all contemporary observers insist that more and more of the 'middle classes' are present in music-hall audiences, it must be borne in mind that the category 'middle class' can include large numbers of government clerks and shop workers whose living conditions were hardly privileged. They might work in offices, keep their hands clean, and feel themselves somewhat more 'classy' than miners or factory workers, but salaries were low and job security non-existent. The histories written of the first trade unions for tax workers or for government clerks suggest that the differences between them and manual workers were often more psychological than material. One tax office clerk wrote that in 1909: 'our work ... was hard and pay and conditions atrocious. I was often working late hours till 10pm for 32 shillings and sixpence per week when I became first clerk in Bradford ... Overtime pay was then practically non-existent and sick leave negligible.'[45] As for government clerks, their starting salary was £45 a year, less than that of a butler, who, moreover, would receive board and lodging free.[46]

Elite groups often continued to feel that the music hall was not for them, despite the occasional royal patronage of variety from 1912 on, and the availability of private boxes in the new variety theatres. Daring acts, such as that of Marie Lloyd,[47] were particularly frowned upon. Nevertheless, the elite would know many of the music-hall hits from pantomime (see below) or from sheet music. The more bohemian members of the elite might go to the music hall looking for an energy and freshness which seemed to them to be lacking in 'legitimate' theatre.[48] At the other extreme of a deeply divided society, the poorest sections of the population could attend music hall only occasionally; but they, too, would know the hits well through street singers.[49]

---

[42] *The Encore*, 4 January 1917.

[43] *Burnley Express*, 19 January 1918.

[44] Andrew Horrall, *Popular Culture in London 1890–1918: The Transformation of Entertainment* (Manchester: Manchester University Press, 2001), *passim*.

[45] A. J. Brown, *The Taxmen's Tale: The First Ninety Years of the Inland Revenue Staff Federation* (London: IRSF, 1983), 7.

[46] Eric Wigham, *From Humble Petition to Militant Action: A History of the Civil and Public Services Association 1903–1978* (London, CPSA, 1980), 18.

[47] Daniel Farson, *Marie Lloyd and Music Hall* (London: Tom Stacey, 1972), 57.

[48] Carter, *Dance and Dancers*, 11.

[49] Robert Roberts, *A Ragged Schooling: Growing up in the Classic Slum* (London: Fontana, 1978), 50.

Turning to the question of gender, music-hall audiences had changed tremendously since their beginnings in the 1860s, when the audience was very much male-dominated. The percentage of women had steadily risen. *The Times* announced itself delighted with this development, proof, it felt, of the increasing respectability of the genre.[50] For the period 1901–1914, Alexandra Carter notes that in the North of England women were able to go to the music hall alone or with female friends without people being shocked, and during the war, we see for example the wife of a clerk in Glasgow frequenting the music hall with her sister without adverse comment;[51] in London this was more difficult, since a woman unaccompanied by a man could well be seen as 'loose'.[52] Indeed, music halls were often accused of being places where prostitutes touted for business. Nevertheless, in all regions, the absence of their menfolk and the higher wages available to women meant that 'unaccompanied' women were becoming a more common sight at the halls.

Much of our information about wartime audiences is anecdotal. Vesta Tilley declared that 'women and girls were almost always in the majority among my audiences,'[53] and that 'the factory and market girls were my great admirers, and many a humble tribute of their appreciation would they nervously hand to me'.[54] We know that Ella Shields, another male impersonator, was popular in Lesbian circles.[55] We know little, too, about the age of the members of the audience; a number of sources, though, suggest a large number of under-sixteens were present. This serves to remind us that adolescence hardly existed at the time for the working class: at twelve, as often as not, the boys were apprentices and the girls domestic servants.

The revue, victory of a new format

The music hall had its rivals and some of them were becoming threatening: the war years saw the rapid rise to prominence of the revue. Several hundred revues were presented during the conflict; some of the biggest variety theatres abandoned traditional music hall to do only revue. From 1913, the London Hippodrome took this road, and the following year the Palace followed suit.[56] In Bristol, the Empire suddenly switched to revue only, in 1914. By 1917, there were 32 major revues touring Britain, as well as those showing in the capital.[57] In September of that

---

[50] *The Times*, 24 January 1910.

[51] Thomas Livingstone, *Tommy's War: The Diary of a Wartime Nobody* (London: Harper Press, 2008).

[52] Carter, *Dance and Dancers*, 10.

[53] Matilda De Frece, *Recollections of Vesta Tilley* (London: Hutchinson, 1934), 124.

[54] Ibid., 113.

[55] Farson, *Marie Lloyd*. 140.

[56] Mander and Mitchenson, *British Music Hall*, 170.

[57] *The Era*, 3 January 1917.

year, of seventeen halls run by London Theatres of Variety, seven were presenting revues and ten traditional music hall. Moreover, those theatres which stayed with the old format often now integrated short revues, occupying half the evening.[58]

Revues drew big crowds; even in the provinces, audiences could be impressive. In Bristol in 1915, the revue *Passing Events* sold 25,649 tickets the first week, a record for the town.[59]

Bevan comments:

> this was an era when the word 'revue' almost ousted 'variety' in the lexicon of the halls. Every show had to have a chorus and a title: the title, if possible, suggesting that the chorus had plenty of sex appeal and not too many clothes. Finally the Lord Chamberlain[60] had to send round a strongly worded circular letter which curbed the excessive display of feminine charms.[61]

If there is truth in what he says about the rapid rise of revue, he is far from being a neutral observer and, in any case, the vast majority of titles of revues which we have found have nothing suggestive about them. From an economic point of view, the revue represents a rationalization of the use of capital. Instead of a constantly changing bill made up of individual turns, each hired for a different length of time according to their popularity, a revue was relatively fixed, and could tour the country as a single unit, thus allowing economies of scale, groups of dancers, and more special effects.[62]

From an artistic point of view, it is also a centralization and the artistic director now has overall control. There is less margin for manoeuvre for the individual artiste, especially if their turn is in the habit of expressing dissent; there is more teamwork and hierarchical management. In her 1915 song 'If You Want to Get On in Revue', Marie Lloyd comments ironically on the discipline needed to join a revue team:

> Where are the ladies? Where are the shadies?
> The Lizas, the Lotties and Lous?
> Where have they gone to? You know they want to
> All go in Revues!
> Girls don't go off to work, all business now they shirk
> They've got in Revue
> On Revue there's now a run, and if you'd like to go in one
> I'll tell you what to do

---

[58] *The Encore*, 11 January 1917.

[59] *The Performer*, 7 January 1915.

[60] The person in charge of theatre censorship.

[61] Ian Bevan, *Top of the Bill: The Story of the London Palladium* (London: Muller, 1952), 46.

[62] Although the touring version of a revue was sometimes a reduced one.

Well, you've got to do this and you've got to do that
If you want to get on in Revue.
Your Maudies and Bessies must wear pretty dresses
And a dainty little shoe!
Plenty of ginger, snap your finger
Let the Johnnies in the stalls get a view!
Have a smile on your face, show a little bit of lace
If you want to get on in Revue.[63]

According to his biographer, the music-hall star George Robey had particular difficulty adapting to the discipline of a team effort.[64]

As so often in the history of popular music, this new format, the revue, was seen by many contemporary commentators as a terrible sign of the decline of popular culture. Macqueen Pope takes this view: 'True music hall was dying, largely because its individualists had sunk their individuality, the very backbone and marrow of Variety, into team work called "revue".'[65]

The specialist press of the time shows that many artistes were somewhat alarmed at the rapid rise of the new format. 'In the good old days it was all single or double turns, now these expensive productions are all the rage' wrote the editorialist of *The Encore* in 1917, expressing the hope that government pressure for less sumptuous special effects would tip the balance in favour of old-fashioned single turns.[66] The Two Bobs, two artistes of US origin who settled in Britain and had a successful career, expressed in their hit 'Get a Job in Revue', the bitterness of music-hall artistes faced with this threat, mixed in with a misogynous tone so common in the music hall. The song recommends ironically that young women should work in revue 'If you've got no talent and you've got no sense... if you are good-looking and you want some pence'. Only the women's physical attributes are of any importance, the lyrics insist; and they claim that revue is an excellent way to find a husband.

Revue took further management strategies which had already existed in some theatre chains. Even before the war, Oswald Stoll, owner of the Coliseum, had frequently chosen himself the songs he wanted singing in his music hall and then engaged appropriate singers to perform them. In this way, he was moving away from the traditional music-hall set-up which had relied on the initiative of the independent individual artiste creating his or her act under pressure from audience and management demand. The revue was a fully hierarchical enterprise. The

---

[63]   In the whole of the present work, the choice of lyrics quoted is very much influenced by copyright issues. If lyricists died after 1944, it is very difficult to quote their work at any length. We have generally then quoted lyricists who died earlier.

[64]   Harding, *George Robey*, 85.

[65]   Walter MacQueen Pope, *Marie Lloyd, Queen of the Music Halls* (Norwich: Oldbourne, 1957), 165.

[66]   *The Encore*, 15 March 1917.

director would adjust, right up to the very last moment, the content of the show, and the song or business which seemed not to please the audience, or appeared to slow down the action, would be cut the following week.

The revue created, as the musical comedy had, new permanent groups of skilled workers such as chorus girls. The music-hall orchestras and the ballet choruses had already been constituted as proletarianized groups over previous decades. It is difficult to know exactly how many dancers there were in this period, since the census classed them with 'actresses'. Nevertheless, it is clear that their numbers were rising rapidly: in 1883, there were 2,368 in London in this category, and by 1911 there were 9,171. [67] These dancers were recruited among the working class, earned about as much as textile workers, and began work on stage at the age of 13. [68]

Many in the music-hall milieu hoped that revue was just a passing fad, and that the reign of individual turns would be back in a few years' time. In the columns of *The Performer*, one commentator remarked in 1915:

> The nondescript entertainment which, no doubt for the want of a better title has been christened 'revue', has shown itself possessed of greater staying power than most folk were inclined to credit it with at the outset ... it is now a more or less serious competitor to the single turn. [69]

In 1917, the editorialist of *The Encore* wrote hopefully 'the public is tired of revue'. [70] But the centralizing logic of revue, which allowed a more coherent and sophisticated entertainment experience created by a team, was, it seems, bound to triumph.

A revue was typically structured around a theme or a narration, even if, as *The Times* pointed out, the plot was rarely very tight:

> The general trend of musical comedy was towards looser technique, the provision of a greater amount of variety with less and less of plot. ... Then came revue, which merely did not trouble about a plot at all. and has lately all but dispensed even with the compere and commere. Revue, in fact, did what musical comedy had never quite dared to do. [71]

Sometimes the theme is clearly announced in the title, as in the case of the revues *Irish, and Proud of It, Too,* (1916), *Hullo, America!* (1918), *Honeymoon Express* (1917), *Jolly Jack Tar* (1918), or *All Scotch* (1915). But this was generally not the case – as in the examples of *Not Likely* (1914), *Zigzag* (1917), *Joyland* (1915), or *Follow the Crowd* (1916).

---

[67] Carter, *Dance and Dancers*, 29.
[68] *Ibid.*, 42.
[69] *The Performer*, 4 March 1915.
[70] *The Encore*, 17 May 1917.
[71] *The Times*, 9 February 1914.

Revue generally eliminated from the stage those music-hall turns which resembled circus acts (acrobats, animal imitators or ventriloquists) and put song and sketches at the centre of the show. The revues recruited artistes who had proved their pulling power on the music-hall stage, and offered them a longer-term contract. Revues toured the country, making use of national advertising and reinforcing the domination of the market by bigger companies. On the social and ethical side, revue was perceived as another step towards respectability for the variety theatres. In her autobiography, Vesta Tilley expressed her satisfaction that 'the theatre was packed night after night with distinguished audiences'.[72]

Each new revue had to offer something original in order to increase its chances of being a hit, and dealing with current affairs was one useful strategy. This was considered so important that one commentator suggested that a revue could be played which changed some of its content every day according to that day's news.[73] Indeed, current affairs often contributed significantly to success. At the end of the revue *Kultur*, in 1915, one could see the actors playing German soldiers 'drowned' on stage in the enormous tank normally used for synchronized swimming displays.[74] The same year another show took as its title *Business as Usual*, a journalistic expression used to underline the hope that the British would not allow their everyday ways to be excessively impacted by the war. *The Better 'Ole*, a tremendous success which continued for 811 shows from 1917 on, took as its subject the life of long-suffering soldiers on the Western Front. The title came from a well-known cartoon by Bruce Bairnsfather in which an older, experienced, sardonic soldier replies to a youngster complaining about their position, hiding in a shell hole in no-man's-land, 'Well if you know of a better 'ole, you go to it!' This revue was well-received by critics, even if *The Observer* felt it was 'unduly spun out, perhaps because there is a limit to the humorous side of war'.[75]

A close look at a revue from the same year with an openly patriotic title, *Follow the Flag*, allows us to see the studied mix which was typical of revue. One song spoke of the pain of separation ('From Somewhere in France to Somewhere in Somerset'), and one song (but only one, the dosing is careful) of love of the flag of the motherland ('Dear Red, White and Blue'). The theme of the girls is present and problematized: you have the song about the angelic girl 'Red Cross Maid' and the comic song about girls who are a little more threatening to established gender roles ('Flappers Three'). In addition, there is one comic song about Lancashire ('Oop to Lancashire') and another about a particular job ('Wig Wag Signal Corps').[76]

A number of other revues are based on a war theme. *Shell Out* from 1915 includes songs such as 'If the Girlies Could Be Soldiers'. The title obviously promises a war theme, though the *London Standard* complained: 'There is nothing

---

72 De Frece, *Recollections*, 94.
73 *The Era*, 12 September 1917.
74 *The Encore*, 7 January 1915.
75 *The Observer*, 12 August 1917.
76 *The Encore*, 7 March 1917.

in the way of a plot or any particular reason … why it should be called "Shell Out". Any other title would do equally well …' The chorus featured 'Some twenty really pretty girls in deep, orange-coloured frocks and black velvet garters emphasising their deep orange-coloured stockings'.[77] The same year, the show *Is That Official?* ironized on the prevalence of rumour in wartime and the lack of confidence in government information, while *Razzle Dazzle*, in 1917, featured on stage a tank recently returned from the Western Front.[78]

Revue was well and truly on its way, and whether it dealt lightly with current affairs or concentrated on tales of romance, it would remain tremendously popular right up to the end of the 1920.

Once a year, the seasonal pantomime

The Christmas show which the British call 'pantomime', and which, I point out for the benefit of non-British readers, has no resemblance to mime, is in fact a topical musical comedy which follows a set of fairly strict rules. It originated in the eighteenth century as a sort of comic opera. During the nineteenth century, it developed into a much more topical show, commenting on the latest fashions and events. The number of accepted storylines was vastly reduced, and the pantomime began to approximate to the type of show still produced in Britain today. Now it was a show based on a fairy story, often taken from Perrault's tales,[79] which incorporated popular song hits from the previous year, and topical jokes. Other rules included that the male lead be played by a young woman, and that one of the old women characters (the 'dame') be played by a man. The pantomime thus continued a long tradition of cross-dressing in popular theatre and carnival.

From the 1860s on, pantomime began to hire music-hall stars to play lead roles, to the disappointment of the more traditionalist sections of its audience. At the beginning of the twentieth century, Vesta Tilley and Violet Lorraine, among dozens of others, played the male lead in different pantomimes; George Formby Senior adapted his character of dour Lancashire working man to the pantomime,[80] and George Robey played the traditional pantomime dame.[81]

Pantomime audiences were more working-class than those of musical comedy, and yet pantomime was more respectable, less likely to shock the elite, than was music hall. In the first quarter of the twentieth century, these pantomime shows played a particular role in the economy of the song industry, as we have explained in the previous chapter. The whole year round a single artiste generally had the right to sing a given song on stage, but during the Christmas season temporary

---

[77]   *London Standard*, 25 August 1915.
[78]   *The Encore*, 4 January 1917.
[79]   Charles Perrault, the seventeenth-century French collector and reteller of folk tales.
[80]   *The Encore*, 4 February 1915.
[81]   Harding, *George Robey*, xvi.

singing rights were sold for songs integrated into a pantomime. A music-hall hit which had sold hundreds of thousands of copies in sheet music would be bought by at least a dozen theatres for their pantomime. Thus, in 1917, the song 'Are we downhearted? No!' was sung by at least 14 stars in different shows around the country.[82]

At the beginning of December each year, the first pantomime of the season went on stage in Glasgow. For the music publishers, it was an occasion not to be missed: a song which excited audiences at this first venue would be bought by many other theatres around the country and would become a best-seller. In Glasgow 'agents from all the popular publishers were at hand to see that their hope of the season was not pushed out by some unscrupulous rival'.[83]

The featured songs, such as 'There's a Girl for Every Soldier', sung in 18 pantomimes in 1917, were generally of the joyful tone so characteristic of the music hall. But pantomime had also to include topical references. A joke about the suffragettes' latest activities, or some minister's latest scandal was de rigueur. The comic actor George Graves explains that he was often asked in pantomime to add a verse to one of his songs to refer to a recent event.[84] Otherwise, pantomimes in December 1917 included a number of songs about Americans, in reaction to the USA joining the war. Conversely, after the Easter rebellion in Dublin in 1916, songs to the glory of Good Old Ireland tended to disappear.

Musical comedy, a more expensive show for all the family

From one point of view the pantomime was a type of musical comedy, but musical comedy was an all-year-round genre of its own. Musical comedies arrived in Britain at the beginning of the 1880s. It is a far more modest sector than the music hall, the revue or the pantomime: only a few dozen musical comedies are produced during the war. The musical comedy is based around a plot, and the songs and action are not mixed in with acrobats, magicians or other circus turns. Musical comedy is more prestigious and respectable, and much more expensive, than music hall or even revue, to such an extent that 'legitimate theatre' feels threatened by it.

Musical comedy audiences have often been described as 'middle-class'. The imprecision of this term, often more a marker of prestige than of social class, has already been commented on. Bailey maintains that the centre of gravity of the genre was 'further down the social scale' than that.[85] As far as the presence

---

[82]   *The Encore*, 7 January 1915.

[83]   John Abbott, *The Story of Francis, Day & Hunter* (London: Francis Day & Hunter, 1952), 59.

[84]   George Graves, *Gaieties and Gravities – The Autobiography of a Comedian* (London: Hutchinson, 1931) 136.

[85]   Peter Bailey, 'Naughty but Nice: Musical Comedy and the Rhetoric of the Girl', in *The Edwardian Theatre, Essays on Performance and the Stage*, ed. M. R. Booth and

of women in the audience is concerned, we have little information, although the family nature of the content is clear. George Graves, who starred in many musical comedies, complained that the matinee audiences were more dominated by women, and more difficult to please.[86]

Musical comedy attracted significant criticism. Its rise did not threaten music hall, but the socially prestigious 'legitimate theatre' in which such playwrights as George Bernard Shaw, John Millington Synge and J. M. Barrie held sway. A well-known playwright, Henry Arthur Jones, complained in 1906 that English theatre was being killed off by musical comedy, and that the audiences were now only interested in seeing pretty girls' legs.[87]

But outright denunciation of musical comedies was a minority viewpoint. The establishment's leading newspaper, *The Times*, analysed with interest each new musical comedy which was staged. George Graves, who spent most of his career in musical comedy, dismissed the critics: 'It is of course the habit [of snobs] to dismiss light musical entertainment as trivial nonsense designed by Philistines to regale the want-wits. Yet I have never seen a vapid musical comedy succeed.[88.]

Musical comedies would sometimes hire tried and tested performers who were already stars in the music hall, and would integrate styles and songs from that genre. Sumptuous decor and costumes were de rigueur, and a wedding finale highly recommended. Intense teamwork served up a highly polished product to enthusiastic crowds.

Unlike operetta and pantomime, musical comedy would often set its stories in contemporary Britain. Without aiming frankly at realism, it would present situations and professions which belonged to the modern world. One smash hit of the very first years of the century, *The Shop Girl*, told the tale of a shop assistant in a department store; in *The Dollar Princess* of 1909, characters include groups of secretaries and businessmen; and in *The Boy*, a 1917 hit, we see the work of financiers and magistrates. During the war years, musical comedy concentrated on producing light entertainment to help people forget, for a few hours, the terrible war. *The Times* explained in 1915 that 'the only new theatrical productions in immediate prospect are of the lighter kind- either musical comedy or revue'.[89] Musical comedy dealt with war questions immeasurably less than did music hall or even revue, and tended to avoid them altogether. Indeed, during the war 'exotic' settings, far from the war, characterized the most popular shows. *Chu Chin Chow*, a 'Chinese' version of the story of 'Ali Baba and the Forty Thieves' broke box-office records in 1916–1917, totalling 2,238 showings. *The Maid of the Mountains* (1917), set among bandits in the Italian mountains, was also a great success (1,325 showings). In a period where few members of the audience would travel

---

J. H. Kaplan (Cambridge: Cambridge University Press, 1996), 53.

[86] Graves, *Gaieties and Gravities*, 150.

[87] Quoted in A. E. Wilson, *Edwardian Theatre* (London: Arthur Barker, 1951), 209.

[88] Graves, *Gaieties and Gravities*, 153.

[89] *The Times*, 1 November 1915.

abroad (except as members of the army), exotic settings could be presented with little difficulty.

The audiences of the time were, at least as much as today, fascinated by the lives of the rich. Only a generation earlier, in the English countryside, 'lowly' people would bow or curtsey when the local elite passed by in a carriage.[90] It is unsurprising, then, to see so many musical comedy plots built around the affairs of the bourgeoisie: in this, musical comedy marks a very sharp break with music hall's interest in everyday working-class life. Many of the plots resemble those of P. G. Wodehouse's novels or Oscar Wilde's plays. The plot of *The Lilac Domino* (1918) presents the story of a very rich 'ladies' man' who must stay away from the female sex for 48 hours or forfeit a million pounds; while in *Yes, Uncle,* a somewhat wild ex-girlfriend from long ago reappears in the life of a man who is now married and settled in polite society. Other shows include good numbers of princesses from distant lands, heiresses travelling incognito and maids who end up marrying dukes.

Peter Bailey explains that the representation of sexuality is a central aspect of musical comedy, and that the nature of the genre is to operate in a 'blithely manipulating mode' with respect to its audience.[91] Thus, sexuality, which was one of the important themes of music hall, expands and moves to centre stage. The representation of the heroine of the musical comedy is characterized by a fierce rejection of those women who are excessively 'respectable' and inaccessible to men, and by a parallel – but far less fierce – rejectionof the 'loose woman'. The heroine should turn out to be 'modern' and 'liberated' while remaining 'respectable'. Seduction tactics may be used to 'catch' a man, with the aim of marriage or for other objectives. The culture of the time frowned on women taking initiatives in their private lives, and one may consider that the more proactive women presented on stage might encourage women to play a more confident role in their own lives.

It was as well for a musical comedy to be in some way topical, and to parody or praise the latest developments in fashion or in manners. In 1912, *The Sunshine Girl* included tango dance numbers, reflecting the very recent arrival of this dance in London. The new public figure of the film star was explored in *The Cinema Star* in 1914.

Competition was ferocious and capital investment very heavy. Musical comedy changed quickly, each producer hoping to find the 'next big thing'. In this business, 'The successful impresario had to be a gambler', explains Pearsall.[92] Even those who managed to produce a hit show, had no guarantee that their follow-up piece would be a success, as Robert Courtneidge discovered when he lost £20,000 on the show *The Mousme* in 1909, which presented a 'Japanese' story

---

[90]   Flora Thompson, *Lark Rise to Candleford* (London, Penguin, 2000 (1945)), 254.
[91]   Bailey, 'Naughty but Nice', 55.
[92]   Ronald Pearsall, *Edwardian Popular Music* (London: David & Charles, 1975), 23.

complete with realistic earthquake scenes. 'No one had the magic touch.'[93] In his autobiography, George Graves recounts the different shows he played in during the Great War. *Mind Your Step* was a success, chalking up 275 showings, but the two of the subsequent shows he played in were failures (*We're All in It* and *Head Over Heels*). The 1914 musical comedy The *Bond Street Girl* had to ring down the curtain after only 40 nights.

A successful show would then tour Britain, or even the USA, South Africa and Australia. Sometimes for financial reasons, the touring show would be a pared-down version of the original production.[94] Occasionally, it would even tour without the original stars, hoping nevertheless to benefit from the reputation forged in the West End. In his autobiography, George Graves gives a taste of the show business atmosphere of opening night:

> Can Miss Somebody change from her morning dress into pyjamas in time, now that the producer has cut the butler's comic business, which was put in earlier to cover the wait but which at dress rehearsal seemed to hang up the action at the vital point?[95]

While music hall, made up of individual, independent turns, and still partly dependent on the local roots of some artistes, could not be dominated by American capital, musical comedy had much more of a modern relationship with the industry in the USA. The arrival in Britain of a number of US shows was not without causing some friction. *The Times* explained that 'The general complaint against American musical comedy is its noise and the breathless speed at which it is played' and congratulated the producer of the musical *Adele* for having avoided these defects.[96] Elsewhere, *The Times* refers to 'the long list' of American productions being staged in London.[97] Indeed, such shows as *The Happy Day* (in 1916) or *Very Good, Eddie* (in 1918) played first in New York before coming to the British capital. It would not, however, be until the 1920s that a true American domination of musical comedy came to pass.

From an artistic point of view, the musical comedy, like the revue, is a team product. From a political point of view, the socially mixed audience and the heavy investment in special effects and, dance troupes tend to impose an even stronger consensus than in music hall, and there is little space for dissenting or radical content. Finally, from an economic point of view, the musical comedy is another instance of the concentration of capital and of economies of scale within the entertainment industry. The money flowed easily, and directors would spend large

---

93 Ibid., 41.
94 *The Encore*, 4 January 1917.
95 Graves, *Gaieties and Gravities*, 146.
96 *The Times*, 4 June 1914.
97 *The Times*, 27 September 1915.

amounts in order to integrate into their production artistes and songs which had already been tried and tested in the music-hall market.

Blackface minstrelsy, the remains of a racist genre

Another type of show, which gave rise to a genre of song, is that of blackface minstrelsy. This was a variety show presented by a troupe of white men in blackface, disguised as caricatures of Black Africans. Blackface minstrelsy originated in the United States, and was imported to Britain in the 1830s, becoming very popular indeed. Many music-hall stars, such as Dan Leno, Little Tich and Harry Champion, began their careers in Blackface. The representation of Black people in the shows was unapologetically racist, in this period when the colonial 'scramble for Africa', and the rise of a literate working class in Britain would combine to produce the imperial 'need' for a new kind of popular racism.[98] But, as Pickering demonstrates, the success of the shows was also due to a real artistic development, which mixed in elements of Irish music, American slave culture and the European clown tradition. As the decades went by, the minstrel shows developed a very precise structure, involving singing, sketches, acrobatics and dance, and were built around the central roles of a pretentious and arriviste Master of Ceremonies and his clownish sidekick playing tricks on him, all of this generally carried on in a stage caricature of Black American vernacular. Pickering explains that the clowns 'supplied a ludicrous element essential to the sense of release, and temporary abandonment of prevailing norms, that made the minstrel show so popular'.[99]

British and American versions of minstrelsy exhibit considerable differences. In the USA, the audience was mostly made up of White working-class men, and the ideological effects of the shows were related to the relations of the audience to an ethnic minority very much present in their everyday lives.[100] In Britain, the audience was considerably more 'respectable' (and the seats were more expensive) than in the music hall, and the absence of a visible Black minority in the audiences' lives reinforced the 'exotic' perception of the representation of Black people.

It was from the 1870s in Britain, that the minstrel show enjoyed a genuine boom in popularity:

> [It] caught the fancy of an amusement starved public and was almost the only alternative to the doubtful humor of the music Hall of the period. Minstrelsy was a form of family entertainment where husband-and-wife could take their children without fear of being asked embarrassing questions afterwards.[101]

---

[98]   John Mullen, 'Anti-Black Racism in British Popular Music 1880–1920', *Revue française de civilisation britannique*,, special issue in memory of Lucienne Germain (2012).

[99]   Michael Pickering, *Blackface Minstrelsy in Britain* (Aldershot: Ashgate, 2008), 15.

[100]   Ibid., 3.

[101]   Abbott, *Francis,Day & Hunter*, 8.

The genre was in a continuous process of professionalization, and its tremendous success lasted twenty years until musical comedy came to be its most serious rival. After 1890, musical comedy attracted audiences away from minstrelsy, perhaps because it was a more flexible format which could deal with more topical themes. It was also true that the all-male tradition of minstrelsy could not deal with male–female relations in a suggestive manner, as musical comedy could. It seems that the decline of blackface minstrelsy in this period was not connected with a rejection of racist representations. There appear to be no records of criticism of minstrelsy on these grounds in Britain; nevertheless it may be that, after the abolition of slavery in the USA in 1865, the theatrical representations of 'stupid black slaves' became little by little to have an outdated feel to them. In the United States, there had been antiracist criticism of the shows: indeed, the great abolitionist Frederick Douglas wrote as early as 1848 that minstrel performers were the 'filthy scum of white society, who stole from us a complexion denied to them by nature, in which to make money, and pander to the corrupt taste of their fellow white citizens'.[102]

Although the full evening minstrel show was clearly in decline by 1900, the genre gave rise to street performers and music-hall turns of blackface singers and comics. These continued to be popular, particularly as open air shows at seaside resorts. Thousands of amateur troupes also existed:[103] during a charity procession in 1907, we see seven separate blackface minstrel troupes in Crewe, which at the time had population of 50,000.[104] In the slums of Salford before the Great War, Robert Roberts informs us that many groups were formed for a local minstrel troupe competition.[105]

During the war years, the best-known professional blackface artistes were G. H. Elliott (stage name 'The Chocolate-Coloured Coon') and G. H. Chirgwin ('The White-Eyed Kaffir'). The latter performer had a novel characteristic: instead of making up the whole of his face in black, he left a white coloured diamond over his right eye, as if the white Chirgwin was peeping out from behind the black mask. This acted as a distancing mechanism. The stage personality of Chirgwin 'was as much cockney as nigger, and in this he contrasted with some other performers who wanted their nigger mask to be "realistic"'.[106] The popularity of Chirgwin was such that one can see in contemporary photos, British soldiers disguised as Chirgwin, with the characteristic diamond over one eye.[107]

---

[102] Quoted in Tracy Ryser, 'A White Man's Inadequate Portrait of a Slave: Minstrel Shows and Huckleberry Finn' (Master's diss., University of Youngstown, 2004), 3.

[103] In the DVD of archive footage, *The Lost World of Mitchell and Kenyon* (London: BFI Video, 2005), examples can be seen from the early twentieth century.

[104] Pickering, *Blackface Minstrelsy*, 57.

[105] Roberts, *A Ragged Schooling*, 63.

[106] Pickering, *Blackface Minstrelsy*, 98.

[107] Claude Ribouillault, *La musique au fusil, avec les Poilus de la Grande Guerre* (Rodez: Editions du Rouergues, 1996), 83.

As well as these star acts, there were at least a dozen other blackface professionals in wartime music halls, as well as many amateurs. In 1915, one could see a novel act on tour of a young 'negro imitator' only eight years of age.[108] In 1919, at the Bristol Empire, one could see Harry Spiers, 'The Unbleached Coon'.[109] A number of revues incorporated blackface performers, and on tour in July 1917, there was even an 'All Black' revue.[110] The performer Jack Woods, 'the imaginary nigger', was a hit in the revue *Miss Paris* in 1915.[111] The revue *Come Over Here*, the same year, included a blackface entertainer,[112] while in the United States the most famous revues such as Ziegfeld's *Follies* included blackface acts.

The blackface artistes were almost all men, though after 1890 there were a few women. Bessie Wentworth, well-known singer of 'Looking for a Coon like Me', died in 1902, but others took up her mantle. In 1917, a certain May Henderson signed a ten-year contract with a music hall for her blackface act.[113]

All in all, then, blackface minstrels constituted only an occasional feature of the shows of the war years. Blackface was not to disappear quickly, however. The seaside version thrived, and famously Uncle Mack's minstrels gave three shows a day in the season in Brighton for several decades beginning in 1900.[114] In *The Times* of 8 January 1932 an article regrets their decline, but television versions of blackface, such as *The Black and White Minstrel Show*, could be seen on television in Britain until 1978.[115] For the television show, racist songs, but not the stereotyped disguises, were taken out.

Musical entertainment on stage was, then, of tremendous variety on the outbreak of war. Minstrelsy had declined radically, and music hall was being successfully challenged by revue, while musical comedy was winning new audiences especially in London. Revue and musical comedy, with their need for socially mixed audiences and high levels of capital investment, seemed to represent the future. As a result, the coexistence in the course of a single evening's entertainment of singing and circus-like acts was becoming rarer, whereas dancing and theatre modes of communication were becoming dominant alongside song.

---

[108] *The Performer*, 18 February 1915.
[109] Hallett, *Forgotten Empire*, 82.
[110] *Burnley Express*, 4 July 1917.
[111] *The Performer*, 4 February 1915.
[112] *The Times*, 30 November 1915.
[113] *The Encore*, 19 July 1917.
[114] When 'Uncle Mack' died in 1949, a monument to him was erected in the town. A clip of one of his shows from the 1930s can be viewed online at http://sasesearch.brighton.ac.uk/view/?film=1018 (accessed 30 July 2014).
[115] Its sister stage-show closed in 1987, after a final tour of Butlins holiday camps.

Amateur shows by and for the soldiers

Entertainment in the towns of the UK aimed at maintaining civilian morale, but wounded soldiers and soldiers on leave were very much present in the halls. Ordinary British soldiers got little leave – three times less than the French, for example. Officers received far more, which was often a source of bitterness.[116] So, as soon as it became clear that the war was going to be a lengthy business, the question of entertainment for troops stationed abroad was raised. Hundreds of thousands of shows were produced, in France, Palestine, Greece and elsewhere. In general, the type of show closely follows existing entertainment which the troops were accustomed to at home, though this entertainment has some particular characteristics. Firstly, the economic motive is almost entirely absent. Secondly, the audiences are almost completely masculine, and living a far harder life than audiences in the UK. It may be also that the audiences were considerably more socially mixed than home audiences. The army reflected a socially divided society in an even more acute form, but during a troop show, all ranks were together in the audience.

In the first 18 months of the war at least 64 of the British Army divisions set up divisional entertainment troupes, and innumerable smaller units established battalion or company troupes.[117] Spontaneous initiatives, at first frowned on by the military hierarchy who feared that frivolity might make their men less virile, these troupes later enjoyed solid support from commanding officers. Their members were excused many military duties and worked full-time to write and rehearse shows. Dozens of theatres were built, or barns converted, generally to make halls with 400 to 800 seats.

Any music-hall professionals in a division were very much in demand, though most performers were amateurs. Costumes and sets were created from locally available resources, or begged from Britain – the music-hall trade press printed requests for donations of costumes, sheet music and gramophone records. This tremendous wave of entertainment activity overtook by far comparable phenomena in the French or German armies. A British soldier stationed near Arras in August 1917 reported: 'within five minutes' walk of our camp no less than four large concert halls had now been erected, and every night concert parties gave first rate concerts, to which all troops were admitted for the sum of half a franc'.[118]

The shows attracted a mass audience. It was said that one pantomime by an ambulance company was presented in front of an audience of 35,000 soldiers. Information on one of the 64 divisional troupes shows that it played 250 shows in its first year. If all the troupes were as busy, that would make a total of 15,000

---

[116] J. G. Fuller, *Troop Morale and Popular Culture in the British and Dominion Armies 1914–1918* (Oxford: Clarendon, 1990), 73.

[117] Ibid., 94ff.

[118] Quoted by Fuller, *Troop Morale*, 97.

shows a year for the divisional troupes alone, and no doubt five times as many if all troupes were counted.

This entertainment was part of a wider drive to amuse the soldiers, and keep them out of trouble. Soldiers would typically spend two weeks 'in reserve' or 'at rest' for each week in the front-line trenches. Even if 'rest weeks' generally included much construction and maintenance work, as well as interminable marching and drill to satisfy the rigid and sometimes sadistic desires of superior officers, a semblance of normal life could be organized. Much alcohol was drunk, and the army organized day trips to the seaside or to the horse races. Football was played constantly, both improvised games and formal tournaments, which could at times attract several thousand spectators. 'Officers against sergeants' games were tremendously popular, not least because the officers, often more accustomed to rugby, almost always lost.[119]

To return to the shows, the most common format was that of the music-hall variety evening. The turns would frequently imitate those of the big stars back home. Performers would sing the hits of Harry Lauder, George Robey or Albert Chevalier, or play Harry Tate's comic sketches. A typical show, from September 1917, included a take-off of Charlie Chaplin, a 'lady singer' (in fact a disguised man) and a 'Scottish' comedian. The 'lady singers' delighted the crowds, singing love songs while they attempted to appear as realistically female as they could. They often had lingerie specially bought in Paris, and were the object of many more or less romantic fantasies. Shows by divisional troupes were well advised to avoid any vulgar material, though precise information is difficult to obtain given the vague nature of the concept. Smaller or more informal shows might be nearer the knuckle, or sometimes frankly obscene.

The Christmas pantomime was much awaited each year, and these shows allowed a freedom of expression which was rare in the army. Horrall notes, concerning the large number of pantomimes at Christmas 1915, that 'pantomime allowed common soldiers to criticise Allied leaders and comment on the predicament of unending war service in a manner that was usually forbidden'.[120]

Shows in prisoner of war camps

During the war, 170,000 British soldiers were captured by the Germans. Their stories have long been ignored by historians, no doubt partly due to negative public attitudes towards their experience, which fitted badly with a heroic narrative. The collection by Richard Van Emden of the detailed testimonies of twenty or so ex-Prisoners of War has gone some way to remedy this lack.[121] The prisoners were in many ways lucky, and their smiling faces in photographs seem

---

[119]   Ibid., 85ff.
[120]   Horrall, *Popular Culture*, 195.
[121]   Richard Van Emden, *Prisoners of the Kaiser* (Barnsley: Pen & Sword, 2000).

to show this.[122] Their life expectancy was far greater than that of the soldiers who stayed on to fight, although it is estimated that 10 per cent of prisoners died in captivity.[123] Living conditions were very hard for 'other ranks' though not so much for officers:[124] prisoners often went hungry, particularly at the end of the war when shortage of food hit the whole of Germany. Otherwise, treatment varied widely, and Van Emden's book recounts many stories of kindness as well as of cruelty by the German guards.

Musical entertainment was universally organized in the camps. In the Munster 1 camp, as one prisoner, Jack Rogers, recounts, each nationality staged theatre or variety shows. The British produced every month a music-hall evening, during which Mr Rogers performed songs from the repertoires of George Robey, Harry Champion and Sam Mayo. The inmates worked tremendously hard producing sophisticated costumes and sets. German prison guards often attended the shows, which no doubt helped to reduce the inevitable tensions in such a situation. In another camp, in Dülmen, a theatre seating 600 was built on the order of the German commander. In 1916, the trade journal *The Era* published a letter from a prisoner who described the shows they were preparing in the camp: a revue entitled 'Don't Laugh', diverse Shakespeare plays and 'a real English pantomime', to which the commandant was invited.[125]

Professional civilian shows for the soldiers abroad

Civilian professionals, moved by a desire to participate in the war, requested permission from the army hierarchy to put on shows for soldiers abroad. Others declined to do so: Vesta Tilley, for example, never went to France, claiming that the transport of costumes and accessories was too onerous.[126] Two leading professionals have left comprehensive accounts of their activities in this respect, which allow us to recover the atmosphere and the polemics of the time. Lena Ashwell, a great Shakespearian actress, recounts in two books her work organizing a series of tours of civilian troupes in France,[127] while Harry Lauder, a somewhat jingoistic Scottish comic singer, wrote three autobiographical works.[128] Written in

---

[122]   Ibid., 20.

[123]   Ibid., 179.

[124]   Ibid., 78.

[125]   *The Era*, 6 June 1917.

[126]   De Frece, *Recollections*, 142.

[127]   Lena Ashwell, *Modern Troubadours* (Copenhagen: Gyldenal, 1922); *Myself a Player* (London: Michael Joseph, 1936).

[128]   Harry Lauder, *A Minstrel in France* (New York: Hearsts, 1918); *Between You and Me* (New York: James A McCann, 1919); *Roamin' in the Gloamin'* (London: Hutchinson, 1928). For more on Harry Lauder, see 'A Star in Focus 1' in the present work.

stage Scots, they narrate his tours of France, during which he sang for the troops very close indeed to the front line.

Lena Ashwell, who was well known before the war for her commitment to the campaign for women's suffrage (she was vice president of the Actresses' Franchise League) and for her fundraising work in favour of impecunious actresses,[129] determined, in August 1914, to become involved in supporting the war. She lobbied government to push for a fuller utilization of women's capacities in the prosecuting of the conflict.[130] Shortly afterwards, she decided that the best support she could give to the Empire would be to organize professional entertainment in France. She viewed this work as almost a crusade, writing 'in our professional capacity we might be of as much use and as real a necessity as the Red Cross or St John's ambulance, for does not the soul of man need help as much as its body?'[131] Or again: 'it is the artists who preserve and express the genius of the race, or the cry of a nation's soul'.[132]

At the end of 1914, faced with the indifference of the army chain of command, she launched an appeal, signed by a number of musicians and several bishops, requesting the establishment of a scheme for touring concerts. The first tour began in January of 1915, consisting of 39 two-hour concerts over a period of two weeks. The troupe was made up of a soprano, a baritone, a contralto, a tenor, a pianist, one other musician, and a music-hall artiste. The composition then shows clearly Ashwell's conception of the entertainment which the soldiers were in need of. Ashwell insisted that no artiste should use the tours for the purpose of advancing their own career.[133] She organized benefit concerts in London in order to raise the necessary funds for the tours, and wrote dozens of newspaper articles, with headlines such as 'Singing them to Berlin'.[134] In October 1916, she explained that £100 a week was required to pay for three troupes touring France, one in Malta and one in Alexandria.[135] Already in June 1915, 300,000 soldiers had seen at least one of the concerts. The YMCA became involved in the organization and soon considered it a central part of its work.[136] In addition to the troupes abroad, others toured Britain to raise funds. In all, Mrs Ashwell organized thousands of concerts, and received the gratitude of Douglas Haig himself, who wrote that the events:

> have been a source of endless pleasure and relaxation for many thousands of soldiers. I am, personally, very grateful for the untiring efforts of those who have contributed to make them such a success, and I know that I am only voicing the

---

[129]   Leask, 'Lena Ashwell', 126.
[130]   Ibid., 150.
[131]   Ashwell, *Modern Troubadours*, 4.
[132]   Quoted by Leask, 'Lena Ashwell', 162.
[133]   Ashwell, *Modern Troubadours*, 6.
[134]   Leask, 'Lena Ashwell', 157.
[135]   *Bristol Times*, 13 October 1916.
[136]   Leask, 'Lena Ashwell', 161.

opinion of all ranks of the army in France in wishing that your scheme may not collapse through lack of funds.[137]

The concerts were varied in content, but were far closer to high culture than were the army's own concert parties. 'We had a quartet from the Gondoliers. Then Schubert music. Of course we had at the end some chorus songs', she wrote.[138] Other concerts included Mozart, and the recitation of poems:

The violin is what the men like most. Handel's Largo, Schubert, dances representing national fetes and folk-songs, and the big simple airs, are more appreciated than any chorus-song ... Perhaps in the future good music and good plays will be part of our national scheme of education. In the meantime it seems possible that our national love of the beautiful has been under-estimated.[139]

Lena Ashwell received many letters of thanks, and the tone of some of them reveals something of the attitudes of elites towards the education of their soldiers. Many officers were delighted to see their men listening to classical music; one wrote to her:

the whole tone of your entertainment, the class of music, and the entire absence of vulgarity are a liberal education to the men. After forty years' service I feel convinced that that is what is sadly wanted for our men – and sometimes for others! Everything should be done to elevate them and alter their tastes.[140]

This concern, to 'raise' the cultural level of the ordinary soldier, was shared by quite a number of rank and file men:

looking around, one can see that we men are lower than when we enlisted, mainly because we are shut off from all refining influences, and are unable to get away from the filthiness of conversation in the huts ... Might I offer you a word of advice: don't in anywise lower the tone of your music. I know there are hundreds like myself, who hunger for the riches which your great gift can supply, and it's so helpful.[141]

Other rank-and-file soldiers were less sure. One journalist recounted that he had met soldiers who felt Ashwell's concerts were too 'straight-laced' and 'patronising'. 'There was also some resentment that officers were given the best seats and priority over ordinary soldiers in meeting the artistes.'[142]

---

[137] *Leeds Mercury*, 17 July 1917, quoted by Leask, 'Lena Ashwell', 193.
[138] Ashwell, *Modern Troubadours*, 19.
[139] Quoted by Leask, 'Lena Ashwell', 162.
[140] Ashwell, *Modern Troubadours*, 137.
[141] Ibid., 138.
[142] Leask, 'Lena Ashwell', 183.

Ashwell was delighted to see classical music listened to enthusiastically by ordinary soldiers. She saw herself as a missionary for classical music among the working-class soldiers and she had to struggle, she says, against many prejudices among the elites, who often believed that the 'lower classes' would never be able to appreciate 'higher' music.[143] Her concerts were planned as a contribution to winning the war, and in some cases they seem to have been effective, as witness this letter she received from soldiers of the third army:

> we beg to express to you our deep appreciation of the concerts ... they have brought to us recollections and suggestions of 'Dear Old Blighty'. We confess that we would rather listen forever to their melodies than go back to the horrid orchestra of war, but they have helped us to realize again that we are fighting for the Empire, Home and Beauty and for all they mean in the life of mankind, and therefore we shall go back from our rest to our work with firmer will and sterner purpose.[144]

During the concerts themselves, soldiers often had to leave, called away for trench or other front-line duty, and Ashwell reports that she received many letters asking for concerts to be organized closer to the front.[145] After several months of negotiations, she received permission to organize concerts closer in. 'Of course the party was to consist of men only, and these men had to be over military age or rejected for the army as medically unfit.'[146] Nine teams were sent out, each of four men and a piano (one of the teams travelled around in a double-decker bus). These teams often played to audiences of well over a thousand. The front-line concerts had to be stopped after February 1917, though, since it was no longer possible to find men in good enough health to tour who had been rejected for military service.[147]

In addition to musical events, Ashwell organized theatre group tours in France, playing both Shakespeare and lighter pieces, and herself participated in many of the concerts and plays. 'I have never felt so proud of being an Englishwoman and I never longed so ardently to be an Englishman. Oh! if I could make the laggards at home see, in their mind's eye, something of what I have seen!' she wrote.[148]

Harry Lauder's concert tours on the Western Front

Harry Lauder became involved in the war drive from the very beginning. He organized in Britain the tour of a military band whose objective was to recruit

---

[143]   Ashwell, *Modern Troubadours*, 138.
[144]   Ibid., 140.
[145]   Ibid., 148.
[146]   Ibid., 149.
[147]   Ibid., 167.
[148]   Quoted by Leask, 'Lena Ashwell', 158.

for the army and navy. While on tour in the USA he campaigned for the States to join the war. His son John, who, he says 'was eager to be at the Huns',[149] joined up, was wounded and later suffered a nervous breakdown. After a few months' convalescence, John returned to the front and was killed at the end of 1916. Lauder responded by working even harder for victory in the war. He pushed to gain permission to give concerts in France close to the front line. 'I wanted to go close to the fronts. I wanted to give a concert in a front-line trench where the Huns could hear me, if they cared to listen,' he wrote.[150] It was in June 1917 that he was able to leave for France, authorization papers in hand and accompanied by a pianist-chauffeur, and a specially made five-octave piano which could fit in his car.

His first concert was in a military hospital in Boulogne:

> I had had enough experience in hospitals and camps by now to have learned what soldiers liked best, and I had no doubt at all that it was just songs. And best of all they liked the old love songs, and the old songs of Scotland – tender, crooning melodies, that would help to carry them back, in memory, to their hames and, if they had them, to the lassies of their dreams. It was no sad, lugubrious songs they wanted. But a note of wistful tenderness they liked. That was true of sick and wounded, and of the hale and hearty too – and it showed that, though they were soldiers, they were just humans like the rest of us, for all the great and super-human things they ha' done out there in France.[151]

The wounded soldiers who listened, wrote Lauder:

> had paid to hear me in the dearest coin in all the world – their legs and arms, their health and happiness. Oh, they had paid! They had not come in on free passes! Their tickets had cost them dear – dearer than tickets for the theatre had ever cost before.[152]

After this auspicious beginning, he criss-crossed France in his car, giving hundreds of concerts, often improvised in the open air. He would give up to seven concerts a day, sometimes presented in bomb craters. His shows were made up of three parts. First, an accompanying civilian gave a speech concerning allowances, pensions and other help available to soldiers and their families. In this way material reassurance accompanied political motivations for pursuing the war. After this, a superior officer would speak about the progress of the war and the relative imminence of victory. Finally, Harry himself came on stage with his warlike, romantic, or nostalgic songs, generally with sing-along choruses. Three song titles will suffice to suggest the tone: 'The Laddies Who Fought and Won', 'The Wee

---

[149]   Lauder, *A Minstrel in France*, 43.
[150]   Ibid., 111.
[151]   Ibid., 132.
[152]   Ibid., 141.

House 'Mang the Heather' or 'I Love a Lassie'. The soldier audience was often joined by French villagers from the area he was passing through. Concerts could be tiny or enormous: 7,000 heard him sing in the chateau at Aubigny. For front-line concerts, Lauder sang unaccompanied since the piano could not be carried so far forward. He wrote that the sound of the guns provided an eerie accompaniment – 'I had to adjust each song I sang to that odd rhythm of the guns'.[153]

Understanding the patchwork

We have examined the whole range of genres of popular musical show in the war years. It only remains to emphasize that the frontiers between the genres were often not hard and fast. The choice of the label 'musical comedy' rather than 'revue', for example, might be made principally for marketing reasons. 'Operetta', 'musical play' and 'revue' were labels used without excessive precision. In 1916, a journalist described the show *The Bing Boys Are Here* as having 'something of a musical comedy about it and something of the light opera'.[154] Such overlaps were accompanied by regular attempts to escape standard nomenclature. So one new show in 1914 was announced as being a 'revusical comedy',[155] and another as a 'musical comedietta',[156] the neologisms showing their dissatisfaction with the fixed genres of the time. The same year, the production *Mixed Grill* was presented as a 'burl-revue-esque'! The perceived importance of the choice of labels is shown by the announcement in block capitals in an advertisement for a show in Burnley in 1918: 'THIS SHOW IS NOT A REVUE'.[157]

We are clearly in the presence of a dynamic and creative industry with a carefully crafted range of products. It corresponds little, however, to monolithic ideas of a homogeneous culture industry generating popular taste. In the world of musical entertainment 'No one had the magic touch' and few were skilled in guessing what the audiences would want to see and hear the following year. In this sense, the situation was not very different to the later history of popular music, a history filled with surprise successes and unexpected turnarounds.

Popular music seems always to have attracted expressions of polemical and ungenerous opinion. For the period we are studying, Pearsall claims that the shows were no longer innovatory, that the dominant theatre chains had found a profitable formula and were unwilling to change: the higher level of capital investment compared to previous decades discouraged, he felt, risk-taking in show business. This is a dynamic which should not be underestimated. Nevertheless, the power of fierce competition, and the creative desires of the artistes tend to be a motor of

---

[153]   Ibid., 204.
[154]   *The Encore*, 4 January 1917.
[155]   *The Times*, 9 February 1914.
[156]   *The Performer*, 7 January 1915.
[157]   *Burnley Express*, 19 January 1918.

innovation. Great flops are seen alongside great hits: a revue or musical comedy might last for 30 shows or 3,000. In some ways the industry can be compared to the cinema industry today. The impression of having found 'the formula' can sometimes lead to the production of a series of highly repetitive films. Yet no one knows when an innovation, sometimes from a creative but low-budget outfit, will buck the trend and open up new themes and methods within production.

The period of the First World War is the last one when live shows are at the centre of the popular music industry. The gramophone is still reserved for a minority and radio is several years off. A series of cultural phenomena generated by the mass technological reproduction and distribution of song are not yet to be seen. There are no amateur fanzines for enthusiasts of one type of music or another; the amount of leisure time and education available for ordinary people at the time forbids them. In addition, the possibilities of palimpsest are infinitely fewer than in later periods. Today, classic versions of many songs are so well known that a new cover version is heard while the classic version is still in our mind. Sid Vicious's 'My Way' has meaning because of our familiarity with Sinatra's version, to take an extreme example for my generation. Yet all the constellation of cover versions, live versions, unplugged versions, retro versions, remixes and mash-ups was inconceivable a century ago: a music-hall star would generally sing their hit in the same way, night after night for years or decades. Lastly, popular music has not yet become what it will be some decades later: a vector of identity for young people. Groupings of young people at the time do not come into conflict, verbal or physical, because of differences in musical taste. Moreover, no one expects of the stars that they should be 'the voice of a new generation' or of a marginalized section of the population.

Our next chapter will examine what the artistes sang about and what conclusions we can draw about popular ideologies and mentalities of the war years.

A Star in Focus 2

Vesta Tilley – the Woman Who Played Men

'Girls – if you'd like to love a soldier you can all love me!'

On stage, Vesta Tilley dressed as a man, in order to gently parody different 'types' of men, from soldiers on leave to social climbers.[1] Born in poverty in 1864, she never went to school and began working on stage at the age of five, quickly becoming the sole source of income for her parents and her twelve brothers and sisters. She was the best-known of the music hall's male impersonators, a genre which included several dozen women artistes until it disappeared in the 1920s.

Tilley was determined to rise in society, and to see music hall recognized by the elite. Towards the end of her career, she could earn up to £1,000 a week. She married the owner of a chain of music halls, who had also been born poor. She became a new type of star, making a fortune through the sale of postcards with her image on, and lending her name to brands of men's waistcoats, of socks and of cigars. Her own advertisements praised her talent over that of serious, 'legitimate' actors:

> Can the stage which is called legitimate show, in England at any rate, a fame which is so rooted in the consciousness of its own times? ... She is the most imitated of all performers on the stage and the most inimitable. She has created a whole school of stage art.[2]

When the great music-hall strike broke out in 1907, Tilley found herself in a delicate position. Her own social milieu was by now that of the theatre owners, who were furious at the strikers;[3] but her fellow-artistes and much of the audience supported the strike, so she dared not distance herself too much from the revolt. In 1912, she was invited to perform at the first ever Royal Variety Performance. The choice of Tilley was considered daring: the press reported that the queen and her ladies averted their gaze during her act, shocked at the sight of a woman wearing trousers.[4]

For her show, she developed very careful staging and spent much time studying the typical gestures, ways of walking and language habits of the men

---

[1]   A number of photos are available at http://www.vam.ac.uk/content/articles/v/vesta-tilley/ (accessed 22 January 2015).

[2]   *The Encore*, 3 January 1918.

[3]   See John Mullen, 'Velours rouge et piquets de grève – la grève du music-hall à Londres en 1907', *Cahiers victoriens et édouardiens* 67 (April 2008).

[4]   Sara Maitland, *Vesta Tilley* (London: Virago, 1986), 47.

she was imitating. When she played a soldier on leave, she carried a backpack of a realistic size and weight. It was said that she changed socks for each character.[5] Many of her hits, such as 'Following in Father's Footsteps' of 1892, 'The Seaside Smile' of 1907 or 'Burlington Bertie' of 1900, presented rather pretentious and smooth-talking young men about town. In this last, Bertie's way of life is described in this way:

> He spends the good oof that his pater has made
> Along with the Brandy and Soda Brigade.

During the war, she earned the nickname 'Britain's best recruiting sergeant' thanks to her speeches at recruiting rallies, and songs such as 'It's a Fine Time for a Soldier' and 'There's a Good Time Coming for the Ladies!'. Her hit 'The Army of Today's All Right'[6] was sung by troops on the march. Yet, unlike many other artistes, she never went to the Western Front to entertain the boys, claiming the transport of her costumes and accessories was too difficult to organize.

Despite her enthusiastic support for the war, she could sing elements of social comment or even mockery. The piece 'Jolly Good Luck to the Girl Who Loves a Soldier' satirizes smooth-talking but unfaithful military men ('I was true to one girl all last week!'). In a more serious vein, the tremendously popular 'Six Days' Leave' deals with the suffering of soldiers who came home to England, knowing they must soon go back to the massacres and unable to communicate to their loved ones the hell they were living through. 'Next time they give me six days' leave, let them give me six months' hard!' she sang. *The Guardian* reported:

> In this song, Miss Tilley is a soldier, straight from the trenches, equipped with a woolly coat, full kit and rifle, and the inevitable German helmet, which dangles inconveniently about his knee. He has discovered that the joyfully anticipated 'six days' leave' is a snare and a bitter delusion. Most of us have heard soldiers talking like it.[7]

For her 1916 hit 'A Bit of a Blighty One',[8] she played a soldier delighted to be being mollycoddled in a military hospital in Britain, rather than having to survive life in the trenches. The tone remains comic despite the grave subject matter.

---

[5]   Ibid., 122.

[6]   Private J. Quigley, *The Slogan – Sidelights on Recruiting with Harry Lauder's Band* (London: Simpkin, 1916), 150.

[7]   *The Guardian*, 10 April 1917.

[8]   'A Blighty one' in soldier slang was a wound serious enough to have the soldier sent back to Britain, but not serious enough to endanger his life. This song is further discussed in Chapter 5.

At the end of the war, Tilley's successful song 'Sidney's in Civvies Again' joked about returning soldiers, and contained some reference to the real difficulties they could face re-adapting to civilian life.

The erotic charge of Tilley's cross-dressing was not discussed at the time, 'in a culture not yet permeated by Freudianism'.[9] In a society where women were supposed to be subordinate, the staging of a woman as a member of the dominant sex was heavily laden with meaning. To the feminist biographer of Tilley, Sara Maitland, 'the act of male impersonation (whatever its radical intention or potential) is an act of collusion, of reaction. It is also an act of self-denial, of self-destruction.'[10] Yet most of her most enthusiastic fans were women who no doubt appreciated the staging of forbidden roles. The woman in trousers who mocked, even if it was without malice, the dominant sex, might well be considered to be transmitting something of a subversive message.

Tilley was obliged to compensate for this subversive potential; she did all she could to not appear 'too' masculine. She hid her hair but did not cut it short. On stage, she kept her high-pitched voice, never wore false beards or moustaches, generally played androgynous young men, and never violent, old or mean characters. Unlike other stars, she did not attempt in her private life to play the role she played on stage. On the contrary, she was careful to wear much jewellery and, having no children of her own, was very publicly involved with children's charities.

After the war, Tilley left the stage. Her husband was standing at the parliamentary elections as a Conservative candidate, and a wife on stage at the music hall would have constituted a significant obstacle for him. At her last performance on the music-hall stage, she would be called back for seventeen curtain calls.

---

[9]   J. S. Bratton, 'Beating the Bounds: Gender Play and Role Reversal in the Edwardian Music Hall' in *The Edwardian Theatre: Essays on Performance and the Stage*, ed. M. R. Booth and J. H. Kaplan (Cambridge: Cambridge University Press, 1996), 86.

[10]   Maitland, *Vesta Tilley*, 9.

Chapter 3
The Songs and Their Content

The following chapters will deal with the songs themselves. First, the way they were presented to and received by the audience will be examined, and then popular themes will be analysed and their connection with people's lives at the time explored. A corpus of over a thousand songs from the war years forms the basis for this study.

As has already been suggested, it is insufficient to see these songs simply as illustrations of social history; they are in fact an integral part of this history. Yet understanding and analysing music-hall songs from a bygone era is not always easy: finding the 'original meaning' of these texts or of these shows is an ambitious and at best approximate endeavour. If Peter Bailey points out the importance of considering how music hall was experienced by its audiences, historians have few tools with which to do so.[1]

Indeed, the value of analysing popular song is not universally recognized. One current of thought maintains that popular song does not deserve to be taken seriously in its own terms. Most of the debates on this question took place in the years after the Second World War, but the arguments put forward can be applied perfectly well to music hall or any other forms of mass entertainment. The influential musicologist Theodor Adorno considered pop songs as purely commercial products, the fruits of blithe manipulation of a stultified population by a cynical and homogeneous cultural industry. His vision has had a very important influence. He claimed that 'Provided the material fulfils certain minimum requirements, any given song can be plugged and made a success'.[2]

On pop song, he continued:

> some of its principal characteristics are: unabating repetition of some particular musical formula comparable to the attitude of a child incessantly uttering the same demand ('I want to be happy'); the limitation of many melodies to very few tones, comparable to the way in which a small child speaks before he has the full alphabet at his disposal. ... Treating adults like children is involved in that representation of fun which is aimed at relieving the strain of their adult responsabilities.[3]

---

[1]   Peter Bailey, *Leisure and Class in Victorian England: Rational Recreation and the Contest for Control, 1830–1885* (London: Routledge & Kegan Paul, 1978), 1.

[2]   Theodor Adorno, *Essays on Music* (Berkeley: University of California Press, 2002), 445.

[3]   Ibid., 450

Elsewhere he maintains there is no difference at all between cultural products and other industrial products of capitalism.

Adorno wrote several decades ago. Since then, this approach has come to be marginal in respects of certain products of mass-cultural production, such as cinema. Cinema has gained a legitimate place in the quality press and in academia. Yet a dismissive attitude has remained remarkably influential for the specific case of popular music, and its serious study still strains at times to gain legitimacy.

The conceptions of Adorno's followers concerning 'mass culture' and 'the culture industry' have been criticized from several different points of view. Firstly, the almost complete lack of empirical studies to support such ideas has been pointed out.[4] Empirical studies tend to contradict their theses. This question cannot be discussed in detail here, but one example is worth noting. A study from the 1990s shows that between 5 per cent and 12 per cent of artistes signed to a record company will make a profit for the company.[5] There is no sign here of an all-powerful cultural industry dictating taste to the masses. Cloonan comments:

> The idea of the industry foisting rubbish more or less at will on a totally passive audience is facile. If it could do so it would, but it can not. Most records are not hits, the industry is notoriously slow in picking up on crazes and audiences soon tire of artists who are hyped into the charts.[6]

Others have suspected there is a heavy dose of elitism behind the theories developed by Adorno and his co-thinkers. Passages such as this one, where Adorno speaks of the popular dance, the jitterbug, seem to back this up:

> in order to become a jitterbug or simply to 'like' popular music, it does not by any means suffice to give oneself up and to fall into line passively. To become transformed into an insect, man needs that energy which might possibly achieve his transformation into a man.[7]

The idea that the mass of the people is less than human is a traditional conservative view of the world, which might seem surprising coming from an author who has been identified with the Left.

A last objection to Adorno's approach lies in the fact that his theories would tend to take popular music out of social and cultural history. If the latest hits are in no way different from the previous ones, one would be obliged to conclude that there is nothing of interest in the history of popular music. That is to say the rise

---

[4]   Dominic Strinati, *An Introduction to Theories of Popular Culture* (London: Routledge, 1995), 49.

[5]   Martin Cloonan, *Banned! The Censorship of Popular Music in Britain* (Aldershot: Arena, 1996), 42.

[6]   Ibid., 31.

[7]   Adorno, *Essays*, 468.

and fall of music hall, rock, or punk, the arrival of rap, techno and world music would be purely commercial fads imposed on people in order to make profit and having no link at all with social political or ideological changes in the real world.

It is no doubt easier to understand Adorno's vision of a stultified and completely alienated population if one keeps in mind his intellectual trajectory. Initially a Marxist, he drew from the political catastrophes of the 1930s the conclusion that the working classes had been definitively neutralized by the development of modern capitalism and could no longer act as engines of social change.

This series of objections has led to a situation today where Adorno's ideas on popular music are 'largely obsolete and unscientific, in the eyes of the cultural historian who is preoccupied with understanding both systems of production and the development of the symbolic landscape of a given society'.[8]

The reader will have noted that the present study of the music industry in the years of the Great War supports the view that these songs emerge from the interaction between a number of different participants – singers, composers, lyricists, investors, managers and members of the audience – and contain richly layered configurations of consensus and conflict. If we maintain, then, that popular music has a history, where do we place wartime music hall in this history? From one point of view this corpus of songs is part of the *prehistory* of modern pop music. They are part of an urban mass culture and contain a number of characteristics which have changed little in the century since: songs are three minutes long; the star who sings them, often from humble origins, is adored by his or her fans; central themes tend to be love, humour, politics and everyday life. Nevertheless, distribution of these songs is radically different to that of modern pop music: the sale of tickets to the music halls and the sale of sheet music are practically the sole vectors of distribution. The gramophone remains a luxury product, and, of course, there is no radio.

How should these songs be read?

Popular songs cannot be reduced simply to their lyrics, nor to their music; staging, communication with audiences and cultural and social context must not be forgotten. The importance of what is left unsaid in popular cultural products is well-established. It is important to keep in mind the objective of the composer and of the artiste. All along the last hundred years one can see a constant evolution of the main objectives of popular music. Some genres, such as choral singing and music hall have as their priority group singing. Others aim above all at accompanying and encouraging dance – big band music or techno, for instance. Others are structured around poetry or around theatricality (as in the cases of progressive rock, punk, glam or heavy metal).

---

8   Ludovic Tournès, 'Reproduire l'œuvre: la nouvelle économie musicale', in *La Culture de Masse en France*, ed. Jean-Pierre Rioux and Jean-François Sirinelli (Paris: Fayard, 2002), 221 [Translation: JM].

The use of character

Hennion and Vignolles, in a study published in the 1970s, deal in some detail with
the question of analysing pop songs.[9] They conclude by declaring that 'variety
songs cannot be reduced to the normal categories of artistic creation' and quote an
artistic director who suggested it was useful to see a pop song as 'a three minute
novel'.[10] In this perspective, they write that the three keys to understanding a pop
song are the music, the lyrics and the 'character' of the singer.

This 'character' can be compared to the narrator in a literary work, and is of
particular interest for the present study, since the use of a carefully crafted stage
character was even more important in music hall than in more recent genres such
as rock. A good number of the best-loved stars of the war years sang 'disguised'
as particular characters, building themselves in this way a narrator figure. Several
presented themselves as 'costermongers' (cockney street sellers of fruit and
vegetables), others as nouveaux riches or declassed aristocrats. There were also
plenty of sentimental and miserly 'Scotsmen' and touching, naive and boisterous
'Irishmen'. Yet others sang blacked up in a 'blackface' negro slave character or
were disguised as a simple farmer from the countryside. Female singers such as
Vesta Tilley dressed up and played different types of male character (the military
officer, the young 'swell' and so on).

Derek Scott of Leeds University has studied the history and development of
these stage characters from the 1840s to the 1890s and suggests that the use of the
characters goes through a series of phases.[11] At the beginnings of music hall in the
1840s it is caricature which is dominant. Later, 'character types' takes over and
we see on stage a 'type': a Glasgow working man, perhaps, or a costermonger,
a village vicar or an elderly Jewish gentleman. There is of course abundant
stereotyping, but the characters are not presented as satirical caricatures. Scott
explains that, during this second phase, the audience see the artiste as an actor or
actress: there remains a distance between the character and the performer.

In a third stage, after 1880, we enter the period of the domination of the 'real
imagined' character. In this final phase, the artiste is supposed to *be* the character.
Marie Lloyd or Gus Elen are praised in the 1890s in part because of their perceived
authenticity, as voices of the poor streets of the industrial towns. This despite the
fact that their characters are in many ways artificial: they use little dialect, for
example (which would cause difficulties for a nationwide audience), and never
swear or blaspheme on stage.

Some of the stars of the war years do indeed correspond to this concept of
'real-imagined' characters: in particular Harry Champion, Harry Lauder and Marie

---

[9]   Antoine Hennion and J. P. Vignolle, *Artisans et industriels du disque – essai sur le
mode de production de la musique* (Paris: CSI-Cordes, 1978).

[10]   Ibid., 198.

[11]   Derek Scott, 'The Music Hall Cockney: Flesh and Blood, or Replicant?', *Music
and Letters* 83:2 (2002), 237–258.

Lloyd. Others such as George Robey or Vesta Tilley change character according to the requirements of a particular song or sketch. Vesta Tilley chooses a different 'type' of man for each song,[12] while George Robey plays both male and female characters (the mayor, the lion tamer, the digs landlady or the merry widow, and so on).

Voice and melody

Voice is tremendously important in pop song. Hennion and Vignolles emphasize that 'Voice, in variety, must not be understood as vocal technique and the systematic mastering of the voice's capacities. It is rather a clue to personality ... it is not a matter of the voice in itself, but of its power of expression.'[13]

This reflection fits very well the singers in the corpus used for the present study. Voices include, for example, the loud and rapid-fire cockney voice of Harry Champion, belting out humorous songs about everyday life, such as 'Never let Your Braces Dangle' from 1910 or 'A Little Bit of Cucumber' from 1915.[14] There is also the plaintive, sardonic voice of an old-fashioned working man in the performances of Gus Elen ('Don't Stop Me 'Arf a Pint of Beer', 1911; 'Wait Till the Work Comes Round', 1906). Marie Lloyd uses a high-pitched voice which almost screeches at times to portray her character as a worldly-wise working-class woman who knows how to have a good time, in songs like 'A Little of What You Fancy Does You Good' (1915) or 'Every Little Movement Has a Meaning of Its Own' (1912); whereas Sam Mayo in 'Bread and Marmalade' (1916) sings in a thick, tired voice[15] and George Robey uses a deliberately pretentious tone. The voices are used theatrically to put over a particular personality or attitude. The absence of microphones on stage at this time makes this loud demonstrative use of voice one of the most appropriate for large music halls.

Many of the songs are relatively difficult to listen to for our twenty-first-century ears: we have absorbed the relative musical complexity of rock and more recent forms, whereas the songs of the time were addressed to audiences whose listening experience was much less varied than our own. Unlike a blues, rock or soul singer, the music-hall artiste had relatively little control over musical expression. The

---

[12] For a study of gender reversal in music-hall performance, see J. S. Bratton, 'Beating the Bounds: Gender Play and Role Reversal in the Edwardian Music Hall', in *The Edwardian Theatre: Essays on Performance and the Stage*, ed. M. R. Booth and J. H. Kaplan (Cambridge: Cambridge University Press, 1996).

[13] Hennion and Vignolle, *Artisans et industriels*, 210 (all translations are my own: JM).

[14] The song 'A Little Bit of Cucumber' is online at http://www.firstworldwar.com/audio/1915.htm (accessed 5 July 2014).

[15] The song 'Bread and Marmalade' is online at www.firstworldwar.com/audio/1916.htm (accessed 20 August 2014), while film of Sam Mayo on stage in the 1930s can be found at www.britishpathe.com.

music was played by the resident orchestra in each hall. If the musicians had to be highly skilled so as to be able to learn very quickly the music of that week's turns, creative ambition was limited. The situation did not encourage the artiste to look for complex musical innovations, and the composers normally wrote the songs very quickly.

The difference between reciting and singing is not always strict on the music-hall stage. We often find recited verses accompanied by a sung chorus; this is the case for the hit 'Silly Ass!' performed by Tom Clare in 1915, and for 'My Word, You Do Look Queer!' by Ernest Hastings. Whether sung or recited, all the lyrics were always clearly heard.

As noted above, the voice in variety singing is often a means of expressing a stage personality. In music hall, this is not the only use of voice, however. A number of performers who do not sing 'in character' use opera or operetta voice registers. This aims both at pleasing the public who can admire the technical mastery, at the same time as it is part of an atmosphere of respectability in the music hall, and a desire to share the values of high culture and high society. Singers such as Gertie Gitana or Zona Vevey, then, use operatic vocal styles, and John McCormack, the famous tenor, became famous in opera before ever singing on the popular stage.[16]

From a technical point of view, the appropriate vocal repertoire was limited by the lack of electrical amplification. The amplifier had been invented in 1909, but was not used on stage before the 1920s. This meant that intimate voices common in modern popular song were not available, and this influenced the type of song in the repertoire.

Given the centrality of sing-along, a catchy tune is important for a music-hall hit. It must be easy to pick up: the audience has not been able to listen to the song many times previously on the radio or the gramophone. Moreover, the theatre orchestra needs to be able to learn all the songs for the week's show at the Monday morning rehearsal: excessive musical innovation is therefore inappropriate. At the same time, a song needs to be a little out of the ordinary if it is to retain the public's attention and become a hit.

What do we know about the music-hall songs?

Most books on the music hall deal with the Victorian period, before 1901,[17] and almost all stop at the beginning of the Great War.[18] Some of them are to be classed

---

[16]   Some of his recordings can be found online at www.firstworldwar.com/audio/1917. htm.

[17]   See, for example, Peter Bailey, *Popular Culture and Performance in the Victorian City* (Cambridge: Cambridge University Press, 1998); Keith Wilson, 'Music Hall London: the Topography of Class Sentiment', *Victorian Literature and Culture* 23 (1995).

[18]   For example Dave Russell, *Popular Music in England 1840–1914: A Social History* (Manchester: Manchester University, 1997); Paul Maloney, *Scotland and the*

as works of nostalgia and lack critical distance.[19] More serious studies have generally covered long periods of time, which allows the identification of long-term trends, but makes a detailed study of songs impossible.[20]

Unfortunately, the lack of work on music hall after 1914 can give the impression that music hall disappeared or went into rapid decline, which is absolutely not the case. As Peter Bailey notes, 'Music hall survived the First World War (despite an entertainment tax and the reintensification of calls for moral surveillance), and took its share of the immediate post-war boom before being confronted with another powerful rival in radio'.[21]

Key song themes before the war

A few authors have studied the themes covered in British music hall songs. Colin MacInnes, in his *Sweet Saturday Night: Pop Song 1840–1920*, presents the main themes of the repertoire as being: Love, London life, Soldiers and sailors, Work, and Holidays. He claims a great deal of emotional power for the best of these songs: 'The music hall songs, at their best, made a formidable and lasting impact on anyone lucky enough to have heard them delivered by the old stars.'[22]

MacInnes notes the important elements of working-class dreaming in the music-hall song: songs speak of winning bets on horses, inheriting from a long-lost uncle, and so on. He also refers to the misogyny and xenophobia of many of the songs. Lastly, he reminds us that tragedy seems to be practically absent from the repertoire, contrary to the case for music-hall repertoires in other European countries in this period.

Peter Davison,[23] in an annotated collection of a few dozen songs, identifies different categories. Naturally the love song is a common type. Songs portraying the everyday life of working-class people are also analysed, such as songs about working-class marriage or ballads about mining accidents. According to Davison, these pieces frequently exhibit 'an acceptance of the way things are. This is not,

---

Music Hall, 1850–1914 (Manchester: Manchester University Press, 2003); Chris Waters, *British Socialists and the Politics of Popular Culture, 1884–1914* (Manchester: Manchester University Press, 1990).

[19]   For example, Maurice Willson Disher, *Winkles and Champagne, Comedies and Tragedies of the Music Hall* (Bath: Chivers, 1974), or Peter Honri, *Working the Halls* (Farnborough: Saxon House, 1973).

[20]   McInnes and Cheshire each cover a period of 80 years, Russell 74, Garret 60, Crowhurst 37 and Horral 28. The work covering the shortest period, apart from the present book, is Pearsall ,who deals with 13 years.

[21]   Peter Bailey (Ed.), *Music-Hall: The Business of Pleasure* (Milton Keynes: Open University Press, 1986), xiii.

[22]   Colin MacInnes, *Sweet Saturday Night: Pop Song 1840–1920* (Manchester: Panther Arts, 1967), 10.

[23]   Peter Davison, *Songs of the British Music Hall* (New York: Oak, 1971).

however, apathetic acceptance ... but a down-to-earth awareness of the real conditions of life lived.'[24]

Then there are the melodramatic songs much prized by the temperance leagues, such as the 1880s song 'Don't Go Out Tonight, Dear Father', which shows a young girl begging her father not to go to the pub but to stay by the bedside of his dying wife. The father ignores her cries and goes drinking anyway. His wife dies, and, returning home at night, dead drunk, the father accidentally falls and kills his daughter!

One of the categories presented by Davison is the motto song, the musical equivalent, perhaps, of the highly popular books of Samuel Smiles.[25] These were very common in the minstrel shows, but also could be heard on the music-hall stage. One example was 'Work, Boys, Work, and Be Contented!':

> *Chorus*:   So Work boys work and be contented
> As long as you've enough to buy a meal
> The man you may rely, will be wealthy by and bye
> If he'll only put his shoulder to the wheel.
>
> You'll enjoy a quiet crust more by rubbing off the rust
> It's a maxim that should never be forgot
> Whilst labour leads to wealth
> And will keep you in good health
> So it's best to be contented with your lot.

Here are some other examples:

- Pulling Hard Against the Stream 1867
- There's Danger in Delay! 1877
- Paddle Your Own Canoe[26] (date unknown)
- Envy Not, Covet Not![27] (date unknown)

If these motto songs were at their most popular in the 1870s, they continued long afterwards, and were soundly denounced by the socialist narrator in Robert Tressell's autobiographical novel *The Ragged-Trousered Philanthropists*, written in 1910.[28] Davison underlines the fact that it is very difficult indeed, a century

---

[24]   Ibid., 248.

[25]   *Self-help, Character, Thrift* and *Duty* were four of his best-known works.

[26]   Lyrics online at http://monologues.co.uk/musichall/Songs-P/Paddle-Your-Own-Canoe.htm (accessed 20 August 2014).

[27]   Michael Pickering, '"A Happy Instinct for Sentiment": A Profile of Harry Hunter', *Cahiers victoriens et édouardiens* 50 (1999).

[28]   Robert Tressell, *The Ragged-Trousered Philanthropists* (London: Flamingo, 1993 (1914)), 375.

later, to see these songs fully in their context. He also reminds us that the audiences who loved to sing along with these melodramatic songs also loved to see them parodied. Harry Champion, for example, parodied the motto songs in his 1910 hit 'Never Let Your Braces Dangle!':

I was one of eighteen boys, all of us wore corduroys
I was roughest of the gang, for my braces used to hang
Dangling all around my feet, and Mother used to bawl
Pointing to the text so neat, she'd hung upon the wall

Chorus: Never let your braces dangle. dingle, dingle, dangle
Never thieve, don't deceive and never row or wrangle
Stick to the right, get away from the bad
Don't get as tight as your poor old Dad
But the greatest motto of the lot, my lad
Is 'Never let your braces dangle!'

Davison then explores the 'suggestive' songs of the music-hall, such a characteristic element of the repertoire. The hit song 'The Swimming Master', which tells of a Don Juan figure who decided to follow a career as a swimming instructor, is examined:

To my manly chest they cling
And their arms around me fling
Oh dear, what a time I have
When I teach the girls to swim!

The high point of the song is when one young woman comes to the swimming class with a home-made swimming costume, which is not strong enough to hold together while she is diving.

Another example presented is that of 'I've Never Lost My Last Train Yet' in which 'missing the last train' is a euphemism for losing one's virginity. Such suggestive songs, as we shall see in the next chapter, will remain frequent during the war years.

Michael Pickering[29] looks at another group of songs, those which sing the praises of the British Empire and sometimes the superiority of the white 'race' over all others; This type of song became more common after 1870. The best-known example, which introduced the word 'jingoism' into the English language, was the 1878 'MacDermott's War Song' written at a time when the British government sent warships to support Turkey in its conflict with Russia. The verse gives a number of arguments for the Turkish cause, and the chorus is made up of these rousing lines:

---

[29]   Pickering, 'Happy Instinct', 78.

> We don't want to fight, but by Jingo if we do
> We've got the ships, we've got the men, we've got the money too!
> We've fought the bear before and while we're Britons true
> The Russians shall not have Constantinople!

Nevertheless, it is to be noted that a parody of the piece, in which the narrator, a deserter, expressed fierce opposition to the war, was also a success:

> Let all those politicians who desire to help the Turk
> Put on the uniform themselves, and go and do the work
> War keeps the population down, the clever people say
> But I would rather stay at home, and try some other way.
>
> *Chorus*:   I'll change my togs, I'll sell my kit, and pop my rifle too
> I don't like this war, I ain't a Briton true
> And I'd let the Russians have Constantinople.

This was only one of a series of anti-militarist songs in late Victorian music halls. [30]

Similarly, if one looks at the music-hall songs which dealt with the Boer War,[31] in particular in 1900, one finds the question treated in many ways other than the purely jingoistic. Songs such as 'Another Little Patch of Red', which directly celebrate imperial expansion, are very rare indeed. Although pieces like 'The Heroes of the Transvaal War' read like straightforward propaganda songs, this was far from the case for many of the hit songs. The 'Absent-minded Beggar' is about the need to help families of the soldiers out 'saving the Empire'. Support for the Empire is take for granted in the song, but the central point is not glorification of the Empire. Songs such as 'When the Boys in Khaki All Come Home' talk of the war, without being imperialistic in tone; others again complain that veterans are badly treated.

Some of the Boer War songs are further still from jingoism. Marie Lloyd, one of the most popular stars of the time, put out a piece 'The Girl in the Khaki Dress' of which the main point was mockery of those who are obsessed with the South African war, coupled with a suggestion that some women had been going beyond the bounds of respectability in showing their appreciation to the soldiers.

> Pa's got a house at Regents Park, he had to have it repainted khaki
> Whim of mine, and dear Papa consented well, of course
> Smiled as sweetly as he was able
> I've just been going through the stable
> Won't let him keep anything except a khaki horse
> Khaki sheets and blankets and, I declare

---

[30]   Davison, *British Music Hall*, 66.
[31]   See John Mullen, 'The Popular Music Industry in Britain in 1900', *Civilisations* 13 (2014).

In every bedroom in the house we've khaki crockery ware
What say? Too much khaki? That's just where the fun begins
What about my sister, eh? Just had khaki twins!

Naturally, in this study of Great War music hall, pro-Empire songs are of particular interest and we shall return to them in Chapter 5.

For Pearsall, the characteristic of music-hall songs in general is that they are close to everyday working-class life and sentiment, in particular as the twentieth century rolls into view: 'the songs somehow embodied the sentiments and feelings of the submerged classes, and the idea that music-hall song was the only true urban folk art gained credence throughout the Edwardian period'.[32]

Robert Roberts, who grew up in a Salford slum before becoming, much later, a sociologist, was of a similar opinion. He refers to the music-hall songs as 'those earthy parodies ... true and only folk songs of the industrial mass'.[33]

This brief survey of writings about music-hall songs in general, though concentrated on an earlier period, lays the groundwork for the present study. The specific corpus of songs of the war years will be the subject of the remainder of this chapter.

Collecting songs from the war years

Our corpus is made up of 1,063 songs from music hall and revue (and occasionally from musical comedy), between 1914 and 1918. Naturally it has been easier to find those songs which were more popular than those which were commercial flops. Over 250 are available in recorded form, most of the others as sheet music in the archives of the British Library, and some are mentioned in the press or in diaries of the time, or in Kilgarriff's catalogue of hits. Our corpus no doubt makes up around a quarter of the total number of songs produced. The corpus includes only songs which were sold. Non-commercial productions (hymns, folk songs or soldier songs) have been kept apart, since they are transmitted by different channels and subjected to different rules: they will form the subject of Chapter 6. In addition, only songs known to have been published or sung in the United Kingdom are included. American songs are only counted if they had some success in Britain, almost always due to their being sung by British artistes.

Dates given for songs are only indicative. Sometimes, only a recording date is available, at other times a date for sheet music publication or a stage success commented on in the press. Change in popular music generally operated more slowly than today: a hit could be sung every day on stage for fifteen years, published in sheet music after a few years, and recorded by a gramophone company years later still.

---

[32] Ronald Pearsall, *Edwardian Popular Music* (London: David & Charles, 1975), 58.
[33] Robert Roberts, *A Ragged Schooling: Growing Up in the Classic Slum* (London: Fontana, 1978), 50.

It was important to be able to distinguish a hit from a flop, and yet sales figures are not available. The presence of a song in the 'Greatest Hits of the Year' collections, brought out by major publishing houses at the end of each year was a key piece of information. A full- or half-page advert for the song in the trade press almost always meant the song was a hit. In addition, the catalogue of music-hall songs put together by music-hall connoisseur Michael Kilgarriff is invaluable. He explains in his preface that he has chosen to include those pieces which were the most popular, the most topical, the most significant in a singer's career, as well as the most remembered.[34] These elements have allowed the relative popularity of songs to become visible and thus allow more representative conclusions to be drawn. When a given song is referred to as a 'hit', this is based on one of the elements outlined above.

Before moving on to wartime song lyrics, it is worth reflecting on the communicative relationship between the artiste and their audience. Singers in the war years do not present themselves as spokespeople for the younger generation, nor as idols who reject the aesthetics and values of a previous generation: young and older people share the same music at the music hall. What then is the position of the artiste in his or her songs? If the strong local roots of singers have been diluted with the development of a national entertainment industry, the position of the singer in many songs is still that of the workmate or neighbour speaking in confidence to someone he or she knows well.

The theatre of complicity

Music-hall singers (around two thirds of them men and one third women) converse with their audience through the songs, frequently using a voice and an accent clearly understood to be working-class. They appear to be confiding in the audience, and invite those present in the theatre to join in a collective game: that of singing the chorus. The narrative procedures in the songs are simple; the narrator is immediately identifiable, and tells a specific story, normally with a beginning, a middle and an end. One of the characteristics of the songs which has most led them to be classified as working-class culture is this neighbourly tone, which is rarer in popular music of later periods. Rather than listening to a poet, prophet, or spokesperson of the zeitgeist, we find ourselves in the theatre of complicity. The staging of this working-class community communication in a theatre whose furniture and decoration imitate grand bourgeois homes is a particularly fascinating aspect of music-hall aesthetics.

In the early decades of music hall, some decades previously, this complicity could be real and local.:[35] 'artists would banter with individuals in the audience

---

[34]   Michael Kilgarriff, *Sing Us One of the Old Songs: A Guide to Popular Song 1860–1920* (Oxford: Oxford University Press, 1999), preface.

[35]   Maloney, *Scotland and the Music Hall*, 95.

who they knew,'[36] and heckling was so common it was part of the show. Such exchanges became rarer as the industry became a national one. In their place, we find a constructed, theatrical complicity between the artistes and an audience they do not know. This can still be found in popular music concerts up to the present day. Rather than confide in the audience about their life as a singer, the wartime artistes sing of fictional episodes in the life of their constructed character, and portray, above all, common experiences of the working-class audiences. Their use of working-class first names, generally familiar diminutives, added to the atmosphere of working-class conviviality. During the war years, among many others, one could hear sing on stage Tom, Gus, Harry, Dick, Fred, Billy, Ernie, Bob, Sam, Jack, Florrie, Elsie, Ada, Gertie, and Lily.

The example of 'Now You've Got Yer Khaki On' performed by Marie Lloyd in 1915, illustrates this construction of neighbourliness:[37]

> P'r'aps you don't know Johnny Brown who sold the flowers and fruit?
> I stood 'im 'cos he used to make me laugh
> The other day he rolled up in Khaki, if you please
> I says, 'Lumme! don't it suit yer, Jack. Not 'arf!'
> … Once or twice, he took me to a moving picture show
> He'd 'old me 'and and all that kind of stuff
> And I don't mind saying this
> I used to let 'im have a kiss
> Until I said, 'Now chuck it, that's enough.'
> Then up he rolls in Khaki – I says, 'Lovely, ain't you grown
> You've altered, but you've altered for the best
> Once or twice I thought you meant to grow a Derby Kell[38]
> But they've took it off, and stuff'd it in yer chest!'

The earthy tone and the use of a moderate amount of dialect reinforces the atmosphere of working-class neighbourliness.

In 'Two Lovely Black Eyes' sung by Charles Coborn (written in 1886, recorded in 1905 and in 1913), we hear:

> Strolling so gaily down Bethnal Green,
> This gay youth you might have seen;
> Tompkins and I with a girl between,
> But, oh! What a surprise!
> I praised the Conservatives frank and free,
> Tompkins got angry quite speedily,

---

[36] Bailey, *Leisure and Clas*, 152.

[37] This song can be heard on line at http://www.firstworldwar.com/audio/1916.htm (accessed 16 July 2014).

[38] 'Derby Kell' is cockney rhyming slang for 'belly' ('Derby Kelly').

And in a moment be handed me
Two lovely black eyes.

Again, the audience is taken into confidence as being part of the same, local peer group, talking of well-known places and characters.

The patter used by George Formby Senior, which often featured chatty monologues addressed to the conductor of the local orchestra in whatever hall he happened to be playing in shows again this construction of complicity: 'Start with me now, boys, when I go … Get ready now, lads. … Have we finished now? Beautiful' (from patter of song 'I Sobbed and I Cried Like a Child', 1915).

The subjects which are brought up in the songs, and the advice given, often correspond in tone to discussions with neighbours over the garden fence. The everyday and even the trivial are very much in evidence. Here are some more song titles which give a flavour of this:

- We're All Happy When the Sun Shines 1914
- A Little of What You Fancy Does You Good! 1915
- We Parted the Best of Friends 1914
- In These Hard Times 1915
- Everybody Is Invited Round to Our House 1916
- On His First Day Home on Leave 1916
- Did You See the Crowd in Piccadilly? 1916
- I Can't' Do My Bally Bottom Button Up! 1916
- Send the Boys a Little Snapshot of the Ones They've Left Behind 1916
- We've Got to Put Up With It Now 1916
- In Grandma's Days, They Never Did the Fox-trot 1917
- We're All Good Until We're All Found Out 1918

Such complicity is not universally present in the popular songs of the war years. It is more a characteristic of the comic songs than of the others. It seems, moreover, to become somewhat less common towards the end of the war, as dreamy tones and romantic tones become more common, in parallel with the rise of the revue, and the psychological trauma of a war which seems endless. The use of this complicity, though, facilitates the treatment by the repertoire of everyday experience of working-class people well into the 1920s. We shall see much more about this when we look at songs on war and society, in Chapter 5.

Lyrics and sophistication

This neighbourly tone influences the song lyrics, which are the subject of the next section. Hennion and Vignolles give this advice for the writer of variety songs:

The words should be simple but not corny, and should reflect current issues, things people are talking about, things which are in the air, but they should not be worn out expressions. To a certain extent, lyricists need to stick to the commonplace, but the commonplace which is still up to date, whose power of association has not been worn away by overuse.[39]

Whereas in *The Era*, during the war, one can read the following recommendations from the successful lyricist Herman Darewski, author of 'Sister Susie's Sewing Shirts for Soldiers' and of 'K-k-k-Katie', among many others:

Writing a song may be likened to making an omelette, there's many a pitfall. Anyone can write a song but few indeed can achieve the perfect omelette … the essential part is the chorus. The opening sentence of the chorus should form a catch phrase … every word must be simple, childish in its simplicity in fact.[40]

Most immediately noticeable on reading the lyrics of the time is their general lack of poetic sophistication; there are few metaphors. Popular song lyrics have followed, through the twentieth century, a parallel path to that of poetry. Narration has been deconstructed; the juxtaposition of different voices and dreamlike images has often come to be used in place of a straightforward chronological narrative. For mainstream popular music, most of these changes happened after the Second World War. From this point of view, music-hall songs seem to be pre-modern in narrative structure; it is very often a matter of 'I was walking along one morning, when suddenly …'

Naturally, there exists no precise scale to measure 'sophistication', but perhaps the following list of song titles, all from 1914 and 1915, will help the reader understand this idea:

- He Misses His Missus's Kisses
- Do You Always Tell Your Wife?
- What's the Use of Ringing on the Telephone?
- Men of England, You Have Got to Go!
- Are We Downhearted? No!
- I Wish I Could Find a Sweetheart Like My Dear Old Dad
- The Germans Are Coming, So They Say.
- When We Want What We Know We Can't Have
- I've Been Out with Johnnie Walker
- All the Boys in Khaki Get the Nice Girls
- Be a Soldier, Lad of Mine!
- Bread and Marmalade
- Cheer Up, Little Soldier Man!

---

[39] Hennion and Vignolle, *Artisans et industriels*, 207.
[40] *The* Era,7 February 1917.

- Dance with Your Uncle Joseph
- Don't Say I Ever Made You Love Me
- Follow the Sergeant!
- Give Me Your Answer, Dear, Before I Go.
- Hearts Are Sometimes More Than Playthings
- I Didn't Raise My Boy to Be a Soldier
- I Like Your Town
- I'm Glad I Took My Mother's Advice
- I've Only Come Down for the Day!
- If you Can't Get a Girl in the Summertime
- If You Want to Get On in Revue
- Just We Too and the Moon
- Keep Your Hands in Your Trousers Pockets

The simple lyrics have sometimes been considered an important reason contributing to the decline of music hall in the more sophisticated world of the 1920s. The website which catalogues the lyrical output of Fred Godfrey,[41] one of the most prolific lyricists of the time and author of 'Down Texas Way' and 'Take Me Back to Dear Old Blighty!',[42] has this to say:

> In the postwar years, recorded music, the cinema, and radio combined to kill off the Music Halls. Popular music itself was also becoming more sophisticated. In the United States, a new generation – Berlin, Kern, Porter, the Gershwins[43] – was replacing the old Tin Pan Alley tunesmiths. The same process was under way in Britain, and Fred Godfrey found it increasingly difficult to sell songs to publishers and artists who wanted the romanticism of an Ivor Novello or the world-weary cleverness of a Noël Coward.

Indeed, the lyrics of Cole Porter's songs, to take that example, are considerably more dense than those of our corpus of songs from the war years. They are characterized by a lively humour, jokey forced rhymes, and many neologisms and cultural references, as well as a certain metaphoric content. It is not unusual to have to listen to his songs several times before fully understanding. This reflects the fact that they are to be listened to repeatedly on a gramophone, rather than, as in previous years, picked up from one hearing on the stage.[44]

---

[41]   See http://www.fredgodfreysongs.ca (accessed 15 July 2014).

[42]   Lyrics and original recording can be found at www.firstworldwar.com/audio/tak emebacktodearoldblighty.htm (accessed 20 August 2014).

[43]   Kern's first hit dates from 1905, but he became famous after 1917. Both Cole Porter and George Gershwin had their first hit in 1919. Ivor Novello, the Welsh composer and singer, rose to success in 1917. Noel Coward recorded hits from 1929 on.

[44]   A few extracts of Cole Porter's lyrics can be found at http://www.coleporter.org/ lyrics.html (accessed 15 July 2014).

Song themes in wartime

The themes treated in our corpus can teach us much about popular attitudes at the time, if it is kept in mind that such attitudes cannot be mechanically read off cultural productions. Some quantitative analysis of themes is necessary, to ward off the risk of a purely impressionistic or even anecdotal analysis. Nevertheless, sorting the songs into categories is surprisingly tricky. It is not rare to find a comic piece which begins as a love song before moving on in a later verse to speak of the war. Should it then be categorized as a war song, a love song or a comic song?

The classification used, then, is by 'main theme', and this is necessarily a little approximate. Since only the year of the song is available in general, this classification was made on the part of the corpus dating from 1915 to 1918 (since songs dated 1914 might be wartime songs or not).

Main theme of song (base 921 songs 1915–1918)

War and life in wartime	25.0%
Love	16.0%
Ireland or the Irish	4.7%
Other geographical locations (Lancashire, Yorkshire, Kentucky, etc.)	9.9%
Women's role in society	4.5%
Type of music or the life of the artiste (fox-trot, ragtime, jazz, etc.)	2.3%
Food and drink	1.8%
Comic songs not in the above categories	12.5%
All other songs	22.8%

Themes absent in this list are as significant as those present. Motto songs, for example, have completely disappeared: Victorian moralism is no longer appropriate, perhaps. Fictional melodramatic pieces also do not figure in the list; no doubt the real melodrama of war gave people little taste for tragic fiction. As for a theme which was popular in previous years – holidays and work – this theme seems to have given way to 'war and life in wartime'.

Almost a quarter of the songs are marked as "miscellaneous", showing how approximate such a classification can be. The following are some examples of songs classified as miscellaneous:

- A Wedding on a Gee Gee 1915
- An Old Fashioned Place Called Home 1915
- Aunt Tilly 1915
- Canoeing 1915
- Frightened to Go to Sleep Again 1915

- Once Upon a Time 1915
- Have You Seen the Ducks Go By ? 1916
- The Right Side of Bond Street 1916
- Don't Blame Me 1917
- Somebody's Coming to Tea 1917
- Luana Lou 1917
- Blackpool 1918
- I'm always Chasing Rainbows 1918

It may be supposed, however, that many of these, too, are in a comic register.

Two further statistical operations allowed confirmation of the conclusions of the first. An analysis by main theme restricted to those songs known to have been successful was followed by a count of key words in song titles.

Theme	Percentage of hits with this main theme (base 264 hit songs 1915–1918)	Percentage of full corpus with this main theme (base 921 songs 1915–1918)
Love	21	16
War/life in wartime	17	25
Ireland and the Irish	2	4.7
Other geographical locations	7	9.9
Women's role in society	4	4.5
Comic song not in above categories	10	12.5
Food and drink	2	1.8
Type of music or the life of the artiste	3	2.3
All other songs	34	22.8

Most of the categories are broadly comparable in size whether we consider the larger corpus of songs produced or the smaller corpus of hit songs. It seems, however, that there was an 'over-production' of songs concerning the war and an 'under-production' of love songs. That is to say, songwriters and artistes overestimated the public's interest in songs about the war, and underestimated their interest in love songs. Were these professions, in the public eye, under more pressure to conform to the priorities of the establishment than were their audiences? This would be one possible explanation.

Presence of key words in wartime song titles (base: 1,143 song titles 1914–1918)

Home 57 + blighty 12 =	69
Girl 62 + lass 6 =	68
Boy 31 + lad 26 =	57
Love	44
Soldier 33 + Tommy 9 =	42
Song 28 + sing 13 =	41
Ireland 6 + Irish 30 =	36
War	18
Mother	18
King	10
Rag or ragtime	0
Dixie	9
Kaiser	8
Fight	7
Wedding	7
Empire	6
Scotland or Scottish	5
Hun	2
Lancashire	6
God	4
Victory	3

The results of the key word search are very striking. The general reputation of wartime music hall as imperialistic and warlike is not justified: they sang more about Mother than about the Empire, and far more about Tommy than about Kitchener. The main groups of song themes will now be examined and analysed one by one, and the integration of the themes in people's everyday wartime life will be explored. Two of the largest groups of themes will each be given a chapter of their own. Chapter 4 will look at love songs and songs about men and women, including the many pieces commenting on women's new roles in wartime Britain. Chapter 5 will be entirely consecrated to songs about war and life in wartime. The other themes will be the subject of the remaining pages of the present chapter.

Diverse comic songs

First, let us look at the comic songs which do not fit clearly into one of the other categories (since love songs, war songs or songs about food are often humorous). Tragedy has little or no place in the repertoire at this time; a jolly tone is almost compulsory.

A number of these pieces rely on tongue twisters, of which here is a selection:

- Sister Susie's Sewing Shirts for Soldiers 1914[45]
- Patty Proudly Packs for Privates Prepaid Paper Parcels 1915
- Pretty Patty's Proud of Her Pink Print Dress 1915
- That Sentimental Ornamental Oriental Tune 1915
- I Do Like a Snice S'mince S'pie 1914
- You Can't Get Many Pimples on a Pound of Pickled Pork 1914
- Nan, Nan, Nan 1915
- Which Switch is the Switch, Miss, for Ipswich ? 1915
- Yaddie Kaddie Kiddie Kaddie Koo 1917
- I Can't Do My Bally Bottom Button Up[46] 1916
- I Saw Six Short Soldiers 1916
- Are Your Sighs the Same Size as My Sighs? 1917

Several were tremendously successful. The difficult sing-along chorus made for good entertainment. The artiste would ask different parts of the audience to sing the chorus separately (the men then the women, or the left of the auditorium followed by the right). Here is a sample of such a chorus:

> I saw six short soldiers
> Scrubbing six short shirts
> Six short soldiers scrubbed and scrubbed
> Six short shirts were rubbed and rubbed
> Six short soldiers sang this song
> Their singing duly showed
> Those six short soldiers
> Scrubbed six short shirts
> Sister Susie'd sewed!

It is to be noted that the war theme when there is one is arbitrarily tacked on: they are not really 'war songs'. The tongue twisters seem to be more popular in the war years than immediately before, and it may be that escaping into the

---

[45] Can be heard online at www.firstworldwar.com/audio/1914.htm (accessed 15 July 2014).

[46] A more recent recording of this song, by Ian Wallace, can be found on Youtube at https://www.youtube.com/watch?v=x0Nw5tDNWo4 (accessed 25 July 2014).

realm of sound without meaning was particularly useful in traumatic times. We are reminded that the primary objective of music-hall songs is to contribute to a 'sweet Saturday night' out, a little fun in lives which were much in need of it. Nevertheless, the words of a textile worker of the time reflect the stress of many in the audience: 'I couldn't enjoy my Saturday night', she said, 'for thinking about Monday mornings.'[47]

More common than the tongue twisters were the comic chorus songs in which each verse presents a different situation, and the repeated refrain takes on a different meaning as the song goes on. 'Cover it over quick, Jemima' from before the war is a typical example. Here are the first and last verses:

We had a chicken yesterday for dinner, yes, we did
And talk about a strong'n, why it raised the saucepan lid
It popped its head up when the missus went to give a stir
It tried to sing, 'The Anchor's Weighed' and so I said to her,

Chorus: Cover it over quick Jemima, cover it over quick
Get the fork and hold it tight
But mind, the bounder wants to bite
Oh, the smell It's getting strong and thick
Now give a tap on the parson's nose
And cover it over quick. …

While working on a scaffold once I tore my corduroys
And soon I was surrounded by a crowd of girls and boys
My missus brought my dinner, nearly had a fit because
I shouted as I showed her what a nasty tear it was.

Chorus: Cover it over quick Jemima, cover it over quick
Put my dinner upon the ground,
While you're making my trousers sound
I'll catch a cold if you're more than half a tick
The dogs will be after my bubble and squeak
So cover it over quick.[48]

George Formby Senior sings a series of songs of a similar structure, such as 'Standing at the Corner of the Street' (1910), 'All of a Sudden, It Struck Me' (1915), 'I Began to Run' (1908), 'I Sobbed and I Cried Like a Child', 'Twice

---

[47]   Elizabeth Roberts, *A Woman's Place: An Oral History of Working Class Women, 1890–1940* (Oxford: Blackwell, 1984), 62.

[48]   On Youtube, one can hear Harry Champion, later in his life, sing a medley which includes an extract from this song: https://www.youtube.com/watch?v=Ng0DsWHnAaA (accessed 25 july 2014).

Nightly' (1916). 'Silly Ass' by Tom Clare in 1915 simply recounts a series of foolish mistakes made by a friend of his. The worst of these is when the narrator asks his friend not to mention to other guests in the hotel that he and his wife are newly-weds: the friend promptly tells everyone that the couple is not married, causing much embarrassment. The songs 'I Shouldn't Be a Bit Surprised' (1917) or 'And Very Nice, Too' (1922) by George Robey work in the same way.

There are songs too, to mock every conceivable scapegoat: mothers-in-law, domineering wives, foreigners, Black Africans, the Irish and, occasionally, Jews, Mormons or suffragettes. They also mock, though less fiercely, soldiers, politicians, fathers, ragtime, new technology and social change of all sorts.

'Irish' songs[49]

Ireland or the Irish constitutes the main theme of almost 5 per cent of the corpus: over 50 songs. Many of the pieces are sung with an Irish or a stage Irish accent, though the singers are often from elsewhere. They are not songs which come from an Irish tradition, and there is no attempt to integrate Irish musical instruments, such as the Celtic harp or the bodhran frame drum, which might have been problematic for theatre orchestras. The songs are not often written by Irish people,[50] and to understand their significance, we need first to look at the meaning of Ireland and its people for the contemporary music-hall audiences.

In the audiences there would naturally be a minority of Irish immigrants and their descendants. Fleeing poverty and employed building first the canals then the railways, or in textile factories and domestic service,[51] the Irish minority was well established. The Great Famine of the 1850s had accelerated the process, even if many maintained close links with their families back in Ireland. When they arrived in Britain, they could be the target of popular racism, sometimes linked to their role as cheap labour which could undercut existing wages, and of racism among the elites. The great Victorian novelist Charles Kingsley was openly racist against the Irish, calling them 'white chimpanzees'![52]

The stereotype of the Irish was complex. As well as stupid and irrational, they were seen as poetic, emotive, playful violent, given to drink and sentimental. In

---

[49]   Those who read French can find a more detailed treatment of the presence of Ireland and the Irish in John Mullen, 'Stéréotypes et identités: Irlande et les Irlandais dans le music-hall britannique 1900–1920' in *Racialisations dans l'aire anglophone*, ed. Michel Prum (Paris: L'Harmattan, 2012).
[50]   The prolific Welsh lyricist Fred Godfrey wrote many Irish songs, but also Scottish songs and many others.
[51]   Most Irish immigrants were women in the period between 1871 and 1891, and again between 1901 and 1911.
[52]   Quoted in Lewis Perry Curtis, *Anglo-Saxons and Celts: A Study of Anti-Irish Prejudice in Victorian England* (New York: New York University Press, 1968), 84.

many ways, Victorian and Edwardian racism saw the Irish as children, a view which was a useful accompaniment to English colonial projects on the island. As Catholics in a Protestant country, most Irish immigrants also experienced religious oppression. Robert Roberts recounts that in the poor parts of town:

> While one saw little open hostility, except among schoolchildren, religious prejudice was deeply ingrained. Protestants held a series of beliefs about 'Micks' which for the most part precluded any genuine friendship between them. People assured one another … that nearly all Roman Catholics were dirty and ignorant and even the cleaner ones could never be trusted. When a member of that faith new to the district came in [to the shop] to buy, customers in the shop would nod and mouth at one another 'catholic!' It was widely held that they went in dread of the priesthood, who had beaten obedience into them in childhood and who now exploited their fear of death.[53.]

This racism was no less sturdy for being based on a difference in faith and not in colour. But Ireland represented something else too: it served as a focus for the nostalgic fantasy of a supposedly simpler and happier rural lifestyle. Imagining a return to rural life was not uncommon among the industrial working class, as well as among bourgeois Romantics. Even the mass Chartist movement of the 1840s, among its many plans to revolutionize capitalism had put enormous energy into the Chartist Land Plan; which aimed at creating a class of smallholder peasants by buying up farms for working-class people to run. In this way they might escape the exploitation by factory owners.

As well as an imagined rural paradise, Ireland was a subject of fierce political controversy. The debates between those in favour of an autonomous Irish parliament – Home Rule – and the unionists were tearing the Liberal party, and indeed public opinion, apart in the immediate pre-war years. The prospect of civil war in Ireland was a very real one. For thirty years now, the question had raged and a number of music-hall songs had been written to defend or oppose Home Rule.[54] Just prior to the war, Home Rule had been voted through by the House of Commons but blocked by the Lords. In 1914, Irish nationalists were sharply divided between those who believed the victory of the Empire against Germany was the first priority, and that the question of Home Rule should be postponed to the end of the war, and those who felt Irish interests to be wholly opposed to British ones. The harshly repressed Easter Rising of 1916 was an initiative of the latter group. Songs about Ireland have also to be seen in this context.

---

[53]   Robert Roberts, *The Classic Slum: Salford Life in the First Quarter of the Century* (Harmondsworth: Pelican, 1973), 170.

[54]   For example, 'New Home Rule Song' of 1893, or 'The Oirishman's Story, a Song of Home Rule,' 1892. Also see *The Era*, 18 July 1917.

One final element contributed to the image of the Irish. Irish people had been significant actors in radical and trade union struggles for many years. Two Irishmen, Daniel O'Connell and Feargus O'Connor, played leading roles in radical movements in the 1830s and 1840s, and Irish workers were important players in the New Unionism of the 1880s and the wave of strikes of 1910–1914. Only a few days before the war, Lloyd George himself expressed anxiety that the strike movement and the Irish nationalist revolt might join forces. The situation would be 'the gravest any government had had to deal with for centuries', he declared.[55]

The image of community cohesion and combativity may have constituted a positive reference for British working-class audiences. The seven-month-long lockout in Dublin in 1913 had inspired an important movement of solidarity among English trade unionists.

This multifaceted complex of popular images of Ireland and the Irish provided the ingredients for the music-hall songs on this theme. It gave rise to three types of portrayal. Firstly there are the songs which present the racist stereotype of the stupid Irishman, well-known in the 'Irish jokes' which remained common in Britain throughout most of the twentieth century.[56] Here is an example from one of the best-known songs of the war, 'It's a long way to Tipperary',[57] which speaks of the homesickness of an Irishman away from home:

> Paddy wrote a letter
> To his Irish Molly-O,
> Saying, 'Should you not receive it,
> Write and let me know!'
> 'If I make mistakes in spelling,
> Molly, dear,' said he,
> 'Remember, it's the pen that's bad,
> Don't lay the blame on me!

Other comic stupid Irishmen appear in songs such as 'Paddy Maloney's Aeroplane' (1915), in which Maloney claims to have invented a plane which has remarkable technology:

> His corrugated iron-plated wonderful machine
> Scatters a thousand frizzly wigs on every submarine
> With telescope and microscope, Maloney says it's right
> That he can see the enemy when they are out of sight!

---

[55]   *Marlborough Express*, 20 July 1914, 5.

[56]   One can still, in 2014, buy allegedly-funny 'Irish mugs', with the mug handle on the inside.

[57]   This can be heard online at www.firstworldwar.com/audio/1914.htm (accessed 15 July 2014).

The comic heroes of these songs succeed in the end through child-like positivity. Paddy McGinty, in 'Paddy McGinty's Goat' (1917) buys a billy goat thinking it is a nanny goat, but the goat manages anyway to sink a German submarine.

Two songs, 'Irish Yiddisher Babies', and 'The Yiddisher Irish', speak of Irish Jews, considered to be doubly hilarious simply because of their communities of origin. In the latter piece, the parents choose for their baby the name 'Levi, Carney, Jacob, Barney, Michael Isaacstein', alternating Irish and Jewish first names. The emotional content of the song appears to be the unease of the dominant culture faced with a perceived strength of identity among vaguely suspect minorities.

But the 'stupid Irishman' songs do not constitute the main presence of the Irish people in British music-hall songs of the war years. Much more common are nostalgic songs where the narrator dreams of the country he has left behind him. Here are a few examples:

- I'm Coming Back to Old Kilkenny 1913
- There's a Cottage in Ballymahone 1914
- My Little Irish Cottage 1916
- For Killarney and You 1916
- A Little Bit of Heaven 1916
- I'll Be Back in Old Ireland Some Day 1916
- My little Cottage Home in Sweet Killarney. 1917
- Come Back to Ireland and Me 1917

A few lines from 'For Killarney and You' will suffice to show the tone:

> For dear old Killarney tonight I am sighing
> In fancy, I wander far over the sea
> To the green fields and dales and the lakes of Killarney
> Back to the land where the skies are the bluest
> And to the fields that I once used to love
> To my fair colleen whose dear heart is the truest
> Who promised me she would wait long ago
>
> Killarney Killarney, the place that I love,
> With its lakes clear and blue as the bright sky above
> Where we told love's sweet story and vowed to be true
> I am singing tonight for Killarney and you

The song titles generally include an easily recognizable town or village name, and may be sung by Irishmen (such as the celebrated tenor John McCormack[58]) or by others, often using nevertheless an Irish accent and a few words of stage Irish dialect.

---

[58]   His fan club website includes a number of recordings: http://www.mccormacksociety. co.uk/ (accessed 15 July 2014).

The Irish sweetheart features frequently in the songs. The rural paradise of Ireland was reflected in her purity, her beauty, and her patience as she awaited the return of her lover. Here are some song titles:

- Molly Mavourneen 1908
- My Dream Maid of Erin Isle 1910
- Sweet Mary O'Neill 1914[59]
- Mary from Tipperary 1915
- My Rose of Erin's Isle 1916
- If She Has an Irish Way with Her 1916
- Oh My Lily of Killarney 1917

An extract from the first of these songs gives a taste of their style:

> A sweet young colleen lived by Blarney Castle all alone
> She'd daily watch the trav'llers come to kiss the Blarney Stone
> One day, that way, a young man she espied
> Who winked a roguish eye at her, and to his darlin' cried.
>
> *Chorus*:   'Molly Mavourneen, Molly ochone
> I came here to kiss the Blarney Stone
> But since I've seen your eyes so blue
> I don't want to kiss no Blarney Stone
> I'd rather kiss you.'[60]

The second is perhaps more typical of the genre. The narrator dreams of his adorable girl who has 'the charms of a rose, though of ways of the world, 'tis but little she knows', praising the 'old-fashioned' Irish girl whom he prefers to sophisticated modern women.

Ireland, then, could be represented as a lost Garden of Eden, and the Irish woman as a paragon of beauty and simplicity, supremely attractive, perhaps, to the urban male worker in a complex world. Another group of songs seemed to be addressed more specifically to the Irish community in Britain, even if they were a small minority of music-hall audiences. These songs expressed different aspects of pride in being Irish:

- When Irish Eyes Are Smiling 1912[61]
- We're Irish and Proud of It Too! 1914

---

[59]   The 1914 recording can be found on Youtube at https://www.youtube.com/watch?v=tgEwbzbmTT8 (accessed 20 August 2014).

[60]   Lyrics C. W. Murphy.

[61]   One of the few which are still well known, this has been covered by a large number of singers, including Bing Crosby and Roger Whittaker.

- It Takes an Irish Heart to Sing an Irish Song 1914
- Ireland Must Be Heaven for My Mother Comes From There 1916
- As Irish As Ever 1917
- A Real Irish Wedding 1917

Others portray community feeling among the Irish:

- Be Sure He's Irish! 1914
- If You're Irish, You'll Remember! 1916
- Long As You're Irish, You'll Do! 1916
- If You're Irish, Come Into the Parlour 1919

In reality, these songs are not addressed specifically to the Irish diaspora. This theatrical portrayal of Irish pride serves to incite in the whole of the audience a nostalgia not only for a simple rural life, but for simple and unanswerable traditional values in a tightly knit community. The Irish communities of London, Manchester and elsewhere were seen as caring for and looking after their own, and this was a key ethical value for working-class communities of this period.[62] Although for Irish people in the audience, pride in being Irish might be linked to a desire for independence from England, this sentiment did not appear in the lyrics.

The song 'Irish and Proud of It, Too!' became a major hit and was rapidly recorded by several singing stars (Florrie Forde 1914, Murray Johnson 1914 and 1915, Stanley Read 1915).[63] Its success gave rise to an entire revue under the same name, which was followed in 1917 by a second revue, *As Irish As Ever*; advertising for the latter review emphasizes that all the actors and singers in the show were authentically Irish.[64] *As Irish As Ever* was produced less than a year after the Easter Rising of 1916, when the Irish Republic had been proclaimed and the insurrection's leaders executed after a week of fighting and much destruction. The event had an effect on the music-hall and revue repertoire. Nostalgic songs about 'Good Old Ireland' became much rarer (they could easily be replaced by songs about Tennessee or Kentucky). The revue *As Irish as Ever* may well have represented, among other things, a reaffirmation of community pride in a time of rising anti-Irish sentiment in Britain.

In a few songs, including 'When an Irishman Goes Fighting' (1914) or 'He's a Credit to Auld Ireland Now' (1916), pride in being Irish was put to the service of the British Empire. One of these, 'Michael O'Leary V.C.' (1915) was inspired by the true story of the first Irishman to receive the Victoria Cross. His photo had been used on a British Army recruitment poster, with the caption: 'An Irish hero! Michael O'Leary VC, Irish Guards. One Irishman beats ten Germans! Have you

---

[62] Roberts, *A Woman's Plac, passim.*
[63] Lyrics and audio extract available at http://www.fredgodfreysongs.ca/Songs/Were_Irish_And_Proud_Of_It_Too.htm (accessed 27 July 2014).
[64] *Burnley Express*, 20 January 1917.

no wish to emulate the splendid bravery of your fellow countryman? Join an Irish regiment [of the British army] today!'[65]

Irish songs, then, are perhaps the most complex group of those music-hall songs which speak of specific communities. This is due to the complexity of the relations between the Irish and the British: a political conflict going back centuries, and a diaspora well-integrated into the British working class but nevertheless subject to prejudice.

Regional songs

Other songs about regions can be divided into two categories: those which speak of a nation or a region of Britain, and those which speak of an exoticized, far-off land. Ten songs in our corpus are about Scotland, seven about Lancashire, six about London, three about Somerset, one about Surrey and two about Yorkshire. Typical song titles are:

*   We All Come Frae Lancashire 1914
*   Destination Lancashire 1917
*   The Heart of Lancashire 1918
*   Remember Where You Come From (Good Old Lancashire) 1915
*   Cockney Bill of London Town 1916
*   Don't Put the Blame on London 1914
*   You're Going Back to Your Girl in London 1915
*   There's Nothing Like London Town 1915
*   Loch Lomond 1916
*   We're All Scotch 1917
*   Auld Mother Scotland 1915
*   Back to Where the Heather Grows 1917
*   The Band Was Playing an Auld Scotch Tune 1915
*   When Sandy Machie Comes Back to Inverary 1916
*   The Green Fields of Somerset 1916
*   In Somerset in Summertime 1916
*   From Somewhere in France to Somewhere in Somerset 1917
*   My Little Surrey Home 1916
*   My Little Yorkshire Rose 1916
*   If You Come from Yorkshire 1916

The absence of Wales in the corpus is significant. We have relatively little information about the place of music hall in Welsh culture at this time. According to the 1911 census, around 43 per cent of the population of Wales spoke Welsh as

---

[65]   Library of Congress online archives, http://www.loc.gov/pictures/item/2003668492/ (accessed 25 July 2014).

their first language, and we can suppose then, that British mass culture may have had less impact than elsewhere. In any case, references to Wales in the corpus are limited to a few references to Welsh soldiers.

The wartime government understood the importance of regional and local loyalties. Lord Kitchener quickly announces that the recruits who came from the same town would be allowed to serve in the same battalion. Within two months, more than fifty of these 'Pals Battalions' were formed. Almost all of them bore the name of an industrial town (Accrington Pals, Barnsley Pals, Newcastle Pals, Bristol's Own, Sheffield City Battalion, and so on); however, a number of 'public school battalions' were also set up.

The songs in music hall refer to regional and not local, town, attachment, though the latter may have been considerably stronger. The national nature of the music-hall market makes it almost impossible to sing songs about attachment to towns, with the exception of large cities such as Glasgow.

It is worth noting that the revue *Irish, and Proud of It Too!* inspired several other revues of a similar type, singing the praises of other communities and identities. *Lancashire, and Proud of It* was a success in the North,[66] and in 1915 the revue *Jewish and Glad of It!* played in London;[67] *Scotch and Cockney* followed in 1917.[68] Each was dedicated then to significant sections of the working-class audience, and followed a similar formula of playing on some of the positive stereotypes of the groups.

As in the case of the Irish songs, a few pieces used the regional identities to reinforce the war drive. The 1915 hit song 'Remember Where You Come From (Good Old Lancashire)!' sees an officer using regional pride to galvanize his troops on the eve of battle. It was also unusually warlike for a 1915 song, with lyrics including the call: 'Remember what you're here for, to do or die for right'.

One last example, sung by the very popular humourist Whit Cunliffe, reminds us that audiences liked to see their own priorities parodied as well as echoed. The song 'In the Dear Old Town that I Was Born In' mocks the idealization of one's home town. The song warns us not to believe the romantic myth made up about home towns and reminds us ironically:

Many leave it with their happy homes tied up inside a sack
Go away and make a fortune but they never wander back!

Singing Dixie

A rather different type of geographically-based song went through a popularity boom during the war: nostalgic songs about the 'Old South', which spoke of

---

66 *Burnley Express*, 19 February 1916.
67 *The Era*, 19 May 1915.
68 *The Era*, 3 January 1917.

Dixieland, [69] Kentucky, Tennessee and other places which of course the members of the British music-hall audiences were never going to visit. Over forty songs in the corpus enter into this category.

From the point of view of the singer, songs about the 'Old South' had two important advantages. The region could be imagined as an exotic rural paradise of open spaces, natural beauty and social stability, as far away as possible from war-torn Europe. And the established tradition of blackface minstrelsy songs, which we described in Chapter 2 had made the imaginary Deep South familiar to the audiences. The wartime songs in this category are occasionally sung with a stage Black American accent or dialect, and may use other aspects of minstrelsy singing such as crosstalk, where a second artiste interrupts the singing with questions or comments. [70] The dreamed-about Dixie is rural, and in this comfortable paradise, the singer of course invites the audience to imagine themselves as White people from the South, not as Black people. The latter appear only as decorative additions. For the years 1914 and 1915, our corpus contains only a few songs of this type, such as the following:

* Off to Carolina 1914
* I Want to Go Back to Michigan 1914
* Just Try to Picture Me Back Home in Tennessee 1915

There are more in 1916:

* Night-time Down in Dixie
* They Call It Dixieland
* My Old Kentucky Home
* Goodbye Virginia
* Are You From Dixie?

And their success continues over the following two years:

* I'm On My Way to Dixieland 1917
* Down Where the Swanee River Flows 1917
* Down Texas Way 1917
* It's a Long Long Way to My Home in Kentucky 1917
* Everything is Peaches Down In Georgia 1918
* They're calling Me in Tennessee 1918
* My Tennessee, Is That You Calling Me? 1918
* When the Sun Goes Down in Dixie 1918

---

[69]   Dixieland is the nickname of the states of the old slave-owning South of the United States.
[70]   A tradition which has continued in gospel singing.

States which were not part of Dixieland could occasionally be worth a song or two:

- Back Home Again in Indiana 1917
- When It's Honeysuckle Time in Maryland 1917

Some of the Dixieland songs could be very popular indeed: during the winter of 1917–1918, no fewer than 62 different artistes sang 'Down Texas Way' in pantomimes around the country.[71]

A short extract from the lyrics gives an impression of the atmosphere:

> Back home in Tennessee just try to picture me right on my mother's knee,
> She thinks the world of me,
> All I can think of tonight is a field of snowy white;
> Banjos ringing, darkies singing, all this world seems bright.
> The roses round the door make me love mother more
> I'll see my sweetheart Flo and friends I used to know.
> Why, they'll be right there to meet me.
> Just imagine how they'll greet me when I get back,
> When I get back to my home in Tennessee!

Apart from questions of fashion which are difficult to pin down, some reasons can be suggested for the rise of Dixie songs in the war years. As the war dragged on, the attractiveness of a distant peaceful paradise could only increase,[72] and the Easter Rising made the evocation of an ideal Ireland more difficult. In addition, it may be that the arrival of US soldiers in Britain made nostalgic songs about America even more topical. After the war, Dixie songs remained popular until at least 1925. The occurrence of racist imagery in these songs is not a characteristic only of Dixie songs. Comic songs of almost any variety in this period will occasionally contain a verse where a denigrated comic stereotype of a Black person is presented; indeed, some are too offensive to quote here, even as illustrations.

No category of music-hall song is complete without its parodies, and several parodies of Dixie songs were produced during the war. In 1917, *The Encore* praised two parodies sung by Ernie Mayne, one about Michigan and the other about Tennessee: they were, according to the paper, 'true laughing hits of a high degree'.[73] In 1918, Harry Weldon tries his hand at a Dixie parody with 'Back, Back, Back, to Alabam'!', while the following year the song 'Where the Dickens Is Dixie?' had some success.

---

[71]   *The Era*, 2 January 1918.

[72]   It was noted in Chapter 2 that the two most successful musical comedies of the war years – *Chu Chin Chow* and *The Maid of the Mountains* – were both set in distant, exotic places.

[73]   *The Encore*, 4 January 1917.

Eating and drinking songs

Over twenty songs have eating or drinking as their main theme. Often they praise the 'simple and wholesome' food of working-class people or defend alcohol and mock the temperance preachers.

'Boiled Beef and Carrots', written in 1909 and still sung during the war by Harry Champion, is one of the few music-hall songs of the time to have not been completely forgotten (cover versions were produced in the 1960s).[74] The song defends the working-class food, and in sung in working-class dialect:

> Boiled beef and carrots,
> Boiled beef and carrots,
> That's the stuff for your 'Derby Kell',
> Makes you fit and keeps you well.
> Don't live like vegetarians
> On food they give to parrots,
> Blow out your kite, from Morn 'til night,
> On boiled beef and carrots.

Champion had a hit in 1916 with 'A Little Bit of Cucumber'.[75] Once again, the message of the song is that 'we' (the narrator and the audience) prefer simple traditional food to pretentious bourgeois delicacies. At the end of the story, the narrator visits the Lord Mayor's Banquet:

> To the Lord Mayor's Banquet I
> Got in one foggy day.
> When I saw the grub it took
> My appetite away:
> 'Sparrowgrass' and chaffinches,
> And pigs-head stuffed with jam!
> I said to the waiter there,
> 'You don't know who I am!'
>
> *Chorus*:   'I like pickled onions,
> I like piccalilli.
> Pickled cabbage is alright
> With a bit of cold meat on Sunday night.
> I can go termartoes,
> But what I do prefer,

---

[74]   Harry Champion's original version can be heard on Youtube: https://www.youtube.com/watch?v=7mIMIUqAa3w (accessed 20 August 2014).

[75]   The song can be heard online at http://www.firstworldwar.com/audio/1915.htm (accessed 15 July 2014).

Is a little bit of cu-cum-cu-cum-cu-cum,
Little bit of cucumber.'

In this story we see both the victory of the canny working man, sneaking into a banquet in the fog, and the defence of working-class tastes against ridiculous and pretentions bourgeois eating habits. Champion sang several more food songs. His 'Potatoes' from 1915 was used in a government campaign in favour of growing vegetables at home. Other singers also contributed to the wartime menu: Charles Coborn sang 'Bread and Cheese and Onions', while Sam Mayo sang 'Bread and Marmalade', and 'Brown Bread Well-buttered' was also popular in 1917.

In a similar tone of defending 'simple working-class tastes', we find songs like Gus Elen's 'Half a Pint of Ale' from a few years earlier:

I hate those blokes wot talks about
The things wot they like to drink
Such as tea and coffee, cocoa and milk
Why, such fings I never fink
I'm plain in me 'abits and plain in me food
And wot I say is this
If a man wot drinks such rubbish at his meals
Well, I always gives 'im a miss.

Chorus: Now at breakfast I never fink of 'aving tea
I likes arf a pint of ale
And me dinner I likes a little bit o' meat
An arf a pint of ale
For me tea I likes a little bit o' fish
An arf a pint of ale
And for supper I likes a crust o' bread and cheese
And a pint and an arf of ale.

If the most obvious pleasure afforded to audiences by these songs is the chance to sing along with working-class singers the praises of simple popular tastes, more basic meanings should not be neglected: a large section of the audience would have known what it was to be hungry. Singing of food helps exorcise the fear of hunger. Indeed, poverty and hunger were not rare. In the single year of 1901, 16,000 people were imprisoned for begging.[76] Robert Roberts, whose parents ran a grocery in a Salford slum, reports that many families owed money to the grocery for several decades,[77] and that women carried shopping in their aprons since they could not afford a shopping bag or basket.[78]

---

[76]   Roberts, *A Ragged Schooling*, 18.
[77]   Ibid., 23.
[78]   Ibid., 67.

In 1906, the problem of hunger was such that the government voted through a law permitting local authorities, if they so wished, to provide breakfast and lunch to those children who were too weak to concentrate on schoolwork through lack of food. In the Commons debate, Mr W. T. Wilson (MP for Westhoughton, Lancashire) 'said he did not think anyone in the House would doubt that a very large number of children went to school without food, or underfed, and the object of the Bill was to provide that meals should be given to such children'.[79] The scheme was to be financed by local charities; in the event, few local authorities decided to provide such meals.

Then again, in 1914 and 1915, a number of commentators remarked upon malnourishment among army recruits, and in 1917 there were hunger riots in London and Liverpool.[80]

Music and show business

The last 'minor category' is that of pieces which deal with a type of music or with the professional life of the artiste. This is a theme which is common in popular music. Over the last century there are many examples, from 'Rock Around the Clock' or 'I Was Country When Country Wasn't Cool', to 'Sheena Is a Punk Rocker'" or 'Best Rapper Alive'.[81]

Ragtime may have been the first musical 'craze' in modern popular music. Born in the United States at the end of the nineteenth century, it swept across Britain between 1910 and 1915. As was to be the case for later styles such as rock, or for modernist innovations in visual arts or in literature, its arrival was often seen as a threat to established cultural values. Ragtime was much denounced, and racist reflections were common. This editorial from *Musical News* was not untypical:

> [ragtime is] the last word in aimless, brainless rottenness. But the ragtime will soon have its day over here, thank goodness, and we shall return to the ditty of the type 'I wonder if you missed me sometimes', maudlin enough in its way but dealing with genuine and homely sentiment. These sort of songs which appeal intensely to the humbler classes do not vary in their sentiments. They are all about the amours of a fellow and a girl but the love is true, and the words perfectly free from offence. [82]

---

[79]   Hansard, online at http://hansard.millbanksystems.com/commons/1906/mar/02/ education-provision-of-meals-bill.

[80]   Richard Van Emden and Steve Humphries, *All Quiet on the Home Front: An Oral History of Life in Britain during the First World War* (London: Headline, 2003), 190; Joyce Marlow (Ed.), *The Virago Book of Women and the Great War* (London: Virago, 1999), 218.

[81]   All these can be found on Youtube.

[82]   Pearsall, *Edwardian Popular Music*, 185.

The Times was more positive: 'there is surely nothing unhealthy or lascivious in the music itself: indeed, its very vigour and rhythm must have a stimulating effect on the popular musical mind'. And for millions of people, like for the novelist J. B. Priestley, the insolent and exciting ragtime rhythms seemed to promise new times: 'hot and astonished in the Empire, we discovered ragtime ... it was as if we had been still living in the 19th century and then suddenly found the twentieth century screaming at us. We were yanked into our own age, fascinating, jungle-haunted, monstrous.'[83]

Ragtime seemed to contain: 'an emotional intensity ... which nineteenth century Britain probably only experienced in a religious context, and its arrival in the world of the Leeds Empire was a disturbing foretaste'.[84] Pearsall emphasized the question of the demands of a new generation: 'ragtime was music for the younger, who were dissatisfied and contemptuous of ballads and the schmaltzes of musical comedy. In particular, the young wanted something lively to dance to'.[85]

By 1912 and 1913, at least 130 ragtime groups from the USA were touring Britain, as well as countless imitators.[86] Whether in town-centre variety palaces, or in small halls in working-class suburbs, the audiences loved them.

Songs about ragtime flooded into the music halls:

- Alexander's Ragtime band 1911
- A Dutch Ragtime Lullaby 1913
- The Ragtime Coppers 1913
- The Ragtime Gollywog Man 1913
- The Ragtime Wedding 1913
- The Ragtime Policeman 1914
- Ragtime Ragshop 1915
- Ragtime in Dixie 1917
- John Willie's Ragtime Band 1917

The revue *All the Winners,* in 1913 aimed 'to make fun of the craze for ragtime',[87] whereas the revue *Hullo Ragtime*, the previous year, intended to sing its praises. Quite a number of music-hall songs on the subject of ragtime mocked the style, in particular in the first few years:

- Don't Drive Me Crazy With Your Ragtime Song 1912
- There Ain't Gonna Be Any Ragtime 1913

---

[83]   J. B. Priestley, quoted by John Baxendale '"... into another kind of life in which anything might happen ..." Popular Music and Late Modernity, 1910–1930', *Popular Music* 14:2 (1995), 136.

[84]   Ibid., 138.

[85]   Pearsall, *Edwardian Popular Music*, 181.

[86]   Russell, *Popular Music in England*, 68.

[87]   *The Times*, 10 April 1913.

- Don't Sing in Ragtime 1913
- Who Killed Ragtime? 1913
- Goodbye Mr Ragtime 1913
- That Ragtime Suffragette 1913

This last song seems to make a parallel between the 'insolence' and 'savagery' of the ragtime rhythms and the 'insolence' of the 'unnatural' women who used direct action in the pursuit of suffrage rights. Both phenomena are seen as a threat to the established order.

Some of the parodies could be quite sophisticated. The song 'John Willie's Ragtime Band', performed by George Formby Senior, saw the dour and supremely unsophisticated working lad from Lancashire forming, incongruously, a ragtime band:

> Talk about your ragtime brass-band,
> Your cigar-band,
> And your 'at-band,
> We've got a band that's over this way,
> It's a band down our way.
>
> Oh, oh, John Willie's ragtime band,
> Oh, oh, John Willie's ragtime band,
> 'Ear us, when we play on Wigan Pier,
> Mill-girls flock around and give a cheer,
> And the colliers, all shout 'by gum,
> 'Ear, 'ear, Itchycoo, Itchycoo, Itchycoo!'
>
> We dress just like the 'orse guards blue,
> We've won gold cups, and saucers, too!
> In Bury, now, they do it grand,
> They 'opp 'round with black puddin's in their 'ands,
> When they hear John Willie's ragtime band,
> Baby, dear, listen 'ear, ZIM!
>
> Oh, oh, John Willie's ragtime band,
> When we play, all the people faint away.
> Oh, oh, John Willie's ragtime band,
> What a mob, when we're out upon the job,
> 'Ear us, when we play on Wigan Pier,
> Mill-girls flock around and give a cheer,
> And the colliers, all shout 'by gum,
> 'Ear, 'ear, Mine's a beer, Mine's a beer, Mine's a beer!'[88]

---

[88]   Can be heard online at https://www.youtube.com/watch?v=jH5h6UKWKbo (accessed 27 July 2014).

One element visible through the mockery of ragtime is a certain conservatism in the music-hall milieu, feeling threatened by the new American music flooding the market. But elite voices too could be heard at times denouncing ragtime. The specialist magazine for gramophone enthusiasts, the *Phono Record*, announced the release in 1918 of a new series of recordings under the series title 'Music for Sundays at Home'. The editorialist spoke of the need to 'raise the level', and complained that he still heard 'so much ragtime and popular music on a Sunday morning'.[89]

Ragtime marched on inexorably, and the criticisms tended to die down. During the war, a ragtime band formed exclusively of soldiers who had lost their sight in battle was formed by the Saint Dunstan's charitable organization for blinded soldiers, a sign of the acceptance of ragtime by respectable organizations.[90] Other musical styles, not quite as influential, followed close behind. The tango was perhaps the first dance to sweep the world in a modern-style fashion craze. A few songs spoke of it:

- She Makes Me Do the Tango Too 1913
- Tango Fever 1914
- A Tango Dream 1914
- Josephine, You're the Tango Queen 1914
- Do a Tango Dance with Me 1914
- Chinese Tango Trot 1916

Two revues, *Hello Tango* and *Hello Miss Tango*, were devoted to the dance craze, and even *The Times* was gradually convinced the tango was worthy of interest, as this extract from a show review indicates:

> She dances a Tango, and for the first time one realizes that a Tango can be danced with meaning and form, a dance that belongs intimately to its music, a dance with ugly movements in it (if any movement of so graceful and so extraordinarily agile a dancer as Miss Levey can be called ugly), but still a dance full of rhythm and often beautiful.[91]

The fox-trot, which was introduced in 1914, gave rise to such songs as:

- At the Fox-trot Ball, That's All 1915
- Everybody's Crazy on the Fox-trot' 1916
- The Hottentot Fox-trot 1916
- In Grandma's Days They Never Did the Fox-trot 1916
- I Want to Fox-trot with You 1916
- The Flapper's Foxtrot 1916

---

[89]   *Phono Record*, April 1918.
[90]   *The Times*, 23 October 1917.
[91]   *The Times*, 14 December 1913.

The arrival of a new dance, the shimmy, in 1918, gave us 'Everybody Shimmies Now!'. At the very end of the war, the word 'jazz' began to be heard. The music-hall songs which spoke of jazz were generally not parodies, as so many about ragtime had been. It may be that the massive cultural dislocations of wartime had finally marginalized those who wished to moan in song that times were changing. In 1918, 'When I Hear That Jazz Band Play' and 'I Went a Jazzing' were both successes, as were 'Jazz!' and 'Stick Around for the New Jazz Band.'

Songs occasionally dealt with the professional life of a music-hall artistes. Already in 1904, in his song 'Twice Nightly', George Formby had commented on the changes in music hall as the one continuous show system gave way to the two-shows-a-night scheme, with the aim of increasing profitability.

Songs about the professional life of an artistes are common throughout the twentieth century such as Simon and Garfunkel's 'Homeward Bound' or Elkie Brooks's 'Pearl's a Singer'. However, these songs in the period of the First War are not psychological portraits; in accord with the general tone of music hall, they are more likely to be ironic reflections on changes in the industry, as demonstrate, for example, the two songs about revue, by Marie Lloyd and by The Two Bobs, which we quoted in the previous chapter.

This category of songs about the life of an artiste serves to remind us of the complexity of the production of popular songs. The artiste is far from being a simple puppet for impersonal commercial interests, and retains a certain capacity to introduce themes of interest to him or her personally.

This chapter has surveyed the range of themes dealt with by music-hall songs of the war years, in an attempt to judge what may be learned about popular attitudes of the time. The two biggest groups of themes have been left to one side. One is a subject omnipresent in popular music and in culture in general: love and the relationships between men and women. The other is specific to these years: total war and how life is affected. The next two chapters will deal in turn with these themes.

A Star in Focus 3
Marie Lloyd – 'Our Marie'

'She'd never had her ticket punched before!'

Born as Matilda Wood in 1870, the eldest of nine children of a waiter and a dressmaker, Marie began working on stage as young as seven years old, singing temperance songs, but she became one of the most popular music-hall stars in history with a somewhat less respectable repertoire.[1] Her three sisters all worked in music hall or in pantomime, and one of them, Alice, became a star in her own right in US vaudeville.

Marie's stage persona was that of a cockney woman, who knew about life and intended to enjoy herself. She was universally known in the working class as 'Our Marie' – one of our people who had made it big. As such, she can be seen, along with other music-hall stars, as a symbolic compensation for the almost total lack of people with visible working-class roots in the elites of the country. 'Social mobility', indeed, had hardly been invented.

Kilgarriff's catalogue lists something over 150 songs in her repertoire.[2] They deal with questions of working-class life (poverty, evictions or drink) in a stoical or joyful tone, or of the love life of young people and honeymoon couples. At a time when strong middle-class pressure was still being expressed in favour of 'elevating pastimes', her songs aiming at defending simple enjoyment were very popular. In 'A Little of What You Fancy Does You Good', she confides:

Now I likes mi drop of stout as well as anyone
But stout you know's supposed to make you fat
Ar And there's many a lar-di-dar-di madam as doesn't dare to touch it
'Cos it might spoil her figure, the silly cat.

Chorus: Now I always hold with having it if you fancy it
If you fancy it, that's understood
And suppose it makes you fat?
I don't worry over that
'Cause A little of what you fancy does you good!

---

[1]   A photograph is available here: http://en.wikipedia.org/wiki/Marie_Lloyd (accessed 22 January 2015).

[2]   Kilgarriff, Michael, *Sing Us One of the Old Songs: A Guide to Popular Song 1860–1920* (Oxford: Oxford University Press, 1999), 269–270.

According to James Agate, an influential theatre critic, 'she depicted the delight of humble life, the infinite joy of mean streets';[3] while another contemporary commentator explained: 'In some indescribable way, she has gathered her audience to her: they are hers, to do with as she pleases. "We are all pals together," she seems to say, and, "strictly as pals, what do you think of this?".'[4]

Some of her lyrics and on-stage gestures could shock, and a number of venues refused to engage her. During a tour of Canada, one of her songs, 'The Ankle Watch', was banned because Lloyd exposed her ankle on stage. In another hit she sang:

> When I take my morning promenade
> Quite a fashion card, on the Promenade
> Oh! I don't mind nice boys staring hard
> If it satisfies their desire!
> Do you think my dress is a little bit
> Just a little bit... Well not too much of it,
> Though it shows my shape just a little bit
> That's the little bit the boys admire!

Along with its optional suggestive gestures, this piece was seen by many as going too far. Another of her songs asked the question 'Should the Sexes Bathe Together?', whereas a piece about travelling on the railway contained the sing-along chorus 'She'd never had her ticket punched before'. Since this suggestive line was part of the chorus, the entire audience was invited to sing it in the tone they chose.[5] Yet another hit, 'Every Little Movement Has a Meaning of Its Own', celebrated the seduction tactics of sophisticated women.

Lloyd was often singled out by moralist associations of the time, and had to perform a number of times in front of censorship committees. She seemed always to be in the press, too, due to her colourful private life: she was twice divorced, and left her adulterous and spendthrift husband to find herself another partner, 18 years younger than herself. Her extreme popularity, despite these, at the time scandalous, events can serve to remind us that moralist ideology did not dominate everyone's thinking all the time.

She had a highly developed sense of showmanship, and was always able to dose the 'daring' content so as to keep the audience with her. Those songs which commence with highly dubious activities tend to end in the two people involved getting married. At the time it was dangerous to defend suggestiveness openly, and

---

[3]   Quote in James Harding, *George Robey and the Music-Hall* (London: Hodder & Stoughton, 1990), 25.

[4]   John Booth, quoted by Richard Baker, *Marie Lloyd: Queen of the Music-halls (London:* Robert Hale, 1990), 48.

[5]   The sheet music to this song was never published during her lifetime, but was included in *The Marie Lloyd Songbook,* (London: Feldman, 1954).

Lloyd felt obliged to claim an unlikely naivety. But at the same time she defended her repertoire:

> They don't pay their sixpences and shillings at a music hall to hear the Salvation Army. If I was to try to sing highly moral songs, they would fire ginger beer bottles and beer mugs at me. I can't help it if people want to turn and twist my meanings.[6]

During one of the moralist campaigns she replied to the critics with a song 'They Can't Stop a Girl from Thinking!':

> I mustn't tell you what I mean, mustn't tell you what I've seen
> Everything that's risqué must be dropped!
> While I've been stopped from winking
> Mustn't tell you what I've heard, mustn't say a naughty word
> So help my Bob, it's a jolly good job
> They can't stop a girl from thinking!

If Marie Lloyd represented a relatively liberated woman for the times, and if her private life may have seemed ahead of the times, her work cannot be considered as feminist in inspiration. One of her most successful hits, 'Oh, Mr Porter', tells the tale of a woman who decided to travel alone by train. Naturally, she got on the wrong train and ended up at the other end of the country. Panicking, she fainted, and was helped by a kindly old gentleman, who found her pretty and asked her to marry him. Another piece, from 1916, 'Women's Opinion of Man', far from being a polemic against misogyny or sexism, mocks those women who think they understand the male sex, and defends the 'natural' position of men and women in relationships.

In 1907, Marie Lloyd threw herself into organizing for the great music-hall strike. She was present at the rallies and pickets, and launched a public appeal for a solidarity fund for the strike. She explained that, although stars like herself were well paid, she had joined the strike to help defend lower-paid performers. In 1912, when the first Royal Command Performance took place, many were surprised to see Lloyd's name omitted from the bill; Lloyd herself was furious and organized a rival show the same evening. It was never clear if her omission from the Royal Command Performance was linked to her role in the 1907 strike or to her scandalous private life.

During the war years, she made almost no change to her repertoire of songs, but added one relatively subtle recruitment song, 'Now You've Got Yer Khaki On', about a man who managed to seduce his girl by joining the army.

---

[6]   Daniel Farson, *Marie Lloyd and Music Hall* (London: Tom Stacey, 1972), 57.

Oh I do feel so proud of you
I do, honour bright!
I'm going to give yer an extra cuddle tonight!
I didn't like you much before you joined the army, John
But I do like yer, cockie, now you've got yer khaki on! [7]

George Bernard Shaw praised her musical talent and T S Eliot, writing on the occasion of her death, paid homage to her art:

Although I have always admired her genius I do not think that I always appreciated its uniqueness; I certainly did not realize that her death would strike me as the most important event which I have had to chronicle in these pages. Marie Lloyd was the greatest music-hall artist in England: she was also the most popular. And popularity in her case was not merely evidence of her accomplishment; it was something more than success. It is evidence of the extent to which she represented and expressed that part of the English nation which has perhaps the greatest vitality and interest. [8]

Towards the end of her life, partly in reaction to her husband's violence Lloyd would drink to excess, and had serious health problems. Taken ill in the middle of a show, she died in 1922 at the age of 52. Her extravagant lifestyle and uncontrolled generosity meant she died penniless. Fifty thousand people lined the streets for her funeral.

---

[7] This song can be heard at http://www.firstworldwar.com/audio/1916.htm (accessed 30 July 2014).

[8] 'London Letter', *The Dial* 73:6 (December 1922).

Chapter 4

'If you were the only girl in the world': Women, Men and Love in Music-hall Song

This chapter will turn to the question of relationships between men and women, and the social position of women, as represented in the industry and in the songs. The practices, ideas and prejudices of the time and how they changed during the war will be at the centre of this section. I will attempt to put together a clear sketch from the masses of information available, while not forgetting what Elizabeth Roberts wrote after having interviewed dozens of working-class women who had lived through Edwardian times. Her work, she insisted, 'continually serves to emphasise the complexity and variety of working-class experience. For every generalisation exceptions can be found.'[1]

What was life like for women in 1914? The legal restrictions on their public life are well known: they could only vote in local elections, and could not sit on a jury. As a rule they would give up any paid work, and certainly any career, upon marriage. Recent changes had allowed small numbers of women to become accountants or doctors, but many other professions remained completely closed to them. A thousand or so women took courses at Oxford or Cambridge in 1910, but were forbidden to receive degrees. A few women, almost always from the elites, managed to overcome all the obstacles and gain recognition in intellectual pursuits, for example: Hertha Ayrton, praised for her discoveries in electricity, published in 1902; Marie Stopes, who was appointed university lecturer in paleobotany in 1908; or Annie Scott Dill Maunder, whose research in solar astronomy was published in 1908.

Working-class women began work young, at 12 or 13 years of age, in domestic service, in textile factories or in shops. When they got married (on average twelve and a half years later), they normally gave up paid work in order to look after house and children. 'Many skilled men did not like their wives to be seen earning money: it reflected badly on their own status as the breadwinner. There is no evidence to suggest that women questioned this point of view.'[2]

Very slowly, new professions were opening their doors to women: 6 per cent of the female workers in Barrow in 1911 were teachers, 14 per cent worked in commerce (in nearby Preston it was 2 per cent and 8 per cent respectively). There

---

[1]   Elizabeth Roberts, *A Woman's Place: An Oral History of Working Class Women, 1890–1940* (Oxford: Wiley-Blackwell, 1984), 38.

[2]   Ibid., 137.

were more and more jobs for lady typists. A trade union for women post-office employees had even been established in 1901.[3]

Generalizations can be overstated: the rate of employment of married women varied very much from one town to another. In 1911, in the port of Barrow (population 64,000) only 6.9 per cent of the category 'married women and widows' were in full-time paid employment, but in Lancaster, a similar town (population 42,000), 11 per cent were, and in the textile town of Preston (population 120,000) as many as 35 per cent of this category worked fulltime jobs.[4] Domestic servants alone accounted for 34 per cent of women workers in Barrow and 25 per cent in Lancaster. In Preston, the availability of work in the textile mills reduced this proportion to only 9 per cent. They dreamed of escaping domestic service through marriage. 'Marriage was the goal of every woman servant ... you were a nobody; marriage was the only way out of it.'[5]

Outside the workplace, the presence of women in public life was growing slowly. In 1903, a press magnate had launched the *Daily Mirror* as 'a paper written by women for women'. Even if it did not last very long in this format, the attempt shows changes in attitudes to women's roles. And women did not spend all their time at home doing housework: in 1914, there were 40,000 arrests of women for being drunk and disorderly in public places, a far higher figure than today.

Separate spheres

Dominant ideology insisted on separate spheres of influence for men and women. Women should never forget that children and the family were their only raison d'être. In working-class parts of town, it was common to see women wearing their apron indoors and outdoors the whole day, a symbol of their role as housekeeper, a role of which they were frequently proud.[6] Robert Roberts tells us that in the poor neighbourhood he lived in just before the Great War, wives referred to their husband as 'my master'.[7] Nevertheless, inside the family they had real power. Of 160 elderly ladies from three different towns, interviewed by Elizabeth Roberts in the 1970s, all except one maintained that in their family, it was the wife who was in charge of finances. The husband handed over his wages intact and received

---

[3]   Eric Wigham, *From Humble Petition to Militant Action: A History of the Civil and Public Services Association, 1903–1978* (London: Civil and Public Services Association, 1980), 15.

[4]   Roberts, *A Woman's Place*, 143.

[5]   Max Arthur, *The Road Home: The Aftermath of the Great War Told by the Men and Women Who Survived It* (London: Phoenix, 2009), 182.

[6]   Roberts, *A Woman's Place*, 168.

[7]   Robert Roberts, *A Ragged Schooling: Growing Up in the Classic Slum* (London: Fontana, 1978), 71.

pocket money in return.[8] It was the wife who made the big budget decisions, such as when to move house, and it was she who managed the – normally extremely tight – budget. She decided what was to be pawned to help survive till pay day, and what to do if there was no money for curtains or netting (using newspaper was a vulgar last resort).[9] The man's role was to work and bring home the money. He who didn't do his bit, but drank his wages away might be stigmatized by the local community.

Most women brought up big families. Family size had begun to fall slightly after 1890, but the main reduction was to take place much later. Women had to do the housework without modern detergents or machines, and generally without the help of their husband. The washtub, the washboard and the manual wringer meant that washing clothes was much harder work than today, and young girls were often kept off school on washing day to help their mothers. Shopping, cooking and cleaning were also much more wearing and time-consuming than they are today.

As for ordinary women's view of their place in society, here is the conclusion of Elizabeth Roberts:

> The oral evidence is complex; it reveals a mass of individual differences, and yet has shown a large section of society following and upholding a clearly understood, if infrequently discussed, set of mores. These produced women who were disciplined, inhibited, conforming and who placed perceived familial and social needs before those of the individual. Women did not seek self-fulfilment at the expense of the family because they saw little distinction between their own good and that of their families. There was a very low level of self-awareness. Women's considerable powers were all exercised, firmly, in the perceived interests of their families – that is how they saw 'their place'.[10]

Clearly, in the public sphere, male domination was very strong indeed. Men had infinitely more freedom. Yet this strict separation of roles had a negative side for men, too. Workplace accidents were frequent and often deadly; the working week was 54 hours on average, and often much longer. Husbands came home exhausted. Moreover, in extreme situations, it was not easy to be a man. When the *Titanic* went down in April 1912, we can see the weight of men's role. Among first-class passengers, 3 per cent of women and 67 per cent of men died. In second class, 14 per cent of women and 92 per cent of men, and in third class, 54 per cent of women and 84 per cent of men. It was more particularly in wartime that men paid

---

[8]   Roberts, *A Woman's Place*, 110. Others have reached the same conclusion: see Catherine-Émilie Corvisy and Véronique Molinari, *Les femmes dans l'Angleterre victorienne et édouardienne: entre sphère privée et sphère publique* (Paris: L'Harmattan, 2008), 55.

[9]   Robert Roberts, *The Classic Slum: Salford Life in the First Quarter of the Century* (Harmondsworth: Pelican, 1973), 33.

[10]   Roberts, *A Woman's Place*, 203.

the price of their dominant position in the public sphere. Demands for women to join in armed combat were non-existent in Britain, despite the wide publicity given to Russian women's battalions. 'Men must fight and women must work' was the slogan of Emmeline Pankhurst. More than 800,000 British men were killed in the war.

As for women, the values of the time held that they should not be told the truth about military life. 'Everyone out here ... considers it only fair to one's womankind to hush up the worst side of the war',[11] reported one soldier, while a nurse explained: 'they look at you with such pathetic eyes and say, "you're a woman, we could not even begin to tell you the things we have suffered"'.[12]

Campaigns for women's rights

At the beginning of the twentieth century, the ideology of 'separate spheres' was being partly called into question, and the movement to extend rights and possibilities for women was a powerful one. In the years since 1860 several organizations had been active in favour of women's rights, using all the traditional campaign tactics: meetings, newspapers, petitions, and so on. Each town had local groups and if middle-class women formed the majority of activists, many working-class women were also involved.[13] Some advances were won by these movements. Married women could own their own property after the law of 1870, and the same year women were authorized to sit on school boards. In 1869, a college for women, Girton College, was founded at Cambridge University, and in 1893, the first female factory inspectors were appointed.

However, on the key question of the right to vote in national elections, no progress had been made. A group of activists led by Emmeline Pankhurst decided that traditional methods had failed, and launched a campaign of direct action. They founded, the Women's Social and Political Union (WSPU) in 1903, soon to be famous under the name 'suffragettes' (whereas the word 'suffragist' was used for the mainstream organizations). From 1905 to 1913, the WSPU went through three stages of direct action and managed to keep the question of women's suffrage on the front page of the newspapers. First, they heckled political speakers, while continuing with traditional methods of political campaigns. Then they moved onto the tactic of damaging property: breaking windows, damaging art works in galleries, setting fire to hundreds of post-boxes in the streets, and so on.

---

[11]   Arthur Marwick, *The Deluge: British Society and the First World War* (Basingstoke: Palgrave, 2006 (1965)), 176.

[12]   Arthur, *The Road Home*, 34.

[13]   Jill Liddington and Jill Norris, *One Hand Tied Behind Us: Rise of the Women's Suffrage Movement* (London; Virago, 1978), *passim.*

By now the organization had 75 full-time organizers, and the demonstration which gathered in Hyde Park in June 1908 reached half a million participants.[14] In a third phase of direct action, the suffragettes set fire to a series of buildings, including the house of Lloyd George, Chancellor of the Exchequer at the time. Their objective was to cause the maximum disorder, without putting human lives at risk. Emmeline Pankhurst explained that the idea was not to persuade more people of the justice of their cause, but to make normal political life impossible until the right to vote was given to women.[15]

Around a thousand women, and a few men, were imprisoned, In jail, from 1909, they went on hunger strike, and the government responded by ordering them to be force-fed, a very violent procedure at this time. The public reaction was very strong.[16] The arrival of the war in 1914 put an end to an intense period of conflict which the Liberal Prime Minister, Mr Asquith, had been finding very difficult to manage.

The feminists support the war

Immediately the war broke out, the WSPU moved to a position of active and enthusiastic support for the drive for victory. The imprisoned suffragettes were freed on the promise that illegal activities would be called off. The National Union of Women's Suffrage Societies (NUWSS), a larger and more moderate organization, and the Women's Freedom League (WFL) also agreed to suspend their campaigns.

Support for the cause of the Empire was the automatic response of the majority of feminist activists. The WSPU went further than the other organizations: it changed the name of its paper from *The Suffragette* to *Britannia* and launched a campaign to bring in military conscription for men. Millicent Fawcett, who had previously been opposed to war, changed her position once the war began. Another leader, Mona Granville, spoke on the platform at army recruitment rallies. One recruiter reported:

> For a time we had Mrs Mona K. Granville, and it was no unusual sight to see women in tears as she urged the country's need and manhood's duty in her intense dramatic way. She laid great value upon the power of women to procure recruits, and she found her sex always most anxious for the men to go.[17]

[14]   Françoise Barret-Ducroq, *Le mouvement féministe anglais d'hier à aujourd'hui* (Paris: Ellipses, 2000), 88.

[15]   See Emmeline Pankhurst's speech online at http://www.guardian.co.uk/theguardian/2007/apr/27/greatspeeches1.

[16]   June Purvis, 'The Prison Experiences of the Suffragettes in Edwardian Britain', *Women's History Review* 4:1 (1995).

[17]   Private J. Quigley, *The Slogan – Sidelights on Recruiting with Harry Lauder's Band* (London: Simpkin, 1916), 150.

In July 1915, the WSPU organized, with government support, a demonstration in London for 'the right of women to serve', and tens of thousands of women were involved.[18]

The NUWSS and the WFL were less enthusiastic in their support for the war, but hoped above all that it would allow women to broaden their roles in society. The two organizations worked hard at relief work for poorer women and for refugees. They were also involved in lobbying for the rights of soldiers' wives. In 1915, when several town councils banned serving alcohol to soldiers' wives, and even introduced curfews, the Ministry of War received a protest delegation from the two organizations.[19]

A section which had been expelled in 1913 from the WSPU, and which was led by one of Emmeline Pankhurst's daughters, Sylvia, took a clearly anti-war position. This organization, the East London Federation of Suffragettes, open to both men and women, published a regular journal, *The Women's Dreadnought*. They set up relief work in the poor parts of East London, opening a series of cost-price canteens, a free health clinic and other such initiatives. They campaigned for higher government allowances for soldiers' wives, at the same time denouncing what they saw as an unjust war. Some of the organization's activists helped hide pacifists on the run from the police.

War, women and change

The first months of the war, and the enrolment of hundreds of thousands of volunteers in the army initially put poorer women in an even more desperate situation than before. The 'separation allowances' paid to soldiers' wives were very low, and often dependent on paperwork too complex for many families. No allowances were paid, initially, for elderly dependants of men away on service, or for children born outside wedlock or less than nine months after their parents' marriage. Many poor families did not have the money to buy the copies of birth and marriage certificates necessary to claim their allowances, and malnourishment was widespread in the poorer areas. Massive orders of food and clothes for the army caused price inflation, too. Lady Frances Balfour denounced as 'deserters' those women who complained about rising prices, while in Glasgow the eviction of soldiers' wives from their houses for non-payment of rent caused a public scandal. It was only after the first year of war that the living standards of the poorer sections of the population began to rise.[20]

Male workers began to be replaced by women workers, in spite of significant resistance at all levels of society. When, at the beginning of the war, one of the first

---

[18]   Marwick, *The Deluge*, 129.

[19]   *The Guardian*, 26 January 1915.

[20]   Sylvia Pankhurst, *The Home Front: A Mirror to Life in England during the First World War* (London: The Cresset Library, 1987 (1932)), 23–30.

women doctors, Elsie Inglis, asked the Ministry of War what contribution she and her fellow women doctors could make she was apparently told 'my good lady, go home and sit still'![21] In a number of situations, women could find that customers simply refused to accept them. A woman who took over the delivery of meat when her father went to war explained that a number of customers, both women and men, initially refused to accept her deliveries.[22] Attitudes changed gradually and, after the introduction of military conscription for men in 1916, the government began to campaign for the employment of the highest number of women possible. Hundreds of thousands left domestic service to work in industry and commerce, where they were better paid, better respected and more independent. Millions of married women went back to paid work, too. Over the four years, 500,000 additional women began work in commerce, 400,000 in agriculture and 800,000 in industry.[23] In the banking sector, which counted only 1 500 women in 1914, there were 30,000 two years later.[24] The first female tram conductors were taken on in Glasgow, and by February 1917 there were 2 500 women conductors on London buses and trams. The newspapers were filled with articles by journalists amazed and impressed by 'the newly acquired capacities' of the female population.[25]

The arrival of so many women on the job market was often not welcomed by trade unions. Some writers have seen a deeply entrenched sexism at work and others have seen it as fear that employers would use women as an excuse to cut wages; no doubt both of these factors were at work. In 1917, 200,000 engineers went on strike to oppose the taking on of unqualified, lower-paid women. For these new women workers, joining the labour movement was not easy. The tax workers' union decided after a fierce debate in 1917, for example, that women taken on during the war could not join the union.[26] But such decisions were not universal: the AUCE shop workers' union, for instance, approved the replacement of men workers by women on condition that they were paid at the same rate as men. The union hired a full-time organizer specifically to unionize women and to encourage them to play an active role in the organization.[27]

Towards the end of the war a new law on suffrage appeared to be necessary: under the existing one, all soldiers stationed abroad would have been unable to vote, a situation which would have been politically inconceivable. The government

---

[21] Joyce Marlow (Ed.), *The Virago Book of Women and the Great War* (London: Virago, 1999), 5.

[22] Ibid., 195.

[23] Marwick, *The Deluge*, 132.

[24] Richard Van Emden and Steve Humphries, *All Quiet on the Home Front: An Oral History of Life in Britain during the First World War* (London: Headline, 2003), 118.

[25] Marwick, *The Deluge*, 130.

[26] A. J. Brown, *The Taxmen's Tale – The History of the Inland Revenue Staff Federation* (London: IRSF, 1983), 18.

[27] William Richardson, *A Union of Many Trades: The History of USDAW* (Manchester: USDAW, 1979), 70.

included in the new law a provision that women over the age of 30 should also have the right to vote. Debate continues as to the reasons for this change of heart by ministers who had so fiercely fought against women's suffrage only a few years previously. Did the authorities, aware that the war was drawing to a close, want to be sure that renewed suffragette militancy did not destabilize a political situation which was already looking to need careful handling? In any case, a number of leading politicians had been convinced, seeing the new roles played by women during the war, that the extension of the suffrage was inevitable, and the law was passed without difficulty by both houses of parliament.

It seems clear that women's new roles had helped change mentalities. Robert Roberts, writing about the poorer levels of society, describes significant change after the war: 'To the shocked stares of the respectable, housewives with husbands away or on night work could now be seen going off in pairs to the pictures or sitting with a glass of stout in the Best Room in the pub.'[28]

After the end of the war, millions of women lost their jobs, in particular in manual trades, yet opportunities in some professions and in secretarial work remained open. One permanent change was the reduction in numbers of domestic servants, who had made up 40 per cent of all women workers in 1911; in 1921, the figure was 32 per cent.[29] In 1919, under pressure from the Labour party which was pushing for wider reforms, the Liberal government decided women could henceforth sit on juries and become magistrates.[30]

Women in the music hall

Let us move on to the situation of women on the music-hall stage, and their representation in the songs. The very first music halls had shown only male turns; the first woman to become a music-hall professional was Ellen Caufield in 1860.[31] Thereafter, the presence of women became gradually more and more common: in 1872, Jenny Hill even had a hit with the song 'Bother the Men!'.[32]

Looking at the music-hall trade paper at the beginning of the war, one can see that of the first one hundred small ads in the column where artistes advertised the dates they were free in the hope of catching the attention of theatre managers, 29 per cent concerned women artistes.[33] Among well-known singers the proportion appears to have been higher still. One of the music publishers boasted in July 1914 of having already brought out 'a hundred and one hit songs' that year. The

---

[28]   Roberts, *The Classic Slum*, 204.
[29]   Corvisy and Molinari, *Les Femmes*, 129.
[30]   Marwick, *The Deluge*, 318.
[31]   Sara Maitland, *Vesta Tilley* (London: Virago, 1986), 15.
[32]   Laura King, '"Matrons, Maidens and Magdalenes": Women's Patronage of 19th Century Music Halls' (Master's diss., Simon Fraser University, 1993), 35.
[33]   *The Performer*, 23 July 1914.

full-page advertisement is illustrated by photographs of the best known singers: 22 women and 34 men.

One might think that the departure of men to the war would leave more opportunities for female singers, in particular seeing that the music halls continued to do a roaring trade throughout the war years. Indeed, all-women orchestras and even all-women shows were to be seen. For music-hall singers in general, though, there seems to be little change. Of 424 songs of 1918 for which the singer is known, only 34 per cent are sung by women.

In a world in which there were precious few opportunities for working-class women to express a public voice, the women on the music-hall stage prepared the way for more active female roles in society. Stars such as Marie Lloyd showed themselves on stage as powerful women, well able to handle their relationships with men, and in no way dupes. In addition, seeing women earning good money in an independent fashion must have impressed both men and women in the audience.

Almost all women who sang on the music-hall stage came from the working class, or from even poorer backgrounds. As models, they were close to the audience and not distant personages, as university lecturers or other intellectuals were. As we have seen, some of the stars worked dressed as men, allowing them to satirize male habits, and in particular those of upper-class men. Nevertheless, we do not find women singers singing songs which defend women's rights or criticize male domination; often quite the opposite.

In other professions within the music-hall industry, new opportunities arose for women during the war, though not without difficulty. The editorial of *The Performer*, in 1917, urged men to agree to work with female musicians in the orchestra, saying that it would be good to release 'a few of the men who play the lighter instruments ... on the definite understanding that directly the war is over, the men should have their positions restored to them'.[34] The same editorial recommended that women should be employed as lighting operators and as prompters. The need for such urgings suggests that there was considerable resistance to the idea. Old prejudices remained strong: in *The Encore* the same year, writers ironized about the danger of employing women as doormen, given their supposed propensity to gossip.[35]

The quasi-absence of women songwriters in the music-hall repertoire deserves some attention. In part, this was no doubt due to the 'non-respectable' pubs in which much selling of songs took place, but in general it fits in with the exclusion of women from many public spaces, and the limitations placed on women's possibilities for public expression. In the music-hall song, the women's authorial voice is extremely rare. Indeed, the authorial voice is in general little developed in the music-hall song compared to later genres of popular music such as rock. This is why, as we have seen for example, 'Irish' songs were frequently written by people who were not Irish. The showman was more present than the auteur in

---

[34]   *The Performer*, 1 March 1917.
[35]   *The Encore*, 17 May 1917.

songwriting in this period, so the presentation of personal philosophy or poetry was not on the menu. Nevertheless one might think that the fact that 95 per cent of the songwriters were men (whereas a third at least of the singers were women) affected the content of the songs. It is certain that, as we shall see below, women do not get treated well in much of the repertoire. One of the important functions of music hall was to bring into the public sphere, for the purpose of collective singing and laughing, the everyday difficulties of working-class life. These could be joys and problems with friends, difficulties in courtship or difficulties in marriage. Men's difficulties and experiences were explored infinitely more than those of women. The women characters in music-hall lyrical content are, with rare exceptions, far more limited in scope, and often examined only in their relationships to men. For example, fantasies of perfect partners, very common in music-hall songs, are, almost exclusively, male fantasies.

Anti-suffragette songs 1908–1914

Turning to the representation of women and women's rights in the songs, we find that before the war, a series of singers included in their repertoire anti-suffragette songs, and that these could be commercially very successful.[36] In 1910, a song performed by Whit Cunliffe, 'Do You Believe in Women's Rights?', portrays a determined and 'hysterical' suffragette who, once she has been seduced by a gallant gentleman, realizes the error of her ways and understands she can find true happiness only in the role of wife and mother. The same year, in the hit 'The Land Where the Women Wear the Trousers', we see men wearing petticoats forced to obey their wives and wash the family's clothes.[37] Cunliffe and two or three other singers specialize in mocking suffragette activists, but they are not the only ones. And, as Russell points out, many female singers felt at ease with such content. Marie Lloyd warns that men who choose to marry a 'suffering suffragette' 'soon will be wearing skirts. And the women will be wearing the trousers.'[38]

Note that most of the songs do not announce as such their opposition to the right to vote for women: by 1908 it is likely that the majority of the audience was in favour of such a reform. The songs prefer to caricature the 'unnatural' and 'hysterical' 'extremist' woman activist, the suffragette. An exception is Wilkie Bard singing in 1909, where a political opposition is expressed:

---

[36]   There were many songs about suffragettes on the vaudeville stage in the USA, particularly in New York. As for the whole of our book, we have only considered here songs published or sung in the UK.

[37]   A version can be heard on Youtube, sung by Billy Williams.

[38]   Dave Russell, *Popular Music in England, 1840–1914: A Social History* (Manchester: Manchester University Press, 1997), 79.

Just imagine how you'd look outside your cottage door
With children three or four, Dame Fortune may grant you more
Your wife she sits in 'Parliament' commanding prolonged cheers
While little Tommy's sticking jammy fingers in your ears!
An angel I shall choose to be, the day that woman's called M.P.

Put me on an island where the girls are few,
Put me amongst the most ferocious lions in the zoo,
You can put me on a treadmill and I'll never fret,
But for pity's sake don't put me near a suffragette!

We should note that the lyrics are directed only at men. The song 'Ragtime Suffragette', a hit in 1913, is particularly interesting. It combines a denunciation, not unusual in the music hall, of ragtime music, seen as disorderly, modernist and rebellious, with a condemnation of the suffragette, presented similarly as a threat to the natural order.

What's that noise upon the avenue?
What's that crowd a-doin' 'round there too?
What's the meaning of that awful crash?
Has a taxicab got in a smash?

Johnny, Johnny run and get your gun.
Get in quick or you'll be dead, my son.
It would make Napoleon quake
And shake his head with fear.
Oh dear, oh dear, just look, look, look who's here

That ragtime suffragette,
She's no household pet,
Raggin' with bombshells and raggin' with bricks,
Haggling and naggling with politics

That ragtime suffragette,
Ragtime suffragette,
For Lordy, while her husband's wait home to dine,
She's just rag-gin' up and down the line.
A-shoutin' votes, votes, votes, votes, votes for women,
She's a ragtime suffragette.

The woman who dares to venture outside her sphere of home and kitchen is presented as a dangerous and violent anomaly. The sing-along experience offered by this song may be, however, more complex than its surface meaning. The whole audience sing along the chorus, shouting 'votes, votes votes votes, votes for women!' at the climax of the melody: the mocking of the extremist is combined with an enthusiastic if ambiguous expression of support for the cause. Not everyone in the audience is singing along in the same way for the same reason!

The same year, in the popular revue *Hullo Ragtime* a suffragette character forces her oppressed husband to go on hunger strike instead of doing it herself.[39]

It is difficult today to measure the effects of these anti-suffragette songs, but it is likely that, presented in the music hall, place of collective relaxation and identity for the working classes, and sung along with by the whole audience, they had a powerful influence. They aim at frightening any woman who might be tempted to follow the suffragettes in wielding influence outside her 'natural field' of home and family. Certainly, any woman or man who, after watching the show with their friends, wanted to argue in defence of the suffragettes and their demands, would have an uphill struggle faced with this expression of theatrical and consensual contempt.

When in 1914 the suffragettes stopped their campaigns, the theme seems to have disappeared from the songs, although Whit Cunliffe makes a reference to a suffragette in a 1914 song. He presents a suffragette who, traumatized by force-feeding while on hunger strike in prison, could no longer bear to wear stockings, since they reminded her of the tubing used for force feeding.[40] These are violent words, though the singer is careful to put them in the verse, and not in the sing-along chorus.

Occasionally a song would promote, somewhat timidly, women's rights: for instance, in 1908, the song 'Give her a vote, Papa', in which we see a boy asking his father to support women's suffrage. And a women living in Newcastle recounts how she was struck by a very popular music-hall song[41] which went:

> Why can't the dear little girls
> Do just the same as the men?
> Why can't the dear little girls
> Have freedom now and then?
>
> Why have the dear little girls
> to be led about by the nose
> And if a girl wants to marry a man
> Why can't she propose?

The demand for a little more equality is expressed, though it is also trivialized, by being reduced to that favourite question of the music-hall repertoire, the difficulties of courtship.

---

[39]   *The Times*, 11 April 1913.
[40]   Original recording of 'Tow the Row Row' at http://www.firstworldwar.com/audio/1914.htm.
[41]   Max Arthur, *Lost Voices of the Edwardians* (London: Harper Perennial, 2006), 382.

Another 1913 song, sung by Jen Latona does not go so far as to defend the suffragettes, but mocks those who seem to want to demonize them:

> You can't blame the suffragettes for that
> When you take your boots off on the mat,
> And the wife, the silly joker
> Greets you with a kitchen poker
> Well you can't blame the suffragettes for that!
>
> The ragtime craze has lately been creating quite a stir
> For everybody's doing it, for they've got it on the brain
> Though we're sick and tired of it
> The fact is very very plain...
> You can't blame the suffragettes for that

In *The Encore*, a few months after the passing of the 1918 law which gave the right to vote to women over 30, a reader complained that he had heard at the music hall an anti-suffragette song. He expressed the opinion that such songs should no longer be sung now the question of the right to vote had been settled.[42]

What conclusion can be drawn from the existence of a few dozen anti-suffragette songs among the thousands of music-hall songs of this period? They do not reflect an attempt by singers to create a particular following: the spectators came to see an evening of variety, not the one singer. But the songs do show that the singers felt they could carry the heterogeneous audience with them with such a song, and in particular get them to sing the chorus. By frequently criticizing a caricature of a 'hysterical' suffragette rather than criticizing the idea of women's suffrage, they were being careful not to alienate too large a section of the audience.

A tradition of sexist songs

The anti-suffragette songs come from the period just preceding the war. More general songs concerning the supposed nature of women – adorable but annoying when single, dominating and unattractive when married, wicked as mothers-in-law – are found over a much longer period and continue throughout the war.

Take, for example, Jack Lorimer's 1914 song 'Gay Ostend':

> Gay Ostend Gay Ostend
> That's the place to spend your holidays
> Beside the silvery spray
> ...

---

[42]   *The Encore*, 5 September 1918.

I'd rather be
Bobbing in the sea
With a little French girl from Paree
Than cuddling the wife who's fifty three
On the banks of the Clyde

It is of course unimaginable that a woman singer would sing on stage a song with such a sentiment.

In 1916, star Tom Clare sings 'Women's Way'. Women are presented as a 'complete paradox' They persuade men to buy them jewels and necklaces, but then decide they don't want to marry the man in question. In town, they are real prudes, but, at the seaside, exhibitionists. Once married, they are incomprehensibly moody. The last verse gives his conclusion: 'mid the horrors of war', women are angels that men cannot do without, who 'fortunately' adhere to their strictly inferior status, even to the point of accepting domestic violence: 'If he's charged with assault, she'll swear it's her fault, just to save her old man from the jail'.

A song from a musical comedy in 1917 is more severe. Its title is 'I'm Absolutely Fed Up with the Female Sex, They Puzzle and Perplex, I'd Like to Wring Their Necks!' However, the words of a song should not necessarily be taken literally. The narrator expresses common prejudices about women, but is presented himself as an object of ridicule, a man who cannot handle women. In the audience, everyone laughs, but not all for the same reasons!

Songs about women's faults were not sung only by men. Vesta Tilley's repertoire included, shortly before the war, a song which complained that women were 'the ruin of man' due to their incessant hunger for jewellery: again it is difficult to know if it is women, or the male narrator who is being mocked more.[43] Marie Lloyd, in a 1915 song 'If you want to get on in Revue', criticizes women with no talent who make a career on stage only by using their feminine charms. The most traditional of sexist prejudices are expressed in the piece (see Chapter 2).

The title of Marie Lloyd's 1915 hit song 'Woman's Opinion on Man' might seem to promise some counter to such frequently expressed negative prejudices about women. This is not at all the theme of the song, which, rather, mocks the women who believe they understand men. The 'woman of seventeen' is a laughable romantic fool, the woman in her forties a long-suffering sceptic, but all in all, women are willing participants in a game where everyone has their natural place.

Great, oh, she's great, is the woman of umpty-eight
She knows what is what for she's been through a lot
She's gone far and might have gone farther
Ah, a lot she has endured from the thing they call man
Still, if to live life o'er again she began
Would she live it again, would she play the same game? Rather!

---

43   Maitland, *Vesta Tilley*, 113.

We see, then, plenty of negative prejudices about women expressed in the music-hall songs. Russell[44] reminds us, however, that we know little, apart from relative sales of sheet music, of how audiences received these songs. We cannot assume their reaction to be homogeneous or unambiguous. The existence of these songs show simply that the artistes believed they could sell them easily and without controversy to a socially mixed if largely working-class mass audience of men and women together.

Ideal women

The other side of the coin of these caricatures is the idealization of women in other songs, and particularly of the loved one. Such content of course remained popular long after the sharp decline of more misogynous types of song. We shall look at love songs a little further on in this chapter. First let us look at the idealization of mothers. Here are a few examples of song titles:

- A Boy's Best Friend Is His Mother 1883
- A Mother Is the Truest Friend Of All *c.*1900
- I Love Somebody's Wife (My Mother) *c.*1903
- I Love To See My Poor Old Mother Work 1908
- Dreaming Of Home And Mother *c.*1914
- Mother's Darling *c.*1914
- Mother Would Comfort Me *c.*1914
- When You've Said Your Last Farewell to Mother 1914
- Any Old Song My Mother Sings 1915
- Mother and Me 1915
- My Mother's Rosary 1916
- Ireland Must Be Heaven For My Mother Comes From There 1917
- How Could I Ever Forget You, Beautiful Mother of Mine? 1919
- That Is What God Made Mothers For! 1919

If the wife, the mother-in-law and 'women' in general are much decried, mothers are idealized. The father of the family can be the target of mockery in songs such as 'When Father Papered the Parlour' (1909), 'When Father Tried to Kill the Cock a Doodle Doo' (1912), 'Father's Got the Sack from the Waterworks' (1915), 'Since Father Joined the Home Defence' (1916) or 'I'm taking the Place of Father' (1916). But no one mocks their mother.

---

[44]   Russell, *Popular Music in England*, 80.

Impressed, intrigued or threatened by women's new roles

The changes in women's roles during the war inspire many song lyrics. In the songs in our corpus from the last three years of the war, one song in twenty comments on these developments: it was an important popular preoccupation. Since an average evening at the music hall included twenty or so songs, it is clear that the majority of people would hear a song on this question almost every time they went to the music hall. In general, the songs do not present a clear position in favour or against women's new possibilities, but reveal an intrigued, amused or sometimes anxious perception of the changes. In this way the content of the song can remain close to consensual. Here are some of the titles of songs which deal with women's new roles:

- Kitty, the Telephone Girl 1914
- The Ladies Football Club 1915
- The Editress 1915
- Which Switch Is the Switch, Miss, for Ipswich? 1915
- If the Girlies Could Be Soldiers 1915
- The Lady Bus Conductor 1916
- Tilly the Typist 1916
- Dance of the Fire Brigade Girls 1915
- Women's Work 1917
- Where Are the Girls of the Old Brigade? 1917
- Polly from the GPO 1918

In 'The Editress' sung by George Robey (in drag), the narrator wants to become editress of a newspaper, and persuades her husband to accept this by beating him. The subtext is that a prestigious public role of this type could only suit a violent, unnatural woman. Another hit song in 1915, 'Which Switch Is the Switch, Miss, for Ipswich', combines different criticisms of new times coming: the new-fangled telephones are difficult to use, and the women telephone operators are incompetent. At the same time it is a traditional tongue-twister song, meaning guaranteed fun with the sing-along chorus in the theatre.

A song such as the 1917 piece 'Women's Work' by Tom Clare reveals a certain unease, and asks if women are really capable of carrying out their new jobs.[45] Female firefighters, according to the song, tend to be otherwise occupied when the firebell rings. In another verse, we hear about postwomen, who understand the importance of not waking babies when they deliver the post. Then a verse talks of the newly popular women's football teams.[46] The last verse, perhaps

---

[45]   This song can be heard online on Spotify, by searching for Tom Clare and Women's Work.

[46]   The history is online at www.donmouth.co.uk/local_history/great_war_football/great_war_football.html.

unsurprisingly, expresses strong reassurance to the spectators that the new roles women have take on will not last further than the end of the war. Feminity will be restored and the women will 'be their own sweet selves once again, when the boys come home in the morning!'

Vesta Tilley sings perhaps a more sophisticated piece, in 1917: 'Where Are the Girls of the Old Brigade?'[47] She plays an army officer on leave, amazed at the changes in women since he went away to war. He presents an ambiguous attitude, both praising and mocking the women workers:

> Have you noticed what the girls are doing now?
> It's simply wonderful, simply wonderful!
> One will drive a motor, while another drives a plough!
> And one will chase a bullock
> When she's told to milk a cow!

And he recounts some perhaps worrying changes

> The barmaid I used to flirt and frivol with
> She's an ammunitions maker so I hear
> Quite a lady since the war and the wages she can draw
> Must be more than she can draw for drawing beer!

The last verse is again reassuring, explaining that these women, so independent now, will become wives and mothers in their turn, and their modern lifestyle will be only a memory. So the song explores social change, and might even provoke discussion, but can be appreciated both by those women and men who welcome the transformation of women, and by those who feel it a pity. Wide appeal remains key to the music-hall hit. It is to be noted, too, that Vesta Tilley's male narrator allows a distancing of the message conveyed. If one wishes, one can consider that it is the narrator who is being mocked. There is something for everyone. Nevertheless, the chorus, by far the most significant section since the audience is asked to adopt its position by singing along, expresses a very traditional masculine attitude to women

> *Chorus*:   Where are the girls of the old brigade?
> The girls of the once upon a time
> I've been looking around
> And there's only one consolation to be found
> The old girl's still there, old girl new style
> And whether it's the old girl or whether it's the new
> It's the same piece of petticoat all the while!

---

[47]   Full lyrics are online at http://monologues.co.uk/musichall/Songs-W/Where-Are-Girls-Of-Old-Brigade.htm.

'Here's to the women!'

As the war years rolled by, and the contribution of women in waged work became more and more visible, we see more positive comments about women's work, even if traditional prejudices remain powerful. In 1917, the magazine *Phono Record* declared 'women have proved themselves as useful as they are ornamental'.[48] Several songs from 1917 and 1918 celebrate the strength of the women who have worked so hard for the Empire's cause. Here are some song titles:

- Here's to the Women, Too! 1917
- We Thank You, Women of England! 1917
- Women of the Homeland 1918
- Raise a Cheer for the Women of Britain! 1918
- What Should We Do without Them (War Girls)? 1918
- Daughters of Britain, Work with a Will! 1918

The tone is radically different from that of the 1914 song 'Women Who Wait', in which the lyrics praise the heroic patience of women waiting anxiously for their heroes to return from the war.

> Women who wait
> Women who wait
> You don't fight with guns at the enemy's gate
> There's no VC for you
> But your duty you do
> And you're none the less heroes,
> You women who wait!

The more active role of women is now recognized.

Some songs bring up the question of the new independence of women even in the domain of sexuality. So, for example, the 1916 songs 'The Girls Know As Much As you Know!' and 'There's a Little Bit of Bad in Every Good Little Girl', and 'Who Taught You All Those Things That You Taught Me?' from 1917, all seem to transmit a certain anxiety about the changes. In 'Be a Good Little Girl While I'm Away', the soldier asks his girl to be 'good' and faithful while he's absent. Naturally, there could be no such song in which a female narrator reminded her fiancé to be faithful while he was away; on the contrary, comic songs such as 'It's in a Good Cause and It's Got to Be Done' portray British soldiers 'kissing French girls' for the sake of the war effort. Even if marital fidelity was a very strong value at the time, there was clearly one law for the men and another for the

---

[48]   *Phono Record*, January 1917.

women, and in some war zones the British army even organized official brothels for their soldiers.[49]

This concludes the sketch of the presentation of changing women's roles in the repertoire. The theme will practically disappear from popular music in following decades, unlike our next theme, love.

What did love mean in 1914?

Love had a different meaning a century ago. Young working-class people generally had to choose a partner from the same part of town, and 'walk out' together for several years, with rare chances for privacy. Finally, the young man would ask the permission of the woman's father before proposing marriage. The low rates of illegitimacy show that sexual abstinence was the rule, and young lovers were often carefully watched. Cinemas, for example, employed people whose job it was to ensure that no indecent behaviour take place.[50]

Attitudes to sexuality had changed little since Victorian times, and ignorance about sexual matters remained common.[51] When Marie Stopes became, almost in spite of herself, one of the first Agony Aunts, answering questions about sex, she received a flood of letters, including some from men who had been married for a number of years and knew nothing about sex, or letters concerning women who were engaged to be married, who believed 'that children were secured as the result of prayers offered at the marriage ceremony'.[52] Robert Roberts paints a similar picture: 'millions went into marriage either ignorant or with ideas utterly distorted'. His teenage friends believed that a woman could become pregnant simply by sharing a bath with a man.[53]

At the same time women were often idealized. Men should not swear in front of women, and, when the Ministry of Food employed women clerks to replace men who had joined the army, the frescoes by Rubens which covered the walls were covered by drapes so that the young women would not be shocked by the paintings of semi-naked bodies.[54]

---

[49]   Clare Makepeace, 'Punters and their Prostitutes: British Soldiers, Masculinity, and maisons tolerées in the First World War', in *What Is Masculinity? Historical Dynamics from Antiquity to the Contemporary World*, ed. John H. Arnold and Sean Brady (London: Palgrave Macmillan, 2011).

[50]   Marwick, *The Deluge*, 181.

[51]   Though some stereotypes about love and sex in Victorian times need challenging. See Françoise Barret-Ducrocq, *Love in the Time of Victoria: Sexuality and Desire Among Working-Class Men and Women in Nineteenth-Century London* (Harmondsworth: Penguin, 1991).

[52]   June Rose, *Marie Stopes and the Sexual Revolution* (Stroud: Tempus, 2007), 184.

[53]   Roberts, *A Ragged Schooling*, 51.

[54]   Marwick, *The Deluge*, 232.

Contraception was becoming a subject of discussion among that minority who dared broach the question. But Marie Stopes, a pioneer in sex education, had to contend with powerful adversaries. The Anglican Bishops' Conference expressed its concern at 'the grave physical, moral and spiritual perils incurred by the use of contraceptives',[55] while Dr Mary Scharlieb, consultant gynaecologist at the Royal Free Hospital in London declared that 'masturbation à deux'[56] (that is, the use of contraception) would lead to degeneration and the destruction of virility in men.[57] Very many women 'found birth control immoral, distasteful, or both'.[58] Attitudes of ignorance were absolutely not restricted to traditionalist or conservative circles. Robert Roberts tells us that adults in the slum he lived in were very much obsessed with preventing masturbation, to the point that school toilets in the boys' school had no doors on the cubicles.[59] And the radical Left newspaper the *Daily Herald* denounced, in 1916, the 'dangers' of masturbation.[60]

Nakedness, and in particular female nakedness, was even more strictly regulated than it is today. Families who had only one room to live in organized their mornings so that boys would never see their sisters without clothes on, and vice versa.[61] In 1915, the new style of 'skirts six inches off the floor' provoked scandalized letters in newspapers. By the seaside, respectable women avoided being seen in relatively revealing costumes by using bathing machines, a sort of wagon on wheels pulled by a horse into the sea, far from prying eyes. This custom was far from being reserved for richer women – collective bathing machines were available for a small fee for poorer people on weekends away.[62]

Many anecdotes from the war years reveal very negative attitudes to undressing in front of the opposite sex. One nurse who worked in France explains:

> most of the new patients were Kitchener's army men and they'd never been in hospital before. They were horrified when I told them that I was going to bath them. One man with a smashed leg assured me that he could easily get to the bathhouse if one of the others helped him. Another badly wounded man actually succeeded in getting to the bath house while my back was turned, but he had to be carried back in a state of collapse. After I had bathed him he was very penitent and promised that he would never funk it again. They didn't funk the battle but they were desperately embarrassed about having a girl to wash them.[63]

---

55   Rose, *Marie Stopes*, 179.
56   Scharlieb uses the French expression.
57   Rose, *Marie Stopes*, 165.
58   Roberts, *A Woman's Place*, 87.
59   Roberts, *A Ragged Schooling*, p. 51.
60   *Daily Herald*, 29 January 1916.
61   Roberts, *A Woman's Place*, 15.
62   John Hannavy, *The English Seaside in Victorian and Edwardian Times* (Princes Risborough: Shire Publications, 2003), 32 and *passim*.
63   Lyn Macdonald, *The Roses of No Man's Land* (London: Penguin, 1980), 108.

Such generalized attitudes are one of the elements which ensure the great popularity of suggestive songs, as we shall see later in this chapter.

The love songs of the war years

'Needless to say, there is one subject which is never stale, love, ... But endeavour to treat it from a completely new angle ... Songs ... which liken the tender passion to birds or the flowers and fruits of the earth are played out – from the purely popular point of view' – such was the advice given to songwriters in one trade paper in 1917.[64] Yet one of the most striking facts about the music-hall repertoire is that the theme of love does not dominate, as it will in many later popular musical genres. Many of the top stars never sang love songs, and the comic song about everyday life is far more common than the love song. Edwardian society did not allow public expression of feelings in the same way as we do today. If D. H. Lawrence was engaged, during the war, in the process of writing his masterpieces of exploration of the unconscious, echoing Freud's work from the very beginning of the century, popular song was worlds away from such visions. In almost all the songs, finding a partner and falling in love was not complex, doubts are never expressed, and the story can only end in happy marriage or in unhappy marriage, this last always represented as grotesquely comic and not tragic.

In any case, in a large theatre and without a microphone, songs of intimate tone are tremendously difficult to sing. Moreover, the singer, wedged in between spectacular acts of acrobats, animal imitation or juggling, had to attract and hold the audience's attention quickly. Tender, reflective ballads were rarely appropriate. Colin MacInnes, in his general thoughts about popular music between 1840 and 1920, writes that love was portrayed as 'a rose capped dream of bliss or [as] a comic disaster' and noted that stars would tend to specialize in one or other of these representations.[65]

One tactic occasionally employed to allow the singing of songs of tragic or unrequited love by male narrators, in a society where being 'manly' involved not expressing feelings in public, was the use of the blackface narrator. A white man blacked-up as a caricature of an African (see Chapter 2 above) could portray himself as heartbroken or sentimental since the racist ideology of the time considered Africans to be like children, and therefore not subject to the same rules of respectability as white men.[66]

---

[64]   *The Era*, 7 February 1917.

[65]   Colin MacInnes, *Sweet Saturday Night: Pop Song 1840–1920* (London: Panther Arts, 1967), 34.

[66]   See John Mullen, 'Anti-Black Racism in British Popular Music 1880–1920' *Revue française de civilisation britannique*, special issue (2012).

Perfect love

Meeting a partner and falling in love has always been a central theme in popular song, even more than the experience of relationships in general. No doubt the biggest grouping of music-hall love songs is that of pieces in which a male narrator announces quite simply that he has met the perfect woman for him. These songs often link the loved one with one particular characteristic, often a (relatively) exotic geographical origin. This origin, or other key characteristic, can then be treated in a sentimental or a comic fashion. These songs were written quickly: songwriters wanting to make a living had to produce large numbers of them, and this is often evident when one listens to them. Nevertheless, as the highly successful lyricist Hermann Darewski commented, one never knew which song was going to catch the public's fancy and become a hit.[67]

Here are some typical song titles:

- My Zulu Loo 1914
- My Dusky Princess 1915
- Normandy Girl 1915
- Portobello Lass 1915
- Mary from Tipperary 1915
- My Girl from Slumbertown 1915
- My Little Pearl from Peru 1916
- My Little Yorkshire Rose 1916
- The Hyde Park Girl 1916
- Oh, My Lily of Killarney. 1917
- My Devon Girl 1918

The upheavals of war open up new possibilities:

- My Little Red Cross Girl 1914
- Little Rosalie, My Pretty Refugee 1915
- The Rose of No Man's Land 1916
- My Little Ammunition Girl 1916
- Red Cross Maid 1917
- My Dapper Little Flapper 1915
- Widows Are Wonderful! 1918

This last song explains why men should prefer widows to younger women who are 'too tame', since 'a merry little widow knows the game!'

All of these songs have a male narrator. A female narrator in love songs is much rarer, but can be found. In 1914, for example, Violet Lorraine sings about 'My Volunteer'.

---

[67]   *The Era*, 7 February 1917.

Other songs take the action forward into rose-tinted views of courtship:

- Under the Honey Moon 1915
- Just We Two and the Moon 1915
- Just One Kiss, Just Another One 1915
- Raining Drops of Love for You and Me 1916
- Paradise for Two 1916
- It's a Wonderful Great Big Love That's Calling Me Back to You 1916

In general, the meeting of the loved one is devoid of psychological complexity, and direct addressing of the loved one in passionate terms is very rare in this period (it is fascinating to see that the only wartime song I have found with the word 'darling' in the title is 'Don't Take My Darling Boy Away').

The avoidance of psychology seems, however, to be slowly changing, and one finds titles like the following, all from 1915:

- Don't Say I Ever Made You Love Me!
- Everybody Loves Me But the Girl I Love
- I Ain't Got Nobody
- Is It Nothing to You That I'm Lonely?

One of the greatest hits of 1915, 'Broken Doll' shows the rise of this new tone. It was sung by many artistes at the time – mostly women, but several men too. It laments a love relationship which has gone sour. The narrator was convinced they were loved, but a year later the person is no longer interested, leaving the narrator to lament: 'For if you turn away, you'll be sorry some day, you left behind a broken doll.'[68] Sad nostalgia of this kind is almost unknown in the repertoire before the war.

The case of the 1916 song 'If You Were the Only Girl in the World', one of the very few songs still known today, is fascinating.[69] It was sung as a duet by George Robey and Violet Lorraine in the revue *The Bing Boys Are Here*. Bing, played by George Robey dressed in a ridiculous sailor suit too small for him, might have been expected to stick to a comic style. Indeed, until a few moments before going on stage, Robey had planned to sing the song in a traditional way, for laughs. He changed his mind and sang the song 'straight' and it became one of the biggest hits of the war years.[70] It may be that his showman's instinct told him that

---

[68] One can find on Youtube a version recorded in 1916 by the US star Al Jolson, at https://www.youtube.com/watch?v=Npji_-Q-sGc (accessed 25 August 2014).

[69] Words and original recording online at http://www.firstworldwar.com/audio/if youweretheonlygirl.htm (accessed 25 August 2014).

[70] James Harding, *George Robey and the Music-Hall* (London: Hodder & Stoughton, 1990), 86.

times had changed, that the immense pain and the generalization of separation in wartime, made new tones of song possible on stage.

The rising revue format (see Chapter 3) also allowed a greater variety of tone since the circus elements of music hall were left aside, and united artistic control over a whole evening's entertainment meant a romantic atmosphere could be set up. The very fact of singing a love song in a mixed duet, extremely rare, moved the performance away from traditional comic modes.

The suggestive song

In the repressed sexual atmosphere described earlier in the chapter, suggestive songs were commercially very successful. Each member of the audience could choose to understand or not the sexual reference in the lyrics. A classic example from before the war was a song which tells of a woman who takes a train alone, and the adventures which befall her with men ('She'd Never Had Her Ticket Punched Before'!) The pleasure of moderate transgression, a constant element of popular music, is, in the music hall, experienced collectively in the sing-along chorus.[71]

Thus, in 1911, Florrie Forde sang 'They're All Single by the Seaside':

> When old Brown at the seaside spends his fortnight's holiday,
> There beneath the moon, a diff'rent girl he'll spoon.
> She says, 'Harold, oh! tell me, have you ever lov'd till now?'
> He says, 'Never, darling, that I vow!'
> Then he feels for his handkerchief to wipe her tears away,
> Pulls out a baby's stocking and the wild waves seem to say –
>
> *Chorus*:   They're all single by the seaside,
> All single by the sea.
> Oh! see them on the pier each night,
> All busy in the twi-twilight.
> They're all single by the seaside,
> All happy as can be.
> When they see a pretty face, or a dainty piece of lace,
> They're all single by the sea.[72]

Whereas, in 1915, Whit Cunliffe had a hit with 'Tight Skirts Have Got to Go', a title which used word play for suggestive purposes, ending: '"Tight skirts have got to go!" Girls, I'm asking you. Why can't the petticoats and blouses, and other little

---

[71]   Songs of moderate transgression can still be successful in the twenty-first century: see, for example, Katie Perry's 2008 single 'I Kissed a Girl'.

[72]   Sheet music available online at http://nla.gov.au/nla.mus-vn3296446 (accessed 1 December 2014).

things, go too?!' That same year, 'The Mormon's Song' invited the audience to imagine the life of a polygamous Mormon. The following year, the hit 'Where did Robinson Crusoe go with Friday on Saturday night?' explains that 'where there are wild men, there must be wild women' and suggests that Robinson must have made the most of their company.

Some more song titles from this category:

- Who paid the rent for Mrs Rip van Winkle? 1914
- I Was a Good Little Girl Till I Met You! 1914
- I'll Make a Man of You 1914
- A Little of What You Fancy Does You Good! 1915
- It's the Girls that Make the Seaside 1915
- I've Tried to Be Good But the Girls Won't Let Me 1916
- Shall We? Let's! 1916
- They Go Wild, Simply Wild, Over Me 1917
- Every Girl Is Fishing 1917
- The Modern Maiden's Prayer 1918
- The Wild, Wild Women 1918

What effect do these songs have? Maitland and others consider, in any case, that 'music hall did a lot ... to challenge the moralistic taboos of the late Victorian era'.[73]

One way of compensating for suggestiveness in songs is by the mention of marriage, and the presence of marriage in the songs is an important difference with pop songs of later periods. Marie Lloyd's suggestive songs such as 'Oh Mr Porter' or 'Now You've Got Your Khaki On' end in a happy marriage. Couples who kiss each other are often presented as being on their honeymoon. And when Harry Lauder refers in song to the end of the war, he declares 'I bet the parsons will be working overtime'. Here are a few other song titles which contain a reference to marriage:

- My Wedding Day Tomorrow 1917
- On Our Happy Wedding Day 1915
- I'm going to Be Married Today 1917
- Sister Susie's Marrying Tommy Atkins Today 1915
- When We're Made One, We Two 1918
- Our Wedding Day 1918

The suffering husband

Marriage too was slowly changing. The idea that a man and a woman should aim at deep communication and affection in marriage, rather than simply at a certain

---

[73] Maitland, *Vesta Tilley*, 126.

economic and family stability based on a traditional separation of roles is slowly on the rise. Very many songs present the situation of a husband and wife as that of a poor oppressed man faced with a tyrannical or even violent scold. Harry Lauder, in his hit song 'That's the Reason Noo I Wear a Kilt', explains that when he wore trousers his wife stole the money from his pockets, and such tropes are very common in the songs.[74]

Billy Merson's 1911 song 'Take an Old Woman's Advice' (which he sings in drag) includes the following sing-along chorus:

> Girls, girls, when you are married
> Take a tip from one who knows
> Treat your old man like you would a pet dog
> Kind words are better than blows!
>
> Don't bark and growl at him, for if you do
> You'll very soon give him the spike
> But treat him with kindness and like a pet dog
> You can train him to do what you like!

In the 1913 song 'Oh Tomorrow Night!', the oppressed narrator recounts:

> My old girl is a wrong one
> Although she's not a suffragette
> For two years I've been wed
> But I've not had the night off yet
> I haven't said a word
> Although I put up with a lot
> But wait until tomorrow night
> And I'll show her what is what!
>
> I scrub the floor and wash the paint
> And even make the bed
> If I was to object
> I'd get a saucepan on my head
> To have a glass of beer she says
> Is money spent in waste
> It's such a time since I had one
> I quite forget the taste!

A 1914 song, 'She's So Jealous', portrays a jealous wife who gives very little pocket money to her husband, for fear he should spend it on drink and women. To guard against any risk of infidelity, she cuts off his ears. George Formby Senior

---

[74]   King, 'Matrons, Maidens and Magdalenes', 55.

sang in 1917 his hit 'Since I've Had a Row with the Wife', in which his wife made him sleep in the kennel with the dog, after having beaten him. Many of Formby's songs present the same deadpan Lancashire working-class man completely dominated by his wife, in particular in a series of songs where the narrator is 'John Willie'.[75] Of course, these songs are very much marked by hyperbole, but the fact that they are not ever balanced by narratives about dominated wives shows that they are part of an ideological structure validating traditional roles.

The theme of the dominating wife can always be brought up to date with current events. In 1918, the piece 'Since My Wife Joined the WAAC' is billed in *The Performer* as a 'bang up to date henpecked husband song'.[76] The theme of the oppressed husband does not disappear with the end of the war. In 1920, The Two Bobs explain, in 'It's a Cert', that all women become terrible scolds once married. And Tom Clare sings, in 1924 and in 1926 respectively, the two, perhaps rather milder, songs 'This Freedom (My Wife Is Away)' and 'At Home, I'm My Wife's Husband, But When I'm Away, I'm Me'.

We have seen then that the repertoire frequently reveals a somewhat misogynous vision of marriage. Male narrators complain about the difficulties of men's role – financial responsibility for example – and also about the power of women in the family, using hyperbole, caricature and fantasy. A few earlier hit songs had even recommended beating one's wife (Gus Elen's 1906 hit, for example).[77]

The dominance of a masculine voice in the discussion in popular song of relations between men and women has remained in place until today, but it was incomparably stronger a century ago. Why did the audiences – both men and women – like this material so much? These are not easy questions to answer. Laura King suggests that portrayals of working-class marriages as conflictual had a wide appeal: 'The middle class could see a life more sordid than their own; the husband could commiserate with his harassed brethren and wives could feel sorry for the woman harnessed to an impecunious partner or a brutish abuser.'[78]

Conclusion

We can see, then, that women are harshly treated in the lyrics of a large number of music-hall numbers before and during the Great War. The portrayals of men dreadfully oppressed by their wives, crazy suffragettes or incompetent women workers show prejudices widely accepted in all social milieux. A minority of songs towards the end of the war express a more positive view about women's

---

[75]   These songs and others by George Formby Senior can be heard online at http://www.monkey-hole.co.uk/formby_senior/downloads/.

[76]   *The Performer*, 25 April 1918.

[77]   In the 1880s this had been quite common: see King, 'Matrons, Maidens and Magdalenes', 49.

[78]   Ibid., 31.

contribution to society, and the fiancée and mother figures are idealized to the extreme.

More progressive ideas about women were not rare in wartime society, but they remained the beliefs of a minority, and, as we have seen, the music-hall stage was not a place for minority ideas.

A Star in Focus 4

Harry Champion – 'the spirit of the poorer parts of London'

'You don't know who I am!'

Harry Champion was born William Crump in 1866, and no doubt chose his stage name because of the slang meaning of 'champion': wonderful.[1] His father was a cabinet maker, and Harry decided young that the stage was to be his career. Nevertheless, at the request of his parents, he followed at the same time an apprenticeship at a cobbler's.[2]

He began his stage career in blackface minstrelsy, disguised as a caricature of a black slave (see Chapter 2). His special novelty act was a turn entitled 'From Light into Darkness' in which he began singing 'as a white man' and in the middle of the act effected a lightning transformation into a blackface minstrel. A few years later he moved on to individual comic turns, and by the end of his career would sing at least 113 different songs – this is the number of songs listed for him in Kilgarriff's catalogue.[3]

Champion represented the ordinary working-class Londoner, and loudly defended the values and the tastes of 'the people'. For Pearsall, 'Champion was all of a piece. His stage persona reflected his real self – beery, red-nosed and loud. When so many of the Edwardian Cockney singers had soft centres, the hard nut that was Harry Champion comes as a refreshing relief.'[4]

According to Macqueen-Pope:

> On stage the words shot out of him like bullets from a gun. He rattled off several songs in a monotonous voice, whirling his arms about with his foot tapping at the same time; he was always audible. He appeared grotesque, but was the embodiment of the spirit of the poorer parts of London; there was no refinement

---

[1] A photograph is available online at http://www.gettyimages.com/detail/news-photo/english-cockney-music-hall-entertainer-harry-champion-news-photo/140482434 (accessed 22 January 2015).

[2] Judith Bowers, *Stan Laurel and Other Stars of the Panopticon* (Edinburgh: Birlinn, 2007), 85.

[3] Michael Kilgarriff, *Sing Us One of the Old Songs: A Guide to Popular Song 1860–1920* (Oxford: Oxford University Press, 1999).

[4] Ronald Pearsall, *Edwardian Popular Music* (London: David & Charles, 1975), 63.

or sophistication in his performance, which was above all a vibrant evocation
of working-class life.[5]

He sang with a cockney accent and some elements of cockney dialect, at a speed
of delivery which was very rapid for the time:[6] all contemporary commentators
mention his rapid-fire delivery.[7] In a series of songs about food ('Boiled Beef and
Carrots', 'A Little Bit of Cucumber', 'Let's Have a Basin of Soup', 'Home-made
Sausages' Baked Sheep's Hearts' and several more), he defended the down-to-
earth tastes of the London working class:

> Now Mrs Potter's got a shop in our localitee
> She'll serve you with a supper a good dinner or a tea
> There's everything you fancy from a salmon to a sav.
> But when the wife and I go there I'll tell you what we have,
>
> *Chorus*:   Hot meat pies, saveloys and trotters
> Something you can talk about
> Something that will blow you out
> Every time we went to supper round at Mrs Potter's
> We had hot meat pies, saveloys and trotters.
>
> Once I went to church I did, while I was sitting there
> The parson in the pulpit went and offered up a prayer
> As I was busy wondering what he'd be doing next
> He said 'This Sunday, brethren, I'm taking for my text,
> 'Hot meat pies…' etc.

In one of his best-known songs, ''Enery the Eighth I Am' he stages himself as
'belonging to royalty':

> I'm 'Enery the Eighth, I am,
> 'Enery the Eighth I am, I am!
> I got married to the widow next door,
> She's been married seven times before
> And every one was an 'Enery
> She wouldn't have a Willie nor a Sam
> I'm her eighth old man named 'Enery
> 'Enery the Eighth, I am!

---

[5]   William Macqueen-Pope, *The Melodies Linger On* (London: W. H. Allen, 1950),
p. 406.

[6]   Several songs can be heard at http://www.rfwilmut.clara.net/stars/champion.html
(accessed 28 July 2014).

[7]   See *The Guardian*, 19 November 1907.

The working-class man is imagining himself as a King, the world is turned upside down: Champion is mocking both pretentious elites and the unrealistic dreams of ordinary people, in a way common in music hall. Elsewhere he takes up the traditional vaguely-misogynistic tirade against his mother-in-law in . 'I'm Getting Ready for My Mother in Law', and his hit 'Wotcher, My Old Brown Son, How Are Yer?' celebrates working-class camaraderie in the atmosphere of a London pub.

Several of his songs belong to the tradition of daring music-hall numbers, open to bawdy interpretations which might be encouraged on stage by appropriate gestures, according to the audience present. 'Cover It Over Quick, Jemima' is a classic example from 1911. In the first verse, the refrain has a clear meaning: put the lid on the saucepan. A verse or two later, unsurprisingly, it is a matter of covering parts of the anatomy which have been inadvertently uncovered. Songs such as 'I Was Holding Me Coconut' (1912), 'The End of Me Old Cigar' (1914) and 'Never Let Your Braces Dangle!' (1910) work in the same way.

> I'm a bit of a sport I am. One day, oh dear, oh Lor'
> I went to Hampstead Heath and I enjoyed myself I'm sure
> I had a go at the coconuts and knocked a beauty down
> I was brimming all over with joy upon me journey back to town.

> *Refrain*:   I was holding me coconut when a lady winked at me
> 'I see you've got it with you' she shouted out with glee
> Up came the hubby. He threw me in the cut
> The only thing that kept me afloat was holding my coconut.

Champion did not hesitate to change the words of the songs according to the nature of the audience. In the case of suggestive songs, one can imagine this allowed him to make the songs more or less rude. In December 1915, the manager of a Birmingham music hall was fined by magistrates after there were complaints about three songs sung by Harry Champion. Champion denied the charge of vulgarity, but admitted that he sometimes changed the words of his songs to make the audience laugh.[8] Nevertheless, Champion was on the bill at the first Royal Variety Performance in 1912, in presence of the Royal Family, while other stars were considered insufficiently respectable to perform that day.

In 1915, he sang a very successful war song, 'Me Old Iron Cross', mocking the Kaiser and the German bravery medal:

> I'm the bloke that broke the bank at Monte Carlo
> I'm the hero of a dozen dirty nights
> I went down in a submarine to give the Kaiser one
> It went off bang and up I went and landed in the Sun

---

[8]   *The Guardian*, 21 December 1915.

There I met the Kaiser and he said, 'I'm up the stick
If you can get me out of here I'll treat you mighty quick.'

Chorus: Me old Iron Cross, Me old Iron Cross
What a waste I do declare
Over there in Germany they're giving them away
You can have a dozen if you shout hooray
The Kaiser said to me, 'Old cock
Me kingdom for a horse.'
I gave him the one the missis dries the clothes on
And he gave me the old Iron Cross!

Harry Champion carried on working until the end of the 1930s, and appeared in a number of films before his death in 1942. He is one of the few music-hall singers whose songs have not been completely forgotten. 'Any Old Iron', a song mocking a working man who comes into an inheritance, was covered by Peter Sellers in 1957, and 'I'm 'Enery the Eighth' by Herman's Hermits in 1965.

Chapter 5

Songs about the War: Elite Voices and People's Voices

We will now move on to songs which speak of the war and of life in wartime, whether the aim be to recruit for the army, to criticize the war machine, to laugh about hard times or to dream of the return of peace. The nature of any social content in music-hall songs has been judged in different ways; some writers have seen music hall as a 'true popular culture', which, unlike high art, belonged to the working classes and could express important aspects of their worries, fantasies and questions about the world. MacInnes writes that, since music-hall songs 'were chiefly written by, and sung by, working-class men and women for working-class audiences, we may hear in them a *vox populi* which is not to be found in Victorian and Edwardian literature'.[1]

Bailey gives a similar view:

> The identification of principal motifs – booze, romantic adventure, marriage and mothers-in-law, dear old pals and seaside holidays, and so on – demonstrates a recurrent emphasis on the domestic and the everyday that supports the most broadly agreed reading of music-hall song as a naturalistic mode that both documents and confirms a common way of life. The great popularity of the songs is said to come from the audience's recognition of and identification with the routine yet piquant exploits of a comic realism that validates the shared experience of a typically urbanized, class-bound world seen from below.[2]

And more recently, Gary Day of De Montfort University has considered that 'The music hall was genuine popular culture. It registered the experience of the working class in an idiom that was at once realistic, sentimental, defiant, resigned and, above all, humorous'.[3]

For ordinary people to see parts of their lives in subjects of song, and hence presented as significant, has been an important dynamic throughout the history of popular music. Yet other analysts have underlined the commercial dynamic which dominated the genre, and the many conservative ideas which the songs

---

[1]   Colin MacInnes, *Sweet Saturday Night: – Pop Song 1840–1920* (London: Panther Arts, 1967), 34.

[2]   Peter Bailey, 'Conspiracies of Meaning: Music Hall and the Knowingness of Popular Culture', *Past and Present 144:1 (*1994), 128.

[3]   *Times Higher Education Supplement*, 24 June 2010.

transmitted. These authors suggest that music hall cannot express working-class interests and that one might consider it to be part of a 'culture of consolation', a palliative to compensate workers for their miserable living conditions, at the same time as integrating them into a patriotic and imperialistic culture. Senelick even goes so far as to say: 'Much of the energy the working man might have directed to ameliorating his own situation was rechanneled by the music hall to the advancement of [the British] empire.'[4]

Gareth Stedman-Jones[5] suggests that this is a form of culture which encourages workers to accept their dominated position in society, while Penelope Summerfield claims that a true working-class music hall declined gradually and was replaced with a commercialized mass culture of consolation, which 'ensured that the view of life selected for projection (even if never totally or even deeply assimilated) would be that of the satisfied customer rather than the angry producer – a culture of consolation rather than confrontation'.[6]

According to the latter analyses, the songs express the voice and the interests of the elite, and in some way deceive working-class audiences. Is it possible to decide between these differing views of music hall? It seems vain, in a society where the working class is in a dominated position, in a society infinitely more cruel and unequal than it is today,[7] to imagine that there could exist a mass culture able to express a voice completely independent to that of the elites. Karl Marx wrote: 'What else does the history of ideas prove, than that intellectual production changes its character in proportion as material production is changed? The ruling ideas of each age have ever been the ideas of its ruling class.'[8] If Marx is right on this, there cannot be a separate proletarian culture able to articulate systematically the interests of the dominated class, though this does not mean that the interests and choices of the working class have no influence on cultural products.

Indeed, it is important to distinguish between the expression of working-class interests and the expression of working-class experience. The former is generally not a characteristic of music hall: there are no waves of songs to support the mass strikes of 1912 or 1919, for example. However, expressing a view of society seen

---

[4]   Quoted by Andrew August, 'A Culture of Consolation?', *Historical Research* 74 (2001), 22.

[5]   Gareth Stedman Jones, 'Working-Class Culture and Working-Class Politics in London, 1870–1900: Notes on the Remaking of a Working Class' in *Languages of Class: Studies in English Working-Class History, 1832–1892* (Cambridge: Cambridge University Press, 1983), 237.

[6]   Penelope Summerfield, 'The Effingham Arms and the Empire: Deliberate Selection in the Evolution of Music Hall in London', in *Popular Culture and Class Conflict 1590–1914*, ed. S. and E. Yeo (Brighton: Harvester, 1981), 237.

[7]   According to the Office for National Statistics, in 1911, the richest one per cent of the British population owned 70 per cent of the country's wealth; in 2001, the figure was 23 per cent.

[8]   Manifesto of the Communist Party, chapter 2, online at https://www.marxists.org/archive/marx/works/1848/communist-manifesto/ch02.htm (accessed 28 July 2014).

from below, and in this way assisting ordinary people in their struggle for survival and dignity, can very much be a part of the genre.

The vision of popular entertainment as 'a culture of consolation' is not a neutral one. Does not all cultural production, whether high or popular serve 'to console', to compensate for the difficulties of living and dying for all social classes, to relieve alienation? High culture cannot be considered to be a pure product, outside society, in contrast with a straightforwardly alienating and commercial mass culture. In addition to their artistic content, opera and theatre, for example, are rooted as concrete activities in the social, economic and ideological structures of their time. Jean-Paul Sartre criticized the bourgeois who went to the theatre purely for social and ceremonial purposes.[9] And when George Graves mocks those members of the elite who hate opera but 'are obliged to go every year because it is the thing to do and the place to be seen',[10] he is reminding us that all cultural activities can be examined from an anthropological point of view.

Several authors have pointed out that music-hall songs do not question the social structure of society, and do not incite workers to rebellion. Rather, they show a certain resignation faced with the hardship and injustice of life. This seems undeniable; yet is that the role of these songs, and is such a question posed to other types of cultural production?

This debate – 'social control or a voice of the people' – has often taken insufficiently into account the specificities of different kinds of cultural product. Music hall neither emerges directly from the lives of working-class people, nor is it created in the brain of Machiavellian bourgeois determined to brainwash the labouring masses. It emerges from a subtle and complex process on which several economic, social and political forces weigh. The result is always an unstable compromise. So the profit motive and the obsessive search for respectability are key factors in the constitution of the music-hall repertoire; and yet the industry must attract a working-class audience by putting on stage artistes who have something in common with that audience and who can, among other things, express its condition and its problems.

In addition, music-hall song is not a series of texts, but a shared emotional experience of listening and singing along, a moment stolen from the struggle for existence which dominates the life of the working-class audience. It is an experience lived in a space which is felt to be ours. Whatever the content of the songs –comic, tragic or resigned – it has been underlined that no one suffers alone at the music hall.

---

[9]   Jean-Paul Sartre, *Un théâtre de situations* (Paris: Gallimard, 1992), 76.

[10]   George Graves, *Gaieties and Gravities – The Autobiography of a Comedian* (London: Hutchinson, 1931), 141.

Expressing dissent

Any form of entertainment has resources which enable an expression of social dissent, and braking factors which make such an expression more difficult. For music hall one of the main resources is, as has been mentioned, the fact that the singers (and indeed the songwriters) generally come from the poorer parts of society, as does their audience. This means that the identification of the audience with the stars is very strong. The stars speak to their audiences in familiar tones, and often sing with working-class accents. Their stage names – Gus, Harry, Tom, Ernie, Jack, Frank, Elsie, Gertie, Maggie or Florrie – mark them out as ordinary folk. Part of their attraction is the joy of the people seeing 'one of our lot' on stage, a feeling which was even stronger in this period, when social mobility was even more restricted than it is today. One might think that this identification would facilitate the expressions of socially dominated voices. Such expression can also be made easier by the use of stage 'characters', as we mentioned in Chapter 3. Harry Lauder appears on stage as a stereotyped Scotsman, Vesta Tilley disguises herself as a series of male narrators, and Gus Elen or Harry Champion play Cockney working men. This character mechanism may allow them to say things which are normally forbidden, just as the King's fool was allowed to in times gone by.

There are two key brakes on the expression of radical or social content; the economic structure of the music-hall industry is the first. Fierce competition forces theatre owners and theatre chains to invest in expensive buildings, luxurious fittings and impressive scenery and special effects. The theatres that cannot make the grade financially go bankrupt.[11] To fill the theatre, content is needed which is exciting *but not too controversial*. A few decades later when the vinyl record dominates the music market, it will be possible to have a hit song by persuading 5 per cent or 10 per cent of the population to buy one's record. The music hall is quite different and is obliged to aim at very wide appeal.[12]

Secondly, the pressure for 'respectability' is extremely powerful, and tends towards the elimination both of 'vulgarity' and of radical political content. A theatre manager, anxious not to have any problems renewing his annual licence, is careful that no offence is caused to magistrates by what is said or sung on stage. In the 1860s and 1870s, the press spoke of 'the political song nuisance'.[13] Singers and other artistes were then obliged to submit all lyrics and patter well in advance to be approved by the theatre manager. A new clause was added to the standard contract forbidding all ad-libbing or improvising outside the approved script.[14]

---

[11]   Paul Maloney, *Scotland and the Music Hall, 1850–1914* (Manchester: Manchester University Press, 2003), 66.

[12]   Andrew Crowhurst, 'The Music Hall 1885–1922' (Ph D thesis, Cambridge University, 1991), 369.

[13]   Peter Bailey, *Leisure and Class in Victorian England: Rational Recreation and the Contest for Control, 1830–1885* (London: Routledge & Kegan Paul, 1978), 166.

[14]   Ibid.

Measures against vulgarity and radicalism are never completely successful, however. A singer like Harry Champion will change the words to his songs to make them ruder when he thinks the audience would appreciate it. Similarly, more radical content may have been present in some halls, though there is little clear evidence for this.

As we have seen, the form of the music-hall show also influences the content. The artiste has a short turn, before they leave the stage to the elephants, acrobats or ballet dancers who are next on. He or she must capture the audience's attention very quickly. This is often done by the use of melodrama and stereotypes, and this fact can work against the introduction of non-consensual material.

Finally, the majority of the songs contain a sing-along chorus. To make this work, a good melody and amusing words are important. If all the audience is to sing along, it will be best to avoid controversial material. This is also the reason that, in those songs where controversial material is present, it is frequently to be found in the verses and not in the sing-along chorus. All of these are powerful braking factors. On the other hand, they allow us to be sure, when protest or dissent is present in the music-hall repertoire, that it represents a widespread view in the working-class audience.

Since the birth of music hall in the 1840s, some songs had spoken of the social condition of the working class. Albert Chevalier's 1892 hit 'My Old Dutch' protested at the fact that people too old to work and with no savings or means of support would be sent to the workhouse, and separated man from wife. Gus Elen mocked, in 1906, the people who 'knuckle down through being out of work' and suggested, in the sing-along chorus, that another attitude was preferable:

> What's the use of kicking up a row
> If there ain't no work about?
> If you can't get a job, you can rest in bed
> Till the school kids all comes out!
> If you can't get work you can't get the sack
> That's a argyment that's sensible and sound
> Lay your head back on yer piller and read yer 'Daily Mirrer'
> And wait till the work comes round![15]

In the verses, the song recommends having a sturdy stick ready in case the bailiffs should arrive.

The 1910 song 'Don't Go Down the Mine, Dad' related a fatal accident at a coal mine. Others sang of being evicted for non-payment of rent or of living in crowded accommodations, or they mocked foremen, policemen and landlords. We shall see shortly what themes dominated in the war years, after a short presentation of the political atmosphere of 1914 and its effect on the repertoire.

---

[15]   Original recording at https://www.youtube.com/watch?v=bQrEmRBN5kw (accessed 28 July 2014).

Popular patriotism

The popularity of warlike songs in 1914 has fomented some debate about the nature of popular support for British imperialism or for militarism. Some writers, such as Richard Hoggart, talking of the beginning of the twentieth century in general, have written that the working class was characterized by a 'general lack of patriotism',[16] while others such as Hobson[17] claimed that deeply felt patriotism was the norm.

Andrew Thompson, in his study of the popular impact of imperialism, points out how difficult it is to characterize popular attitudes with any precision: 'There are ... real problems in reading from imperial propaganda – however widespread or commercially successful – public acceptance or approval of the opinions therein expressed.'[18] He insists that the very need for large amounts of propaganda may be a sign of lack of popular adherence to elite priorities and he warns that 'What the empire meant to the masses cannot simply be read from the words of a music hall song'.[19]

Robert Roberts describes the poor workers of his part of town before the war as very much patriotic: 'the indigent remained staunchly patriotic ... they knew the empire was theirs and they were going to support it'.[20]

The very frequent presence of British flags at popular festivals in Edwardian times, the annual celebrations of Empire Day, and the nature and popularity of the Scout Movement, founded in 1909, would tend to suggest that the working classes were by no means impermeable to imperialist discourse. Sylvia Pankhurst, who was active in London opposing the war and organizing to defend the interests of poor women, writes that even women activists in her own radical organization would sometimes encourage the men around them to volunteer for the army.[21]

The figures for numbers of volunteers in the first few months of the war have generally been seen as revealing a deep popular patriotism, even if enthusiasm was far from being the only reason that men decided to join up. The prisons and homeless hostels were emptied by the recruitment drive, and many male workers elsewhere were given the choice: join the army or lose your job. An unemployed man of military age could no longer hope to receive any government allowance

---

[16]   Richard Hoggart, *The Uses of Literacy: Aspects of Working-class Life* (London: Chatto & Windus, 1957), 110.

[17]   John Atkinson Hobson, *The Psychology of Jingoism* (London: Richards, 1901).

[18]   Andrew Thompson, *The Empire Strikes Back?: The Impact of Imperialism on Britain from the Mid-Nineteenth Century* (London: Pearson, 2005), 39.

[19]   Ibid., 84.

[20]   Robert Roberts, *The Classic Slum: Salford Life in the First Quarter of the Century* (Harmondsworth: Pelican, 1973), 144.

[21]   Sylvia Pankhurst, *The Home Front: A Mirror to Life in England during the First World War* (London: The Cresset Library, 1987 (1932)), 23.

if he did not 'choose' to join the forces.[22] In Sylvia Pankhurst's personal view, 'patriotism flamed high; the best and the worst of it, service and sacrifice, love of excitement, desire for advertisement, fear and prejudice'.[23]

One might consider nevertheless that patriotic ideology was in some ways fragile, since it required daily reinforcement by all the physical and ideological forces of the state. And the determination to act as the fatherland seemed to require was far from universal: the majority of soldiers who fought in the Great War had to be obliged to do so by the 1916 conscription laws. Most of these men had resisted the pressure of a huge propaganda campaign, and of moral and economic pressures at historic levels.

The result of these contradictory ideological forces will give rise to massive popular efforts in support of the war drive, as well as many popular strikes to ensure that workers are not the only ones to pay the price of the war while employers make record profits. Popular acceptance of the need to win the war could co-exist alongside deep mistrust of the government and of the employers.

The reputation of the Great War music hall

If we move onto the songs themselves and the reputation they have, we see J. B. Priestley denouncing the repertoire of the period: 'The first war, unlike the second, produced two distinct crops of songs: one for patriotic civilians, ... the other, not composed or copyrighted by anybody, genuine folk song, for the sardonic front-line troops.'[24]

Priestley is not alone. The poet and soldier Siegfried Sassoon expressed his bitterness against the music-hall treatment of the war in his poem 'Blighters' written in February 1917, in which he imagined with delight the idea of a real tank crushing in their seats the foolish civilians who were singing enthusiastic songs about the war, mocking, he felt, 'the riddled corpses round Bapaume'.[25]

The 1963 musical comedy *Oh What a Lovely War*, which played some role in popularizing an anti-imperialist view of the First World War, also presents music-hall songs as jaunty warmongering to be contrasted with the bitter and cynical soldier songs. And the very influential historian Arthur Marwick claimed that 'popular patriotic songs or songs like the nostalgic "Tipperary" ... accounted for the bulk of the records pressed during the war'.[26]

---

[22]   Ibid.,47.

[23]   Ibid., 39.

[24]   J. B. Priestley, *Margin Released: A Writer's Reminiscences and Reflections* (London: Heinemann, 1962), 111.

[25]   Can be read online at http://www.bartleby.com/135/16.html.

[26]   Arthur Marwick, *The Deluge: British Society and the First World War* (Basingstoke: Palgrave Macmillan, 2006), 187.

As we have seen, this vision of music-hall songs as mostly made up of warmongering patriotism is quite false, and these judgements must be seen in the context of the fact that the archival work on a large corpus of music-hall songs had not been carried out.

Joining the war drive

The outbreak of war saw a general mobilization of civil society for the imperial cause. For the government, Lloyd George waxed lyrical about 'the great peaks we had forgotten, of Honour, Duty, Patriotism, and, clad in glittering white, the great pinnacle of Sacrifice, pointing like a rugged finger to Heaven'.[27] And he claimed that the war would both purify the nation and bring much greater social justice in its wake. Trade union leaders such as Ben Tillett, a working-class hero who had led the great dockers' strike of 1889, threw themselves into the war drive, too. Tillett later wrote: ' Despite our former pacifist attitude, the forces of Labour in England have supported the government throughout the war. We realised that this is a fight for world freedom against a carefully engineered plan to establish a world autocracy.'[28]

The leaders of the young Labour party, with very few exceptions, supported the war and, as we saw in Chapter 4, the vast majority of leading feminists did too. The best-known intellectuals of the time followed suit. Rudyard Kipling had always been a convinced imperialist, but was now accompanied by many more. Novelists G. K. Chesterton and Arthur Conan Doyle formed a team along with six historians from Oxford University to write propaganda pamphlets. Even authors such as H. G. Wells or George Bernard Shaw, who criticized certain aspects of the running of the war, desired victory for the British Empire.[29] And the Church of England, as we shall see in Chapter 6, saw support for the war as its sacred duty.

The music-hall stars joined then, quite naturally, the war drive. Harry Lauder, one of the most enthusiastic, organized a tour of the country accompanied by a military band in order to recruit soldiers in the music halls.[30] Vesta Tilley was soon nicknamed 'Britain's best recruiting sergeant' and the title of one of her songs – 'The Army of Today's All Right' – was used for recruiting posters.[31] Theatre managers also did their bit: groups of wounded soldiers were soon invited up on stage to help recruitment, and theatres were printing on their programmes the

---

[27]   Quoted in *The Times*, 20 September 1914.

[28]   Ben Tillett, *Who Was Responsible for the War and Why?* (London: Whitwell Press, 1917), 3.

[29]   J. L. Wisenthal and Daniel O'Leary, *What Shaw Really Wrote about the War* (Gainsville: University Press of Florida, 2006), 5.

[30]   Private J. Quigley, *The Slogan – Sidelights on Recruiting with Harry Lauder's Band* (London: Simpkin, 1916).

[31]   Matilda De Frece, *Recollections of Vesta Tilley* (London: Hutchinson, 1934), 142.

reassuring piece of information 'No man of military age appears on stage in this theatre'.[32]

One nurse, who was invited to a theatre along with a group of wounded soldiers towards the end of 1914, explains how at one point they were all ushered from their seats:

> Abashed, but not displeased with the applause, they were ranged across the stage. The curtain rose behind them to reveal a spectacular representation of the burning of Rheims Cathedral, with realistic flames that spurted dangerously through an open trapdoor on the stage. In front of them strutted Hetty King, and as the orchestra played the opening bars she started to sing the hit song of the year.[33]

Propaganda songs and their effectiveness

Many 1914 songs echoed the war fever. They played an important role, because the music-hall stars were adored by their audiences, and their words could carry much more weight than sermons by bishops or speeches by intellectuals or politicians. In addition, the place of the singing was key. To hear a pro-war message among friends on a relaxing night out could move people in a particular manner. Messages carried by music, moreover, have a special emotional power, and active participation in collective singing involves more commitment than does passive listening. Music hall professionals were proud of their speed of reaction to current events, and the first war songs appeared only hours after the declaration of war. In the trade press, lyricists placed adverts promising to add a 'war verse' to any existing song, for a small fee.[34]

For the whole of the war years, around a quarter of the songs take the war or an aspect of it as their main theme. In the category 'recruitment and other warlike songs', we have such titles as the following:

- Three Cheers for the Red White and Blue
- Be a Soldier, Lad of Mine!
- The Army of Today's All Right!
- Won't You Join the Army?
- We Don't Want to Lose You but We Think You Ought to Go
- For the Honour of Dear Old England
- Boys in Khaki, Boys in Blue[35]

---

[32]   Terry Hallett, *Bristol's Forgotten Empire: The History of the Empire Theatre, Bristol* (Westbury: Badger Press, 2000), 74.
[33]   Lyn Macdonald, *The Roses of No Man's Land* (London: Penguin Books, 1993), 52.
[34]   *The Encore*, 13 August 1914.
[35]   In khaki for the army, blue for the navy.

- Men of England, You Have Got to Go!
- You Ought to Join!
- Let 'em All Come, We're Ready!
- March On to Berlin!
- Our Country's Call
- Be a Soldier, Be a Man!
- I'd Like to Be a Hero, Too.
- Bravo, British Volunteer!
- Tommy Is As Good a Man As Any Knight of Old
- It's a Grand Sight to See them Going Away

Several 1914 songs mobilize seductive and even suggestive discourses of women artistes to persuade men to volunteer for the army. Here is the sing-along chorus of the hit song 'Your King and Country Need You':

> Oh, we don't want to lose you
> But we think you ought to go
> For your King and your country
> Both need you so
> We shall want you and miss you
> But with all our might and main
> We shall cheer you, thank you, kiss you[36]
> When you come back again![37]

Another hit[38] exhorted women to refuse to go out with civilian men:

> The Army and the Navy need attention
> The outlook isn't healthy you'll admit
> But I've got the perfect dream
> Of a new recruiting scheme
> Which I really think is absolutely it.
>
> If only other girls would do as I do
> I do believe that we could manage it
> For I turn all suitors from me but the sailor and the Tommy
> I've an Army and a Navy of my own!
>
> On Sunday I walked out with a soldier,
> On Monday I'm taken by a tar,

---

[36] Sometimes 'bless you' was sung instead of 'kiss you', considered daring.
[37] Full lyrics and 1915 recording at http://www.firstworldwar.com/audio/yourkingand countrywantyou.htm.
[38] *Phono Record*, April 1915.

On Tuesday I choose a baby boy scout,
On Wednesday a hussar!
On Thursday I go out with a Scottie
On Friday the Captain of the crew,
But on Saturday I'm willing,
If you'll only take the shilling,
To make a man of any one of you![39]

This song combines the traditional music-hall taste for 'the naughty' (a woman
who has a different man each day) and the patriotic needs of the war.

The theme of seduction would be used to encourage soldiers in later songs
which did not speak of recruitment. In 1915, 'All the Boys in Khaki Get the Nice
Girls' was a smash hit, and in January 1918, the trade press reported that the
song 'There's a Girl for Every Soldier' was performed by 18 different artistes in
pantomimes around the country.[40]

Moral ideas of childhood and fatherhood were also mobilized in songs like the
following:

- Daddy's Going to Fight for England! 1914
- For the Sake of the Motherland, Goodbye Daddy! 1914
- Farewell, Daddy! 1914
- God Bless My Soldier Daddy! 1914
- The Empire Now Will Be Your Daddy 1915
- Daddy's Had to Go to War 1916
- God Bless My Sailor Daddy 1916)
- Sergeant Daddy, VC 1916

The publication in 1915 of the song 'Our Daddy in Khaki – a War Action Song for
Infants', which was written to be sung at home rather than at the music-hall, shows
once again the depth of the war atmosphere.

Songs to help unite the nation

A number of pieces dramatize the unity of the nation and of the empire, and
the loyalty of its allies. 'Then They All Sang "God Save the King"' presents an
Englishman, an Irishman, a Welshman and a Scot, 'the night before the war':

'Should auld acquaintance be forgot'
The Scotsman sang with pride
'Men of Harlech, march to glory'

---

[39]   Full lyrics at http://lyricsplayground.com/alpha/songs/o/ohwhatalovelywar.shtml.
[40]   *The Era*, 2 January 1918.

> The gallant Welshman cried
> 'God save Ireland' sang a hero
> With a real old Irish swing
> Then every mother's son proudly held a gun
> And sang 'God Save Our King!'

The message is that being proud of one's particular people in no way contradicts being a proud member of the British nation and contributing to its war effort. It is to be noted that the Englishman's pride in his country does not require separate reinforcement, since England and Britain are so closely identified. The ideological work attempted by this song was very necessary. Recruitment was extremely slow in Wales, in particular in the mining regions where the socialist movement was influential.[41] In 'Red Clydeside', the industrial heartland of Scotland, recruitment was also problematic.[42] As for the Irish population, if the unionists supported the Empire automatically, the nationalists were split down the middle between the position that supporting Britain in the war would lead to Irish interests being better respected after the conflict, and the idea that, now that the British Army was bogged down in France, this was the perfect time for opposing British domination.

'Sergeant Solomon Isaacstein', a 1916 hit, shows the will to include Jews in the national community, at the same time as it reveals frank and unapologetic anti-Semitic prejudices. The chorus proposes to toast the health of 'the only Jewish Scotsman in the Irish Fusiliers'. but the verses repeat all the old stereotypes of cunning and avaricious Jews. Isaacstein opens a usurious lending bank ('with money lent, at 90 per cent') in the trenches, at the same time as showing an admirable enthusiasm for fighting the Germans. In the last verse, he is almost killed when the bombs he is using to make a pawnbroker's sign explode. This is presented as hilarious:[43]

> He hadn't any three brass balls
> To hang out for a sign,
> So he found three bombs and gilded them
> And my word they looked fine!
> But one of them fell wallop from the chain
> And nearly sent him back to Petticoat Lane!

Britain's allies are praised in pieces such as 'Our Brave Colonials' in 1914, or 'America Answers the Call', released after the USA declared war on Germany. A few, somewhat paternalist songs praised European allies, such as 'Three Cheers

---

[41]   Gavin Roynon (Ed.), *Home Fires Burning:The Great War Diaries of Georgina Lee* *(Stroud: Sutton,* 2006), 25.

[42]   Harry Mcshane, *No Mean Fighter* (London: Pluto Press, 1978).

[43]   1916 recording at http://www.firstworldwar.com/audio/1916.htm.

for Little Belgium!',[44] 'Well Done, Little Ones! Bravo, Belgian Boys!' or 'Good Luck, Little French Soldier Man!' (all from 1914).

One 1915 song, 'John Bull's Little Khaki Coon', blends a celebration of the participation of Black African regiments alongside the British Army with condescending racist content. The narrator is a Black soldier:

Germany has found that the colours won't run
No matter how you shoot
We always stand our ground
And John Bull's very proud of his little khaki coon

Chorus: I'm not a common darkie
That's why I'm dressed in khaki
One of the boys that helped to bear the brunt
We've been very very busy at the front
William thought he had us cornered
But we've made him change his tune
I'm an absent minded beggar
But everybody's proud of
John Bull's little khaki coon!

The previous year, music-hall audiences had heard sung the praise of Indian soldiers:

The hindoos with their knives
Are offering up their lives
For the honour of the empire's glorious name!

If all these songs worked at reinforcing the spirit of imperial unity, a few others aimed at constructing the rejected Other who did not deserve to belong to the nation. The pacifist conscientious objector is presented in 'The Conscientious Objector's Lament'. When the conscription laws were passed in 1916, British law allowed those who had religious objections to fighting to be assigned, once a court had so decided, to non-combatant duties. Sixteen thousand men applied to be conscientious objectors.[45]

Few sympathized. It was felt that these people were simply 'slackers' and unwilling to participate in a common endeavour, though the soldiers who worked with the conscientious objectors often came to respect their principles.[46] 'The Conscientious Objectors' Lament', sung in a tearful voice by Alfred Lester,

---

[44]   1914 recording can be heard at http://www.firstworldwar.com/audio/1914.htm

[45]   Felicity Goodall, *We Will Not Go to War* (Stroud: The History Press, 2010), 1.

[46]   Will Ellsworth-Jones, *We Will Not Fight..: The Untold Story of World War One's Conscientious Objectors* (London: Aurum Press, 2008), 127; Alan Wilkinson, *The Church of England and the First World War* (London: SCM Press, 1996), 53.

presents a comic picture of an effeminate, cowardly, intellectual and no doubt homosexual pacifist.[47] The cowardly narrator explains that he doesn't 'object to fighting Huns but should hate them fighting me!' His use of the word 'conscience' at all is presented as ridiculous:

> Non-combatant battalions are fairly in my line
> But the Sergeant always hates me for he calls me 'baby mine'
> But oh, I got so cross with him, I rose to the attack
> And when he called me 'Ethel' I just called him 'Beatrice' back.
>
> *Chorus*:   Send out the army and the navy
> Send out the rank and file
> Send out the Brave old territorials
> They'll face the danger with a smile!
> Send out the boys of the old brigade
> Who made old England free
> Send out my brother, my sister and my mother
> But for God's sake don't send me![48]

Several other songs and sketches expressed similar sentiments[49]. Ironically, the chorus of 'The Conscientious Objector's Lament' became used as a soldiers' song expressing frustration with the pointlessness of the war. It is also interesting to see that, although the general tone of the song is very much anti-pacifist, the conscientious objector-narrator is allowed a little legitimate protest against aspects of the war in the last verse, when he sings 'Send out the bakers, and the blooming profit-makers, but for Gawd's sake don't send me!' Ambiguous and contradictory messages in songs were not of course unusual. This song provides at least two different pleasures to the audiences: in the verses, the audience can watch the pacifist (whose world view is perceived as threatening) being reassuringly reduced to ridicule; but in the chorus the audience is encouraged to take on the dissenter's voice and sing all together of the desire not to be involved in the war.

The rapid decline of enthusiastic songs

Songs of warlike enthusiasm declined very rapidly. Every one of the recruitment songs cited earlier in this chapter was released in 1914. The collection of 'Greatest

---

[47]   Full lyrics available at http://monologues.co.uk/musichall/Songs-C/Conscientious-Objectors-Lament.htm and a 1916 recording at http://www.firstworldwar.com/audio/1915.htm (consulted 27 November 2014).

[48]   The 1915 recording of this song can be heard at http://www.firstworldwar.com/audio/1915.htm (accessed 25 August 2014).

[49]   See, for example, Bransby Williams in *Phono Record*, February 1915.

Hits of 1915' published at the end of that year by Francis & Day, biggest of the music publishing companies, contains not one recruitment song. For the remaining years of the war, warmongering songs were rare and a far more ambivalent tone dominates. One of the successful songs directly about the war, in 1915 emphasized not the glory of dying for empire, but the responsibility to care for the families of those that had died (this in a period where welfare was all but non-existent): 'Let old England guard the widows and the orphans that remain. Then will England guard her honour and escutcheon free from stain!'

The decline of enthusiastic songs is to be seen in the context of the fact that the nature of the war in the popular imagination had changed tremendously. Early illusions that the soldiers would be 'home for Christmas' quickly faded; the lists of dead and wounded grew ever longer. The First Battle of Ypres in October and November 1914 left 7,960 British soldiers dead, 17,830 missing and 29,562 wounded. Numbers volunteering fell from 350,000 for the month of September 1914 to 120,000 a month in 1915. The desire for victory over Germany remained strong, but it seems it was no longer possible to get a music hall audience to sing all together in favour of recruitment.

Getting morale back up

The carnage continued. Even after the disastrous Dardanelles campaign in 1915 and the terrible numbers of casualties on the Somme in the summer of 1916, most of the population still saw the war as 'a job to be done' and no one wanted to think that all those young men had died for nothing. Songs to help people carry on despite the suffering became more important in the music-hall repertoire where they fitted into a long tradition of 'cheer-up' songs which began long before the war. In 1914, two major hits were already of this nature: 'It's a Long Way to Tipperary'[50] and 'Pack Up Your Troubles'.[51]

Of course, the very many wartime songs about seaside holidays or the joys of courting play a similar encouraging role, but we now see quite a number of titles which attack the question of demoralization directly. The best known is 'Are we Downhearted – No!', a title which recognizes that demoralization is the main subject of reflection.[52] The chorus exclaims, 'While we have Jack upon the sea, and Tommy on the land we need not fret' Nevertheless, the last line states that demoralization has not arrived 'yet'. The tension is clear.

---

[50]   Full lyrics and early recordings online at http://www.firstworldwar.com/audio/ itsalongwaytotipperary.htm (accessed 1 December 2014).

[51]   Full lyrics and original recording online at http://www.firstworldwar.com/audio/ packupyourtroubles.htm (accessed 1 December 2014).

[52]   1914 recording can be heard at http://www.firstworldwar.com/audio/1914.htm (accessed 1 December 2014).

Here are some other such song titles:

- Cheer Up, Little Soldier Man! 1915
- Our Whistling Tommies 1915
- Jolly Good Luck to Everyone! 1916
- Now Cheer Up, Everybody! 1916
- Send the Boys a Little Snapshot of the Ones They've Left Behind 1916
- We've Got to Put Up With It Now 1916
- Slog On, Slog On for 1917 1917
- On the Other Side of a Big, Black Cloud 1917
- At the End of a Vale of Shadows 1918
- It's No Use Worrying Over Yesterday! 1918
- Every Day Is One Day Nearer 1918
- We Must Keep On Keeping On 1918

Warlike enthusiasm seems to have given way to a sort of smiling fatalism, and war is treated in a similar way to the manner in which music hall had for a long time dealt with other catastrophes of working-class life.

Black humour

Towards the end of the war, we also find songs marked by a dry, black humour, which encourage the audience to laugh at the war (we shall see in Chapter 6 that this attitude is general in soldiers' songs). The 1917 music-hall hit 'Whizz Bang Lane'[53] is a jaunty song about life in the trenches:

> Way down communication trench,
> In the middle of Whizz Bang Lane,
> I've got a nice little sandbag pillow,
> Where the Crumps and the Johnsons[54] rain
> Very very close to the sniper's post
> Where the aerial torpedoes worry us most;
> Where old Fritz gives us egg on toast
> Away down Whizz Bang Lane

At the end of the song, the narrator is wounded and relieved to be going home.

The 1918 hit song 'Oh, It's a Lovely War', set to a joyful marching tune, mocks the official myth that all is going well. The soldier narrators are enjoying the war so much that they exclaim 'Don't we pity the poor civilians, sitting around a fire!'

---

[53]   In soldier slang, a whizzbang is a small, high-speed shell.
[54]   'Crumps' and 'Johnsons', in slang, were types of heavy shell.

and describe the luxury lifestyle in the trenches – 'we never get up till the sergeant brings our breakfast up to bed'.[55]

Another hit song, 'Goodbyee!', seemed to strike a chord with the public, and was performed by a number of different stars in 1917. The first verse and the sing-along chorus went:

> Brother Bertie went away
> To do his bit the other day
> With a smile on his lips
> And his Lieutenant's pips
> Upon his shoulder bright and gay
>
> As the train moved out he said,
> 'Remember me to all the birds.'
> Then he wagged his paw
> And went away to war
> Shouting out these pathetic words:
>
> Goodbye-ee, goodbye-ee,
> Wipe a tear, baby dear, from your eye-ee,
> Though' it's hard to part I know,
> I'll be tickled to death to go.
> Don't cry-ee, don't sigh-ee,
> There's a silver lining in the sky-ee,
> Bonsoir, old thing, cheerio, chin chin,
> Nah-poo,[56] toodle-oo, Goodbye-ee![57]

It is not easy to analyse this song, with the terrible repetition of a deformed 'Goodbye' (pronounced in baby talk, perhaps), the jaunty melody, jokey references to death and forced rhymes. One has the impression of a pain which cannot be described, where farce is the only option for emotional survival. The signs of his grade (lieutenant's pips) count for little in the context of his pathetic and helpless farewell. He uses upper-class slang and is being mocked, yet the audience is singing along this chorus and revisiting, in comic tone, the many Goodbyes they have each had to live through.

---

[55] 1918 recording online at http://www.firstworldwar.com/audio/1918.htm (accessed 1 December 2014).

[56] 'Na-poo' was soldiers' slang for 'all gone', a corruption of the French phrase 'il n'y en a plus'.

[57] Full lyrics and original recording online at http://www.firstworldwar.com/audio/goodbyeee.htm.

Dreaming of the end of the war

By far the biggest category of songs about the war is that of those which express
the dream of the end of the war and the return of 'our boys'. In Chapter 4, we saw
that 'home' was the single most common word in song titles during the war. Here
are some examples from this category:

1914

- When Tommy Comes Marching Home
- The Homes They Leave Behind
- Keep the Home Fires Burning
- It's a Long Way to Go Home
- Johnny O Morgan With His Little Mouth Organ, Playing 'Home Sweet Home'

1915

- Save Your Kisses Till the Boys Come Home
- Tell My Daddy to Come Home Again

1916

- The Road Back Home
- I'm Longing to Go Back (Your Prodigal Son is Coming Home)
- When Tommy Comes Home Again
- When You're a Long Way from Home
- Blighty, the Soldiers' Home Sweet Home

1917

- Back to My Home Once More
- I Love That Dear Old Home of Mine

1918

- It's the Welcome Home That Makes It Home
- As the Boys Come Home Again
- My little Holborn Home.
- Way Back Home
- The End of the Journey: Homeland and You
- Home, Home, So Dear To Me
- Welcome Home, Brave Lads
- Where The Milestones End, It's Home
- When My Soldier Boy Comes Home

Some of the songs say in so many words that the priority is not patriotism, but going home. In the hit 'Johnny O'Morgan on His Little Mouth Organ, Playing "Home Sweet Home"', the narrator explains to his sweetheart that, although back in Britain military bands are playing to civilians like her tunes such as 'Rule Britannia' and 'God Save the King', these songs have no resonance for the soldiers at the front. For 'there's one tune only [which] cheers us when we're sad and lonely', which is of course the 'Home Sweet Home' mentioned in the title of the song. The voice of the ordinary soldier is explicitly preferred to the voice of the establishment.

The biggest seller from the last years of the war was 'Keep the Home Fires Burning':[58]

> They were summoned from the hillside,
> They were called in from the glen,
> And the country found them ready
> At the stirring call for men.
> Let no tears add to their hardships
> As the soldiers pass along,
> And although your heart is breaking,
> Make it sing this cheery song:
>
> *Chorus*:   Keep the Home Fires Burning,
> While your hearts are yearning.
> Though your lads are far away
> They dream of home.
> There's a silver lining
> Through the dark clouds shining,
> Turn the dark cloud inside out
> Till the boys come home.[59]

It is to be noted that the verses of this song are patriotic in tone, and defend explicitly British intervention in the war, but the chorus, which all the audience will be asked to sing along with, speaks only of the dream of the end of the war. The drive for victory has by this time been fairly comprehensively replaced in the repertoires by the desire for the return of peace.

Life in wartime Britain seen from below

The major events of the war from the point of view of ordinary people were the following: the recruitment campaign, the introduction of conscription, the 400,000

---

[58]   Actually written in 1914, but rising in popularity throughout the war.

[59]   Lyrics and original recording at http://www.firstworldwar.com/audio/keepthehom efiresburning.htm (accessed 25 August 2014).

victims of the Battle of the Somme, the brief impression that peace was possible in 1916, the very late introduction of rationing in February 1918, and the ups and downs of the military campaigns of the last summer of the war. Some of these events would give to rise to songs which clearly rejected the priorities of the wartime state.

Open opposition to the war was very much on the margins in Britain, particularly in England, except for a short period in 1916. The Empire's objectives, revealed in the treaties of 1918, were little understood.[60] Protest concerning inequality of sacrifice in wartime was, however, frequent, and the campaign against conscription gained considerable support. In September 1915, the Trades Union Congress, grouping together almost all British trade unions, voted against conscription. At the end of 1916, a strike by engineers succeeded in giving trade unions the right to choose which workers should be exempted from military conscription because their work was essential to industry.[61] Indeed, some employers had wanted to take the opportunity of the war to get rid of trade union activists.

During 1916, a Stop the War campaign was built. It remained a minority opinion, but was strong enough to organize meetings in practically every town, large or small, across the country. As for the No Conscription Fellowship, this organization counted only 350 members at the beginning of 1915, but by April 1916, its national conference in London brought together 1,500 local delegates.[62]

More powerful protest arose concerning the effect of the war on workers' living standards. Though unemployment fell sharply, and there were far more opportunities for women in particular to get jobs, inflation was high and profiteers were very active, in particular before the introduction of rationing in 1918. There was a big strike wave between 1915 and 1918 accounting in total for 18 million strike days, a far higher figure than for the period 1911–1914. The most important disputes were the dockers' strike of 1915, and the engineering strikes of March 1916, April 1917 and April 1918. Numbers of trade unionists rose from 4.1 million in 1913 to 6.5 million in 1918, despite the fact that 5 million men were in the army, and so not able to join trade unions.

Anti-war songs

As we have seen, the economic structure of music hall does not easily allow dissenting opinions to be expressed in the songs. This means that when dissenting

[60] The treaties of 1919–1920 added 4.6 million square kilometres of territory and 13 million people to the British Empire. Among the elite, these objectives were better understood (Roynon, *Home Fires*, 14).

[61] Marwick, *The Deluge*,124.

[62] Thomas Cummins Kennedy, *The Hound of Conscience: A History of the No-conscription Fellowship, 1914–1919* (Fayetteville: University of Arkansas Press, 1981), 114.

songs do reach success, we can be sure that they represent a powerful current of popular opinion. This is why there are practically no anti-war songs on the music-hall stage, even in 1916, if one excepts such comic songs as 'If They'd Only Fight the War with Wooden Soldiers' of 1915. Before the war was declared, such songs were possible. One of Little Tich's hits in 1911, 'The Twenty-Third', is anti-militarist in tone: it has the form of a regimental anthem expressing pride, but it describes a regiment filled with drunks and idiots, most of whom end up on the gallows. Another example of anti-militarism in popular commercial song is given in the autobiography of a socialist activist in Glasgow:

> Just prior to the outbreak there was a music hall song which really caught on –
> You could hear it sung everywhere, in the workshops and on the streets. It went:

> > 'Little man, little man
> > You want to be a soldier [...]
> > You are your mother's only son
> > Never mind about the gun
> > Stay at home
> > Fight for her all you can.'

> In the socialist movement we were surprised and delighted by the song's popularity. But the day war was declared that song just died; it was amazing the way that nobody was whistling it.[63]

Anti-war songs appear on the stage and on records in the United States until the country joins the war, and some became well-known in Britain. Irving Berlin, to his later embarrassment, penned the hit 'Stay Down Here Where You Belong' which recounts a conversation between the Devil and his son. It includes this reference to humans: 'To serve their king, they've all gone off to war /And not a one of them knows what they're fighting for'. Another success was entitled 'Don't Take My Darling Boy Away' and presents a mother who has seen her husband and three of her sons leave for the war. She begs the recruitment officer not to take her last son into the army. One can note that the story is careful to present a protest through the words of a mother who cannot be accused of being unpatriotic. The aim for a consensual discourse is clear.

Even more famous, and more radical, was a song which also uses the figure of a mother to help gain the sympathy of the audience. This is 'I Didn't Raise My Boy to Be a Soldier', [64] a rousing ballad which declares that victory can be of no importance to a mother who loses her son. The mother-narrator asks, concerning her son 'Who dares to place a musket on his shoulder, to shoot some

---

[63] McShane, *No Mean Fighter*, 61.
[64] There is a recording at http://en.wikipedia.org/wiki/I_Didn't_Raise_My_Boy_to_Be_a_Soldier.

other mother's darling boy?' and declares that mothers should stand together to insist that arbitration and not war be used to solve international conflicts.

Certainly it would have been difficult, in Britain, to persuade theatre managers to allow the singing of this song on stage. Yet the song is included by Kilgarriff in his list of the thirty or so most remarked-upon songs of 1915.[65] It may have been sung in smaller music halls or in parts of the country like Glasgow where the war was unpopular, but there is no clear evidence of this. In any event, the piece was well-enough known to inspire the production of a very successful reply, set to the same melody, the following year: 'I'm Glad I Raised My Boy to Be a Soldier'. The anti-war version became the anthem of the peace movement throughout the war. In Australia, it was sung in anti-war rallies led by Adela Pankhurst, one of Emmeline's daughters who had, like Sylvia, broken off relations with her ultra-patriotic mother.[66]

Criticizing war priorities

A few songs, as we have seen, criticize the war fever without questioning the need for victory. Such content is extremely common in non-commercial soldiers' songs, as we shall see in the next chapter, but can also be heard on the stage, as in this hit from 1917:

> We don't want a lot of flags a flying
> When we come marching home
> We don't want your big brass bands ...
> We don't want a lot of speechifying
> And we don't want a lot of waving hands
> We don't want a lot of interfering
> But we do want to find the girls we left behind!

Other lyrics mock the excesses of the recruitment machine. 'Forty Nine and in the Army!'[67] suggests that conscription has gone too far, and is taking men who are too old:

> I'm forty nine and in the army
> 49 isn't it fine
> Though I'm weakly across the chest
> And gouty about the knees

---

[65]   Michael Kilgarriff, *Sing Us One of the Old Songs: A Guide to Popular Song 1860–1920* (Oxford: Oxford University Press, 1999), 587.

[66]   June Purvis, *Emmeline Pankhurst: A Biography* (London: Routledge, 2002), 277.

[67]   It is as well to remember that the average state of health of a 49-year-old British man a century ago was very much inferior to what it is today.

I'm learning to shoulder arms
But I'd rather be standing at ease!

49 and in the army.
And soon I will be in the fighting line,
If somebody holds me rifle,
While I borrow a pair of steps,
I'll be over the top and at 'em at 49!

The introduction of conscription in 1916 produced a number of protests in song, and reminds us of the capacity of music hall to react immediately to current political events. While the conscription bill was still being debated in parliament, music-hall audiences were listening to 'Conscription on the Brain'.

Asquith take back your bill
It really makes us ill
For we are all real volunteers today, sir
We are our good king's own
In flesh and blood and bone
And we're going to wipe out the blessed Kaiser

The shirkers may be weeded,
But conscription is not needed,
We only want the king to say 'Come on, sirs!'
Then you'll find we've quite enough
Of downright bulldog stuff
To double up at least a dozen Kaisers

A few months later a comic song by Ernest Hastings protested against the fact that it seemed to be almost impossible to be exempted from military conscription.[68] Local civilian tribunals were set up to decide on cases where exemption had been requested; 750,000 men submitted applications to be excused.[69] In each tribunal, a military representative, who had overwhelming influence, was present. This song 'The Military Representative', which was greeted with rapturous applause in the theatres,[70] tells the story of a tribunal who refused to exempt a man of 91, a conscientious objector, and a dead man:

They called upon the next case
Then a woman rose and said

---

[68]   Ilana Bet-El, *Conscripts: Forgotten Men of the Great War* (Stroud: The History Press, 2009), 44.
[69]   Ellsworth-Jones, *We Will Not Fight*, 64.
[70]   *The Encore*, 27 September 1917.

'I'm very sorry, gentlemen
But my poor husband's dead.'

The chairman said 'Well, he's exempted, he needn't come again'
'Oh, thank you!' said the widow as she ran to catch a train
But the military representative got up and shouted 'Hi!!
How dare your husband die?!
He was A1 in July!
What say, ma'am, he's in heaven now?
Well you just let him know
I'm sending a Sergeant to fetch him back
For of course he's got to go!'

They called on Rip Van Winkle next and smiling all serene
He mumbled 'Gents I'm 91, you've got me down 19!'
... but the military representative got up and shouted 'Say!
Don't let him run away though he's 91 today!
There are men down at the War Office as old as he, I know
And I'm sure they're a damn sight sillier,
So of course he's got to go!'

Rationing, applied from early 1918, and other wartime restrictions, gave rise to a number of songs such as 'Sugar', which tells of the antics of a man in desperate search of a bag of sugar, 'Lloyd George's Beer', and 'Never Mind the Food Controller, We'll Live on Love'.

'Lloyd George's Beer'[71] complains of the decision by the new prime minister to reduce by law the maximum alcohol content allowed in beer, since he believed that working-class drinking habits were a major obstacle to the war drive. One might think that a chorus criticizing Lloyd George for this symbolic attack on working-class lifestyles might not cover for other kinds of criticism. Singing along against Lloyd George in 1917 could be comforting to audiences who had other, inexpressible, reasons to be angry with the man.

Other songs on rationing expressed frustration, always in a comic tone; for example:

You'll find the coupon system
Ruling all your daily life
And when into the barber's shop you'll go
If you haven't got a coupon he'll refuse to cut your hair
But he'll make you give him three to let it grow

---

[71]   Full lyrics and recording at http://www.firstworldwar.com/audio/lloydgeorgesbeer.htm.

Songs about life in the army became more common. Vesta Tilley's 1916 hit 'A Bit of a Blighty One' shows a discourse far removed from the official, heroic line.[72] The narrator is a wounded soldier, delighted to have been saved from life in the trenches by his 'misfortune'. Being fed expensive desserts and plenty of meat, he declares himself delighted to have been wounded. *'When I think about my dugout, where I dare not poke me mug out'* he sings, he's pleased to have been hit with a *'Blighty one'*.

Again we see the almost obligatory comic tone. A 1918 song, 'Back to Blighty', has a slightly more serious tone:

> When you get sent back to Blighty
> With a ticket on your chest
> There's a nice clean cot
> And lord knows what
> Where a bloke can be at rest
> And there ain't no shells
> And there ain't no smells
> And there ain't no liquid flame
> There's no place like Blighty
> With a bullet in your what's its name

The songs do not of course accuse the soldiers of having inflicted the wounds on themselves deliberately, but it was an open secret that such things were not unusual. Four thousand British soldiers were court-martialled for self-inflicted wounds during the war, and the confusion of trench warfare meant it must have been fairly easy to hide such events. Thinking about the best way to get oneself wounded was an everyday conversational topic for many soldiers.[73]

These are just some examples of songs which distance themselves sharply from war propaganda and seem to find a way of defending ordinary people sucked into the destiny and massacre machine. Another title, 'I'm Sick of This Blooming War', has a soldier narrator complaining of the danger of life under shell fire, the interminable boredom of square-bashing, and of the fact that the army insists he take a regular bath. The audience sings along with the chorus: 'I'm sick of this blooming war'. Naturally, the word 'blooming' was easily replaced by stronger or unprintable adjectives.

Notable absences

What is not sung about can be just as significant as what is sung about. The most remarkable absence in the repertoire is that of songs of hatred against the

---

[72]   1917 recording at http://www.firstworldwar.com/audio/1917.htm.
[73]   Macdonald, *The Roses*, 95–97.

Germans: there are practically none. Kilgarriff's list of music-hall hits of the war years contains no song title at all containing the word 'hun' – the slang insult word for the Germans – and this despite the fact that the word is easy to find rhymes for.

There do exist a few songs mocking the Kaiser and his institutions, such as Harry Champion's 1916 hit 'My Old Iron Cross', denigrating the famous German gallantry medal.[74]

'Hoch, Hoch, the Kaiser' from 1914 mocks German patriotism and 'The Day', the same year affirms:

> We do not fight for glory
> Nor are we out for swank
> It's Kaiser Bill, the gory
> We're setting out to spank
>
> *Chorus*:   Oh, Kaiser Bill oh Kaiser Bill
> What price that fateful day?
> For Britons now are Britons still
> And ready for the fray!

The informal appellation 'Kaiser Bill' is to be noted. In a similar tone, popular discourse often referred to enemy soldiers as 'Fritz': not quite friendly, but not hateful.

Why are there no songs of hate against the Germans? There was an active and violent xenophobic minority in Britain during the war: dozens of shops run by Germans were burned down, even if the German owners had taken British nationality. At least seven Germans were killed in Liverpool in anti-German riots in 1915, after the sinking of a civilian ship by a German U-boat,[75] and anti-German sentiments were present on the music hall stage in the form of anti-German sketches. But it is, perhaps, one thing to show an anti-German sketch and something quite different to get the whole audience to sing xenophobic choruses. Before the war, the many German immigrants in the big towns had been very well integrated with the native population. It may well be that anti-German xenophobia was not consensual enough for sing-along purposes. It is also the case that music-hall songs have very rarely expressed aggressive or negative emotions. Singers preferred in the war years to put forward songs which dreamed of the end of the war, or generic cheer-up songs.

There are one or two exceptions, which were not a great success. The song 'The Khaki Tramp' exhorts soldiers to:Stick to your guns!

---

[74]   For more on Harry Champion, see 'A Star in Focus 4' in the present volume. Full lyrics and original recording are online at http://www.firstworldwar.com/audio/my oldironcross.htm.

[75]   Richard Van Emden and Steve Humphries, *All Quiet on the Home Front: An Oral History of Life in Britain during the First World War* (London: Headline, 2003), 70.

Wipe out those Huns!
Remember we're proud of the empire's brave sons!
Make no mistake, the Germans will quake!
Kaiser and Moltke their armies you'll break!

And the 1914 song 'John Bull's Catechism' spoke very negatively of Germans:

Who gives his hand to the strangers as they come? John Bull.
Who opened the door to the horde of German scum? John Bull
Now they've had to take their hook, the vaterland to gain
From baron down to German cook will number in the slain
But who'll stop to think before he welcomes them again?
John Bull!

Popular song in France and in the USA included far more anti-German songs. The following are all US songs from 1918

- Big Chief Kill-a hun
- Run the Hun
- Bury the Hun
- Old Satan Gets the Hun
- Don't Quit till Every Hun Is Hit!
- Hunting the Hun[76]

In the French piece 'Le chien des boches'[77] a German dog helps a French prisoner of war to escape because 'a dog has more heart than a Hun'.

The other major absence in the repertoire is songs about death and killing. At the end of the nineteenth century one could hear melodramatic songs at the music hall about death through drinking. It seems that the omnipresence of tragedy in the war years put an end to death in the songs. British war poets such as Wilfred Owen or Siegfried Sassoon gave graphic details in their work about death and battle, and propaganda books such as Rev. Hardy's *The British Soldier* spoke of the enjoyment of killing with bayonets,[78] but music-hall numbers leave the subject almost completely alone.

One rare exception is the star Harry Lauder. 'Boys don't cry here when they die, they smile' he recited in his piece 'Granny's Laddie' in 1918. A similar sentiment was expressed in an 1897 song, revived during the Great War without

---

[76] Full lyrics and recording at: http://www.firstworldwar.com/audio/huntingthehun.htm (accessed 25 August 2014).

[77] Lyrics online at http://shihtzupassion.fr/autre/chien_du_boche.htm (accessed 25 August 2014).

[78] Rev. E. J. Hardy, *The British Soldier, His Courage and Humour* (London: T. Fisher Unwin, 1915), 42; 200.

great success, 'Break the News to Mother'. It tells the story of a young man killed gloriously on the battlefield while trying to save his regiment's flag.

Naturally, a number of other aspects of the war such as desertion, summary execution of prisoners,[79] suicide or soldiers shot at dawn to reinforce morale[80] have no place at all in the music-hall repertoire.

A freer tone once the war was over

The end of the war changed the repertoire. First of all, the word 'Victory' reappeared in the titles of a number of songs, such as these from 1918:

- Victory Bells Are Ringing
- The Voice of the Victory Loan
- This Christmas Brings Us Victory
- Our Day, Victory Waltz
- The Allies' Victory March Song
- Thank God for Victory

Nevertheless, for every 1918 British song whose title includes the word 'victory', there are ten whose title includes the word 'home', and this is also the case for the following year. And another phenomenon is to be noted: once the armistice had been signed, the national patriotic consensus was not so constraining. In the army and the navy, pent-up frustrations, and anger about demobilization, led to a number of mutinies. In 1919, a huge wave of strikes took place (35 million strike days), including a major strike in the police force. In the music hall too, there were some signs that it was easier to sing songs which broke with the wartime consensus.

A few hit songs criticized the myth of a heroic national unity. The piece 'First I Went and Won the DCM'[81] mocked those soldiers who invented stories of their courageous exploits in the trenches. On the theme of the Home Front, top singer Tom Clare presented a cynical 'What did you do in the Great War, Daddy' in 1919.[82] In each verse, we meet some British citizen and his contribution to 'the great Great War'. Here are some extracts:

---

[79]   Richard Holmes, *Tommy: The British soldier on the Western Front 1914–1918* (London: Harper Perennial, 2005), 549–551; Wilkinson, *The Church of England*, 98.

[80]   A comprehensive study of British military executions was carried out in the 1990s, once the archives had at last been opened to the public: Cathryn Corns and John Hughes-Wilson, *Blindfold and Alone: British Military Executions in the Great War* (London: Cassell, 2005).

[81]   Distinguished Conduct Medal.

[82]   The song can be listened to at http://www.firstworldwar.com/audio/1919.htm (accessed 25 August 2014).

Come and sit beside me, Daddy
Tell me the tale once more
I often asked you to tell me, Daddy
What you did in the great Great War. …

What did you do in the Great War, Bertie?
'I' said the young man from the grocery store
'Took no coupons from the woman next door
Whose husband was on the Tribunal!'

What did you do in the Great War, Frederick?
'I' said the special, 'From ten to four
Guarded the local reservoir and saw that no one drank it' …

What did you do in the Great War, Jane?
'I' said the lady with the voice pathetic
'Sang songs without giving an anaesthetic
I sang to the soldiers.
I sang to wounded Tommies with their beds all in a row
We do not want to lose you but we think you ought to go.
And that's what I did in the Great War, Daddy.'

…And all the profiteers who had been so long in clover
Fell a-sighing and a-sobbing when they heard the war was over
For they'd all made their 'bit' in the Great War, Daddy.

A few 1920 songs, some very popular, demanded punishment for profiteers: 'What Shall We Do with the Profiteers? Shoot Them All!' was the most aggressive of them.

'Now Bottomley's Words Are True' ironizes on the speeches of the warmongering orator Horatio Bottomley, and paints a picture of post-war priorities:

We'll all be friends, we'll have no foes
And many a sergeant they'll punch on the nose
Now Bottomley's words are true

No more we'll go down on our knees
Before the medical board MDs
And hope they'll find we've got heart disease
Now Bottomley's words are true

One hit is particularly striking. It sold enough copies to be printed in the hits of the year collection by leading publisher Francis & Day, and was entitled 'Pop goes the Major', the 'pop' representing the sound the Major would make when burned to death.

When the first the Armistice was signed
We took an oath, made up our mind
When we got home we'd try to find
Our Late S.M. or bust …

He thinks he's been forgotten quite
We'll soon see him in a different light
We're going to set fire to his house tonight
Pop goes the major!

Some chaps we knew spent two weeks leave
In hunting Sergeant major Reeve
They all had something up their sleeve
A bayonet or gun!
We swore we'd be the first to do the major in, one said 'not you!'
You will have to line up in the queue
And take your turn my son!

We've heard it said that he
Has got the OBE
But his next decoration
Looks like being the RIP
And him I'm going round to see
I'm taking a hand grenade with me!

That such a song should be a popular hit says much about the inexpressible suffering of ordinary soldiers under their superior officers.

To end with, consider the song 'Stony Broke in No Man's Land' in which the narrator, an ex-soldier, complains that life is even harder than it was during the war, given that ex-soldiers have been abandoned by society. Unable to find a job, saddened to see many others 'a lot worse off than me', ignored by his friends, he end up being nostalgic about the war experience. The sing-along chorus claims: 'I must confess, I was contented more or less when I was stoney broke in No Man's Land'.[83]

Conclusions

This chapter has concentrated on the themes of the songs and how they are dealt with; in particular, themes of war experience, social suffering and political understanding. However, it may well be that the weight of the social effect of

---

[83] Full lyrics and recording at http://www.firstworldwar.com/audio/stonybrokeinno mansland.htm (accessed 1 December 2014).

music-hall song does not reside in the themes. The form and the atmosphere – community singing, listening to people of our own class on stage – may well have been more significant, in a society where the pressure to 'better oneself' and reach for a taste of high culture in the hope of gaining a little social respect was very strong indeed.

When bourgeois society was working so hard to instil values of work and respectability, suggestive songs or the praise of hedonism may be considered to be transgressive. Far from the codes of high culture where audiences sit in silence at concerts watching musicians who are dressed up as bourgeois, the music hall often remained a working-class 'home from home'.

The use of a large corpus of songs has made it possible in this chapter to assess and contextualize the messages within them. We see that the music-hall milieu mobilized comprehensively for the war drive, as did so many other groups, but that the priorities of the working-class audiences had to be taken into account, even in the absence of a mass anti-war movement. The majority of songs sung in the war years were not about the war, and the majority of songs about the war are very far from patriotic warmongering. Comic and tragic aspects of the war experience took a far greater place in the music hall. 'Home' swiftly overtook 'Empire' or even 'victory' as the key value to be celebrated.

The songs of our corpus cannot be simply characterized as part of a 'culture of consolation', nor as purely 'authentic popular culture'. They no doubt have elements of both. Other song genres, less influenced by theatre managers under the dual pressure of economic competition and moralist censorship, could express more rebellious and less respectable attitudes to the war drive. Soldier songs are the main example, and will be at the core of the next chapter.

Chapter 6
'I want to go home': Soldiers' Songs and Other Non-commercial Songs

The songs we have looked at all along the previous three chapters had to be sold to a publisher, a singer or the director of a musical revue, and this fact had a strong influence on their content. This chapter concerns pieces which did not have to be commercialized. What was the role of such songs in the war years? Religious hymns will be our first port of call. They were immeasurably more influential then than they are now. If in the Church of England one heard many complaints about the decline of religious practice in urban areas, this impression was often exaggerated by being based on an idealization of religious practice in a rural past in which going to church was as much a social necessity as a sign of strong faith.

So, in 1909, a Liberal member of parliament, C. F. G. Masterman, in his book *The Condition of England*, expressed concern that religion 'is slowly but steadily fading from the modern city race'.[1] Yet there were still millions of children at Sunday schools in London and elsewhere, and the country still boasted a priest or vicar for every 1,457 inhabitants. Further, the Roman Catholic Church which served millions of citizens of Irish descent, and the Nonconformist churches, particularly well-represented in Wales, had higher rates of churchgoing than did the Anglican Church.

The Church of England felt itself very much to be part of the establishment and provided enthusiastic support for the war from the very first days. Dissenting voices among the clergy were rare. Soldiers were sometimes welcomed to the Western Front by religious sermons urging them to kill as many Germans as they could.[2] The Church mobilized itself fully for victory, and also for the cause of safeguarding the moral purity of young soldiers: two million pamphlets from the Army Chaplain, warning of the dangers of lust, were distributed among the troops.[3] The cause of the British Empire was directly identified with the cause of God. The Bishop of London, Arthur Winnington-Ingram, announced 'this is an Holy War. We are on the side of Christianity against anti-Christ';[4] while the

---

[1] Alan Wilkinson, *The Church of England and the First World War* (London: SCM, 1996), 5.

[2] Ilana R. Bet-El, *Conscripts: Forgotten Men of the Great War* (Stroud: The History Press, 2009), 76.

[3] Wilkinson, *Church of England and First World War*, 125.

[4] Will Ellsworth-Jones, *We Will Not Fight...: The Untold Story of World War One's Conscientious Objectors* (London, Aurum Press 2008), 43.

chaplain for the House of Commons wrote: 'to kill Germans is a divine service in the fullest acceptance of the word'.[5]

The use of hymns was an integral part of this mobilization. During the conflict, 40 million religious books and pamphlets were provided to troops. A typical example was a booklet containing Saint John's Gospel along with the words of six of the most popular traditional hymns[6]:

- Rock of Ages
- Sun of My Soul, Thou Saviour Dear
- Oh God Our Help in Ages Past
- Abide with Me[7]
- Onward, Christian Soldiers
- Eternal Father, Strong to Save[8]

Hymns have certain characteristics in common with the popular songs of the time we have been studying. They are sung in large groups, themes are often melodramatic in nature, and they must be set to fairly simple melodies in order to allow people to learn them very quickly (before the generalization of radio and gramophone, audiences would often be singing songs they had never heard before). Nevertheless, there are obvious differences: hymns are never comic or racy, do not concentrate on realistic detail of everyday life, and contain far more classical poetic imagery than do popular songs. Lastly, popular hymns remain so for decades or even centuries, which was rarely the case of popular commercialized songs.

One of the major historians of the Church of England during the Great War, Alan Wilkinson, tells us that almost all soldiers knew by heart a dozen or so hymns they had learned as a child and which held then particular emotional and nostalgic power.[9] Wilkinson suggests that 'The Church's teaching had come over [to soldiers] as externalized dogma: only hymns lasted and gave delight'.[10] It is therefore not surprising to find hymn-singing was an important part of the work of the 4,000 Army chaplains. For example, the evangelical meetings during the 'National Mission' of 1916, everywhere on the Western Front, were always preceded by half an hour of singing.[11] The clergy, according to Wilkinson, had

---

[5]   Ibid., 42.

[6]   Wilkinson, *Church of England and First World War*, 153.

[7]   It can be heard online at http://songsandhymns.org/hymns/detail/abide-with-me-fast-falls-the-eventide (accessed 1 July, 2014).

[8]   Online at http://songsandhymns.org/hymns/detail/eternal-father-strong-to-save (accessed 1 July, 2014).

[9]   Wilkinson, *Church of England and First World War*, 156.

[10]   Ibid., p. 162.

[11]   Bishop L. Gwynne, *Religion and Morale: the Story of the National Mission on the Western Front* (London: Society for Promoting Christian Knowledge, 1917), 19.

nevertheless to be attentive, since soldiers were 'easily sickened by too many martial hymns, and especially when they were urged to sing them by clergy who did not fight themselves'.[12]

In Britain, new collections of hymns were published. The first months of the war saw the appearance of *Twenty Hymns for National Use in Time of War from Old and New Sources*[13]. The contents page lists eight themes:

- the justice of the cause;
- the moral and spiritual equipment
- confession of personal and national sin
- prayer for divine and heavenly aid
- the endurance of those on active service,
- the natural instinct to review the course of past life in presence of death;
- the need of patience in time of adversity;
- the expression of grief, and then again the duty of refraining from it[14]

These were considered by the editors 'to cover the ground of the psychology of war from the Christian point of view'.[15] This book and others dig into the Church's stock of traditional hymns for ones pertaining to war, of which there were many. 'Onward Christian Soldiers' is of course one of the most famous:

> Onward, Christian soldiers, marching as to war,
> With the cross of Jesus going on before.
> Christ, the royal Master, leads against the foe;
> Forward into battle see his banners go!
>
> At the sign of triumph Satan's host doth flee;
> On then, Christian soldiers, on to victory!
> Hell's foundations quiver at the shout of praise;
> Brothers, lift your voices, loud your anthems raise.[16]

Draper's collection also includes compositions such as the following, seemingly written specially for the world war:

> Never at any time
> Hath baser wrong been done

---

[12] Wilkinson, *Church of England and First World War*, 156.

[13] William H. Draper and Edward C. Bairstow, *Twenty Hymns for National Use in Time of War from Old and New Sources* (London: Stainer & Bell, 1914).

[14] Ibid., 6.

[15] Ibid, preface.

[16] A recent version of this hymn can be heard online at http://songsandhymns.org/hymns/detail/onward-christian-soldiers (accessed 1 July, 2014).

Beneath god's blessed sun
Than this you see
Gird on your sword, nor let it rest
Smite where you find the weak oprest
And set him free!

Never at any time
O, England was revealed
A juster cause to shield
With all thy might
The Lord is with thee, fear thou not
And he against thy foe's dark plot
Defends the right

Or on a similar tone, this song written during the American Civil War:

God of all nations, sovereign Lord
In thy dread name we draw the sword
We lift the flag of freedom high
That fills with light our stormy sky

From treason's rent from murder's stain
Guard thou its folds till peace shall reign
Till fort and field till shore and sea
Join our loud anthem, praise to thee

Naturally the appeal to the 'God of all nations' should not mask the conviction that God had taken sides in this particular war.

A new hymn book was published to accompany the National Mission, a major evangelizing campaign organized by the Church of England in collaboration with the military hierarchy in 1916.[17] It included pieces like the following, from the 1860s:

Thy kingdom come, O God
Thy rule, O Christ begin
Break with thine iron rod
The tyrannies of sin!

'The tyrannies of sin' were naturally understood, in 1916, to be those of the Kaiser and his allies, but hymns generally remained at this level of abstraction. Another popular hymn from the National Mission songbook was:

---

[17]   *The National Mission Hymn Book* (London: Society for Promoting Christian Knowledge, 1916).

Stand up stand up for Jesus
Ye soldiers of the cross
Lift high his royal banner
It must not suffer loss
From victory unto victory
His army shall he lead
Till every foe is vanquished and
Christ is Lord indeed.

If most hymns come from collections approved by the hierarchy of one of the major churches, there were also some compositions put forward by other enthusiasts of the new holy war. A Salvation Army newspaper published in 1917 this more warlike hymn, written some decades earlier:

Jesus give thy bloodwashed army
Universal liberty
Keep us fighting, waiting calmly
For a worldwide jubilee
Hallelujah
We shall have the victory!

Thou hast bound brave hearts together
Clothed us with the spirit's might
Made us warriors forever
Sent us in the field to fight
In the army
We will serve thee day and night

Neath thy sceptre foes are bending
And thy name makes devils fly
Christless kingdoms thou art rending
And thy blood doth sin destroy
For thy glory
We will fight until we die![18]

And in the local Catholic journal from the town of Burnley, we find the following, which does not assert the justice of the imperial cause, but just demands the intercession of the mother of Christ.

Our Lady of the trenches
Oh how sad is the refrain

---

[18] *Social Gazette - Official Organ of the Salvation Army's Social Operations*, 17 February, 1917.

Our Lady of the trenches
It is born from hearts of pain
Midst the booming of the cannon
And the bullet's warning hiss
Our Lady of the trenches
Is there fitter name than this?[19]

Other uses for hymns

If hymns were generally used to improve morale among civilians and soldiers, for soldiers, the hymns they knew served at least two other purposes. Firstly, since some were part of a common international culture, they could help to communicate with enemy soldiers. Accounts of the 1914 Christmas truces in many places across the Western Front often indicate that hymn-singing began the truce or was part of it. Such songs as 'Silent night'/ 'Stille Nacht', 'O Tannenbaum'/ 'O Christmas Tree' or 'O Come Alle Ye Faithful'/ 'Herbei, o ihr Gläubigen' could be enjoyed and sung in unison, a symbol of a fragile community spirit while the truce lasted. At Christmas 1915, also, joint carol-singing concerts were sometimes organized with German or Austrian soldiers.[20]

Secondly, the solemnity of hymns lent itself particularly to the production of parody songs by sardonic 'other ranks', well-known for irreverent and black humour. Wilkinson points out that:

> To sing bawdy verses to hymn tunes was an example of that sceptical wartime humour which enabled men to cope, because by mocking the whole hierarchy of God, politicians, the Church, military authorities, and the romantic picture of soldiers as heroic knights, they were all cut down to size.[21]

So the well-known soldiers' song 'When this Bloody War is Over':

> When this bloody war is over
> No more soldiering for me!
> When I get my civvy clothes on
> Oh how happy I will be!

was sung to the melody of 'What a Friend We Have in Jesus', of which the original words were:

---

[19]   *Burnley Catholic Herald*, 10 February, 1917.
[20]   Malcolm Brown and Shirley Seaton, *Christmas Truce* (London: Pan Books, 2001), 49, 201.
[21]   Wilkinson, *Church of England and First World War*, 158.

What a friend we have in Jesus,
all our sins and griefs to bear!
What a privilege to carry
everything to God in prayer!

This may be seen as particularly ironic since one of the first advantages of civilian life mentioned in the song was 'no more church parade on Sundays'! Similarly, the words of 'Onward Christian soldiers', a rousing cry inviting to valorous battle, contrast sharply with the bitter anti-militarist lyrics soldiers put to the hymn tune:

Forward Joe Soap's army, marching without fear,
With our old commander, safely in the rear.
He boasts and skites from morn till night,
And thinks he's very brave,
But the men who really did the job
Are dead and in their grave.

A number of accounts indicate that the (compulsory) Sunday church parade was an opportunity to sing their own words to the hymns. This insubordination in the face of obligatory piety was difficult for officers to prevent, seeing that a religious ceremony is generally an unsuitable atmosphere for a disciplinary crackdown. So soldiers were free to carry on replacing words like

Our God, our help in ages past,
Our hope for years to come,
Our shelter from the stormy blast,
And our eternal home.

with

John Wesley had a little dog
It was so very thin
He took it to the Gates of Hell
And threw the bastard in![22]

In conclusion, then, hymns were an important element helping emotional survival and military morale during the war years, even if their influence cannot be separated out. It was not only a matter of encouraging the rank and file troops. Senior officers also appreciated the support of church ceremonies, as did civilians

---

[22]   Richard Holmes, *Tommy: The British Soldier on the Western Front* (London: Harper Perennial, 2005), 508.

of all classes, but particularly of elite groups.[23] Hymns, however, remained wedded to the general treatment of emotional and spiritual adversity. They did not change through the war in parallel with development in popular attitudes, as music-hall songs did. The content was linked to the position of religious hierarchies as part of the establishment. So we see that the warlike content in hymns was as much present in the 1916 *National Mission Hymn Book* as in the publications of 1914, whereas music hall had moved away from war enthusiasm by this date.

Folk songs

Let us move on to another non-commercial genre, the folk song. These songs, generally from a centuries-old rural tradition, had little influence among the working class at the beginning of the twentieth century, even if a few well-known traditional songs might be sung on the music-hall stage or in choral societies. The traditional repertoire of folk songs and folk dances attracted, however, significant interest among sections of the intelligentsia. Schools, compulsory for all children after 1870, began to teach folk song in the hope of contributing to a feeling of national pride. A number of organizations, of which the best-known were the Folk Song Society, founded in 1898, and the English Folk Dance Society, founded by Cecil Sharp in 1911, worked hard at transcribing folk songs and dances in rural villages, and tried to popularize them in the towns by means of lecture tours. Such lectures, in which choirs would illustrate the explanations of the expert speaker, continued throughout the war years.

In the early years of his work promoting folk song, Sharp had managed to involve a few high-profile composers such as Elgar, Dvorak and Greig. It was Sharp's views that became dominant in the English Folk Dance Society, despite differences with other, now-forgotten collectors such as Lucy Broadwood and Frank Kidson.[24] Sharp considered urban culture to be 'nothing but common rowdyism and sordid vulgarity. Folksong was contrasted to the got up glitter, sham and vulgarity of music hall. It was idealised as unsophisticated, primitive, genuine – simple beauty and common emotion.'[25] In Sharp's view, folk music belonged to 'a great tradition that stretches back into the mists of the past in one long, unbroken chain, of which the last link is now, alas, being forged.'[26] He was

---

[23]   Gavin Roynon (Ed.), *Home Fires Burning: The Great War Diaries of Georgina Lee* (Stroud: Sutton, 2006), 154.

[24]   John Francmanis, 'National Music to National Redeemer: The Consolidation of a "Folk-Song" Construct in Edwardian England', *Popular Music* 21:1 (2002), 7.

[25]   S. A. Sczelkun, *The Conspiracy of Good Taste: William Morris, Cecil Sharp, Clough Williams-Ellis and the Repression of Working Class Culture in the Twentieth Century* (London, Working Press, 1993), 46.

[26]   Quoted in John R. Gold and George Revill, 'Gathering the Voices of the People? Cecil Sharp, Cultural Hybridity, and the Folk Music of Appalachia', *Geojournal* 65 (2006), 59.

very much influenced by the ideas of the great folk song collector, Francis James Child (1825–1896), who had hypothesized that true folk songs came a different society in the distant past: 'a condition in which the people are not divided by political organization and book culture into markedly distinct classes, in which consequently there is such community of ideas and feelings that the whole people form an individual'.[27]

The movement to promote folk music felt that rediscovering traditional musical forms would help to clean away the artifices of modern life. It also aimed at reinforcing national identity at a time when art music was dominated by German and Italian composers (Brahms was reputed to have dismissed England as 'a country without music'). In 1910, *The Times* published a long defence of folk song:

> the folk-song is both old and new. It comes to us from long-forgotten times, and in that sense it belongs to the past, but it has been constantly remodelled by the minds of generation after generation, passing from father to son by oral tradition, never stereotyped by the stiffening process of print, but always in a state of flux, adapting itself to the needs of each successive generation.

It continued with specific recommendations:

> The folk-song may be introduced into a music-hall programme in many ways. Our popular singers, who are probably finding that the stock humour of the mother-in-law and the stock pathos of the starving child are wearing a little thin, might well turn to the folk-song for pretty tunes and humour, romance and vigour in the words.[28]

Later the same year *The Times* suggested again that, rather than denounce music hall, folk enthusiasts would do better to produce folk song and dance turns on the music-hall stage.[29]

In the early part of the war, Cecil Sharp continued his lecture tours in Britain. In Burnley, in October 1914, he was guest speaker at the Mechanics' Institute.[30] But he was soon convinced that the war was going to eradicate the last traces of 'authentic' popular music in Britain, and he decided to travel to Canada in 1915, and again in 1916. In the villages of the Appalachian Mountains, he was convinced, there could be found the genuine traditional English folk music, which had survived unsullied by urban industrial life. One of his assistants, Maud Karpeles, commented:

---

[27]   Quoted in David Harker, *Fakesong: The Manufacture of British 'Folksong', 1700 to the Present Day* (Milton Keynes: Open University Press, 1985), 109.

[28]   *The Times*, 15 January 1910.

[29]   *The Times*, 15 October 1910.

[30]   *Burnley Gazette*, 3 October 1914.

there was not, as in England, the tiresome business of having first to listen to popular music hall or drawing-room songs of 50 years ago, before extracting the genuine traditional music ... the whole time we were in the mountains, we never heard a poor tune.[31]

Far from the ordinary lives of the population of Britain, torn apart by the war, Sharp had found his 'true' English people. In 1917, he published the first volume of *English Folk Songs from the Southern Appalachians*, unnoticed by the masses of British people.[32] It had been an illusion to think that the urban masses could be 'converted' to folk music, persuaded to leave behind the sardonic and earthy music-hall comic songs and embrace songs about passing seasons, harvests and village fairs. And the folk songs could not be adapted month by month to fit the mood of an audience whose lives were being constantly revolutionized. For all its faults, music hall could reflect the upheavals of the war years where folk could not.

Soldiers' songs

The remainder of this chapter will be concerned with a genre of song which gives a particularly sharp insight into life in the war years – the British soldiers' song. It is not entirely a new genre – soldiers' songs existed at least as far back as the eighteenth century – but the genre was particularly prolific during the First World War. The long months of immobility, and a mass army raised on collective singing in music-hall, church and school, produced a rich repertoire. The analysis of the genre poses important questions and has become, as we shall see, somewhat polemical.

   This section is based on a corpus of 160 songs. After a short presentation of the soldiers who were singing them, favourite themes and dominant tone will be examined.

Who were the British soldiers?

The British army was recruited in towns and mostly among manual workers. The urban population became the majority in Britain as early as the 1850s; unlike the French peasant army, the British was made up of urban wage-earners. The soldiers can be divided into three groups. First, there were the professional soldiers who had enlisted before 1914; often from poor families, they had joined an army which had little prestige, which had fought in Africa against the Zulus (in 1879) and against the Boers (in 1880 and again in 1899–1902). At the outbreak of war,

---

[31]   Gold and Revill, 'Gathering the Voices of the People?', 61.

[32]   Olive Campbell and Cecil Sharp, *English Folk Songs from the Southern Appalachians* (London: G. P. Putnam's Sons, 1917).

there were, including non-combatant units, 710,000 of these professionals (half of whom were stationed in the different colonies), and 80,000 left for France in the first week of the war.

Secondly, there were the 2,467,000 volunteers who responded to the biggest propaganda campaign in the history of Britain. Their reasons for joining were diverse. Some ached to escape from poverty or boredom, many felt that Germany would be beaten in very few months, and the chance for travel and manly adventure would quickly evaporate. Others acted under the pressure of family or fiancée, or saw a chance for a little prestige in a life which was sorely lacking in this commodity. The majority believed that the cause of the British Empire was that of justice and freedom. 'There were a myriad reasons for enlisting. Everyone had their own.'[33]

In theory, these volunteers had to be at least 18 years old, and 19 before they could go to fight abroad. Many were in fact only 16, or less, but managed to sign up, assisted by a bureaucracy willing to turn a blind eye, and sometimes by recruiting sergeants and doctors paid per recruit signed.[34] Not everyone was shocked by their young age: soldiers only 14 years old were praised in the pages of the *Daily Mail,* which printed interviews with their proud parents.[35] On the first day of the battle of Loos, two of the British soldiers killed were only 15 years old, and 86 were 17 years old or younger. During the four and a half years of the conflict, 28,000 British dead and 70,000 wounded were under 18.[36]

The number of men volunteering varied with the news of the development of the war. In the two months of August and September 1914, 700,000 volunteered. After the huge death toll of the Battle of the Marne, and the realization that the war was likely to last for years, numbers fell. October and November together brought 300,000 volunteers. From then on recruitment stabilized around 120,000 men a month until the end of 1915, with the exception of a brief rise after air bombardments by Germany of British coastal towns.

Thirdly, and this is often forgotten, there were the conscripts who were to make up the majority of British combatants in the war. From January 1916 on, 2 504,000 men were obliged by law to join up. The work of Ilana Bet-El, which studies conscripts in great detail, serves to remind us that the official heroic narrative of enthusiastic volunteering moving onward to inevitable victory hides the history of those who were forced to fight. Moreover, most memoirs and collections of letters published have been by volunteers, and this has also served to reduce the space for conscripts in the national memory.

---

[33] Richard Van Emden amd Steve Humphries, *All Quiet on the Home Front: An Oral History of Life in Britain during the First World War* (London: Headline Books, 2003), 12.

[34] Bet-El, *Conscripts,* 34.

[35] Richard Van Emden, *Boy Soldiers of the Great War* (London: Headline Books, 2005), 131.

[36] Ibid., 157.

Reflecting soldiers' experience

The misery and danger of trench life, the irrationality and injustice of the treatment of lower ranks, and the attitudes and behaviour of superior officers are among the most common themes in soldier songs. To understand the songs, we must first look at the experience of the soldiers concerning these subjects.

Hundreds of books, diaries, interviews and collections of letters have attempted to communicate what the soldiers went through. The publishing success of such books is impressive and seems permanent, and our image of life in the trenches remains one of the most emblematic pictures of twentieth-century history . If these books are so successful, it may be because we remain fascinated by these men who could live through such trauma and remain for the most part sane. Many soldiers have related that, once they returned home, they hid their experience from everyone including their immediate family. Men often felt it was their masculine duty to hide the truth from wives and mothers. The refrain of one of the soldiers' songs says in so many words: 'They'll never believe us'. Many kept silent: one of the four soldiers present at a commemoration in 2004 reported that he had never spoken of his war experience before.[37]

Other sources underline the inexpressible nature of the trauma. In 1917, when signs of discontent were showing in the navy, a group of sailors was asked to spend a week in the trenches so as to be able to later give talks, each on their own ship, concerning the situation at the front. Before leaving, they asked to be allowed to write down what they had seen and have it signed by a senior officer; without such a document, they felt, their comrades might not believe what they had to say.[38]

Expressing the inexpressible being one of the functions of poetry, it has often been the poet that we have asked to put into words the trench experience. Wilfred Owen wrote in a poem that has since become a classic:

> What passing-bells for these who die as cattle?
> Only the monstrous anger of the guns.
> Only the stuttering rifles' rapid rattle
> Can patter out their hasty orisons.
> No mockeries now for them; no prayers nor bells;
> Nor any voice of mourning save the choirs, –
> The shrill, demented choirs of wailing shells;
> And bugles calling for them from sad shires.[39]

---

[37] Ibid., 308.

[38] E. W. Hermon and Anne Nason, *For Love and Courage: Letters Home from the Western Front 1914-1917* (London: Preface, 2009).

[39] Wilfred Owen, *The Poems of Wilfred Owen* (Ware: Wordsworth Editions, 1994), 56.

Faced with this terrifying vision, Owen asks in another of his well-known pieces whether this war does not invalidate the whole of humanity's history and evolution:

Was it for this the clay grew tall?
– O what made fatuous sunbeams toil
To break earth's sleep at all?[40]

Mud and blood

Soldiers' narratives are full of profoundly shocking anecdotes. Some speak of a dead body built into the walls of a trench; one arm protruded out of the wall, which soldiers used to shake in macabre humour when passing by. Others tell of the use of enemy bodies to reinforce earthworks.[41] Still others relate having had parts of their friends' bodies and brains falls on them, a few moments after the conversation they were having with these friends when a shell hit, or listening all night long to the cries of dozens of dying men in no-man's-land. The soldiers' stories explore a mountain of distress and terror: officers threatening soldiers with revolvers if they refused to attack, men executed *pour encourager les autres*, others drowned in mud at Passchendaele.

A date often cited is 1 July 1916, the great attack on the Somme where in one morning 20,000 British soldiers are killed and twice as many wounded. During the whole of the war, 800,000 will die and 1.6 million will be wounded. But since the telling of a single episode can sometimes portray better than statistics, let us hear what Lynch recounts he saw in France in 1916:

Just outside the wood, we came to a well-constructed trench. In it there's a British soldier to every yard, killed on the parapet in trying to hop off. Twenty yards in front, a row of dead British soldiers in perfect line as if on parade, NCOs in position, and a half-dozen paces ahead, their platoon officer, a rusty revolver in one outstretched hand, his whistle still clasped in the other, mowed down by machine guns … we see two men, a Fritz and a Tommy, dead within a yard of each other; the Fritz has a British bayonet through his throat whilst the Tommy lies doubled over a Fritz bayonet whose point protrudes from his back.[42]

Death in battle was far from the only danger. Hunger, cold, mud, insects and rats, all contributed to the misery of much daily life. Many soldiers reported never eating to satiety; food parcels sent by parents or spouses, for those who could get them, often constituted a vital supplement.

---

[40]   Ibid., 90.
[41]   E. P. F. Lynch, *Somme Mud* (London: Bantam, 2008), 115.
[42]   Ibid., 89.

Live and let live

The lives of the soldiers cannot be reduced to such traumatic experiences; equally important, and reflected in the content of soldiers' songs, is 'ordinary' life for the troops when there was no battle in perspective – a fair part of the time, and no doubt the time when singing was more common. Historians have examined this 'ordinary time' in the trenches, and have discovered a vast, informal system of 'live and let live', a series of practices which were well known in anecdotes but ever overshadowed by the more dramatic narratives of battle and strategy.

The soldiers found ways to refuse the war that was dominating their lives. The most extreme example, now well known, was the Christmas truces of December 1914, when thousands of British and enemy soldiers met in no-man's-land to talk, play, eat and smoke together – to the horror of their superior officers. A few dozen individual initiatives, mostly from the German side, led to a truce which held over two-thirds of the British front.[43] But during the rest of the war too, soldiers on all sides organized themselves to make the war a little easier to bear, and to avoid fighting when it was possible to do so. On a 'quiet' section of the front, a battalion of a thousand men might see 'only' three deaths a month, whereas an 'active' front might see seventy.[44] It was often an implicit agreement between enemies which determined whether a sector was 'quiet' or 'active'.

Daily truces at mealtimes, and the ritualization of bombing, are two examples of this 'live and let live' system. Enemies agreed to bomb each day, at a fixed hour, a particular part of the trench. In this way, soldiers could show visiting 'brass hats' that offensive action was being taken, but casualties were kept to a minimum, since each side's troops were forewarned about the time and place of shelling. Another instance: night patrols who came across enemy patrols in no-man's-land tended each to avoid them rather than engage them in fighting, despite orders to be offensive. Groups of soldiers imposed, moreover, their own bottom-up discipline. When a soldier was excessively combative and thus put his comrades at risk of being hit by reprisals, he was quickly brought to heel. During the whole of the war, superior officers battled against this tendency of the 'lower ranks' not to fight when not directly ordered to do so immediately. Night raids by small groups of soldiers, for example, which had been left to local initiative in 1914 and 1915, were carefully controlled from above through bureaucratic accounting from 1916 on. Officers who were 'insufficiently offensive' were replaced by new ones, and each battalion had to send back to Headquarters samples of German barbed wire to prove that the announced raids had actually happened.

Similarly, Headquarters gradually realized that tunnelling in order to place explosives under enemy lines had become a little-used tactic, since it was incompatible with an implicit agreement between adversaries to 'live and let

---

[43]   Brown and Seaton, *Christmas Truce*, 82, 103.
[44]   Tony Ashworth, *Trench Warfare 1914–1918: The Live and Let Live System* (London: Pan, 1980), 16.

live'. Mining, then, was organized centrally from the end of 1915, whereas it had previously resulted from local decisions.[45]

Such practices, which underlined the divergent priorities of army leadership and ordinary soldiers, help to explain the dissenting character of a good number of popular soldiers' songs. The British army, unlike the French, saw few mutinies during the war years. A small number of local mutinies were organized, and the end of the conflict led to much bigger ones in 1919,[46] but in the main, military discipline was maintained. This should not blind us to the deep bitterness often present among those faced with an interminable war and an inhuman military machine.

Hierarchy and the army

For twenty-first-century readers, it can be difficult to conceive how deeply inegalitarian the British army was a century ago. Armies are never noted for the respect accorded to the interests and opinions of 'lower ranks', but in 1914–18, the army was the emanation of a society infinitely crueller and less democratic in spirit than it is today. It was not just the fact that only a minority of the population could vote (all women and a third of men could not), but that the whole set of egalitarian ideas which have slowly emerged in the twentieth century, along with the welfare state, progressive income tax and relative social mobility, is simply absent. They said of Kitchener that he had never spoken to an ordinary soldier.[47]

The welfare of the soldier was far from being a priority. The soldier who wanted good boots, gloves or socks asked his family to send them, if they could. Bulletproof jackets were not provided, but were only available for private purchase by families.[48] The newly invented parachute was banned in aircraft, since superior officers felt it might encourage airmen not to fight as vigorously.[49]

In 1914, officers were recruited mainly on social criteria, among those who felt they were 'born to rule'; the young man straight out of Eton or Harrow was automatically made an officer if he so wished.[50] Although front-line officers died at least as often as ordinary soldiers, their life was very different. They were transported in passenger coaches rather than cattle wagons, their food was far

---

[45]   Ashworth, *Trench Warfare*, 200.

[46]   See Chanie Rosenberg, *1919: Britain on the Brink of Revolution* (London, Bookmarks, 1995).

[47]   Ronald Pearsall, *Edwardian Life and Leisure* (Melbourne: Wren, 1973), 201.

[48]   An advert in the *Burnley Express* of 27 January 1917 proposes 'a shield worn like a bullet-proof jacket' which 'deflects revolver bullets and shrapnel. We pack and post to any front. Single, 35 shillings, double 70 shillings. Recommended by a Major General.'

[49]   Arthur Gould Lee, *No Parachute: A Fighter Pilot in World War I* (London: Jarrolds, 1968), 219–225.

[50]   Holmes, *Tommy*, 144.

better, their hospital wards, if wounded, quite separate and superior, they could march without the 100 lb pack of the soldier – enormous inequality marked every hour of life in the army.

Senior officers left for war with a servant or two,[51] and could benefit from far more periods of leave than their men. Their memoirs contain many references to continuing the ordinary habits of the Edwardian gentleman: dressing for dinner, playing polo,[52] or receiving daily parcels of luxury food from Harrods or from Fortnum and Mason's.[53] If they were captured by the enemy, their experience in no way resembled that of the 'other ranks'.

Officer cruelty was not rare and is well documented. The tremendous harshness of the Edwardian workhouse, prison or lunatic asylum was reproduced in the army at a time when even at civilian work, as one historian points out, the foreman might commonly impose discipline with his fists.[54] A soldier who had broken discipline might have to suffer 'field punishment number one'. Kept on a diet of bread and water, he would then be tied to a gun carriage, in a crucified position, for an hour every morning and evening. This punishment was hated by British soldiers, and there are even recorded cases where horrified Australian or Canadian soldiers intervened to free the crucified soldier.[55] As for disciplinary executions, the detailed study carried out by Cathryn Corns and John Hughes-Wilson underlines that the main criterion for deciding whether to carry out a death sentence imposed for 'cowardice' or desertion was the perceived need by senior officers to intimidate the rest of the division at that particular moment or not.[56]

This overview of the life of a soldier is all there is space for in this book. Much more has been published on the subject, the most complete volumes being *Tommy* (2005) by the late Richard Holmes[57] and *The Soldier's War* (2008) by Richard Van Emden.[58] A century after the war, three or four new books are appearing every month on aspects of soldiers' lives in the Great War. The last few pages have given a brief summary of basic facts without which the contents of the soldiers' songs cannot be appreciated.

The songs invented by rank-and-file soldiers reflected all the experiences described above. They contain an indirect reflection of life at the front, filtered through a sarcastic humour, forged to help men survive and not to explain to future

---

[51]   Hermon and Nason, *For Love and Courage*, 3.

[52]   Ibid., 84.

[53]   Ibid., 187.

[54]   Cathryn Corns and John Hughes-Wilson, *Blindfold and Alone: British Military Executions in the Great War* (London: Cassell, 2005), 85.

[55]   Bet-El, *Conscripts*, 156–157.

[56]   Corns and Wilson, *Blindfold and Alone*, 97.

[57]   Richard Holmes, *Tommy: The British Soldier on the Western Front* (London: Harper Perennial, 2005).

[58]   Richard Van Emden. *The Soldier's War* (London: Bloomsbury, 2008).

generations their experience. Intended for singing along to, their content had to be not individual, but consensual with respect to the group of 'lower ranks' present.

'I want to go home'[59]

As has been pointed out, a long and often immobile mass war gave more chance for soldiers' songs to be produced and to spread. The singing of these songs was part of a front-line culture which included sport, memento-hunting, the use of a particular slang, and the entertainments which were described in Chapter 2. There was also an impressive production of front-line amateur newspapers. J. G. Fuller has studied a hundred or so titles by British and Empire soldiers.[60]

What are the specific characteristics of soldiers' songs? If they were no doubt generally written by individuals, they are practically all anonymous. They will mostly be put to existing well-known tunes, they tend to be short, and often exist in several slightly different versions, due to the fact that they are spread by oral, sometimes approximate, means. Soldier songs do not represent the total repertoire of sing-along activity in the army; they constitute an additional repertoire, to add to the music-hall songs and hymns soldiers might sing. They might then be expected to deal particularly with important subjects the other repertoires do not cover. The soldiers do not invent love songs, for example, because the songs they know from the music hall cover that theme thoroughly.

Soldier songs have attracted in many ways more attention than have the music-hall songs. During the war years already, some of these songs were collected and published,[61] while other songbooks were produced of songs which their authors thought the soldiers *ought* to be singing. Some soldier songs made it to the music-hall stage: in 1916, singing star Hetty King toured with a turn entitled 'Songs the Soldiers Sing'. The following year an act called 'Songs in the Trenches in Seven Tableaux' was a hit in the halls,[62] and in 1918, famed tenor John Coates recorded a selection of soldiers' songs.[63]

During the 1930s, two ex-soldiers, Eric Partridge and John Brophy, published a collection of soldier songs after enquiring around ex-soldiers for memories of

---

[59] The lyrics of a series of these songs are online at http://www.oucs.ox.ac.uk/ww1lit/education/tutorials/intro/trench/songs.html (accessed 2 July 2014).

[60] See, for example, J. G. Fuller, *Troop Morale and Popular Culture in British and Dominion Armies 1914–1918* (Oxford: Clarendon, 1990); Malcolm Brown (Ed.), *Suffering from Cheerfulness – the Best Bits from The Wipers Times* (London: Little Books, 2007).

[61] F. T. Nettleingham, *Tommy's Tunes* (London: Erskine Macdonald, 1917); *More Tommy's Tunes* (London: Erskine Macdonald, 1918).

[62] *The Encore*, 27 September 1917.

[63] *Phono Record*, November 1918.

the songs. This collection was again published in the 1960s and in 2008.[64] In 1963, the influential anti-militarist musical comedy *Oh What a Lovely War* included a number of soldiers' songs,[65] while in 2001, Max Arthur published a new collection.[66]

An initial repertoire proposed by the elite but rejected by the ranks

The history of songs sung by soldiers in the First World War does not begin with the amateur repertoire which will later become well known, 'the songs of an itinerant community, continually altering within itself under the incidence of death and mutilation'.[67] It begins with the proposals, made from the very beginning of the war, by members of the elite, concerning songs which they felt soldiers ought to be singing. In 1914, Arthur Campbell Ainger, a retired teacher from Eton, published, at the very low price of twopence a copy,[68] a collection of *Marching Songs for Soldiers, Adapted to Well- known Tunes*, and at the end of September it provoked a lively exchange of letters in the columns of *The Times*[69]

Ainger suggests firstly that the Kaiser should be roundly denounced in song:

> He tore the scrap of paper,
> The Belgian scrap of paper,
> He tore the scrap of paper,
> And bade the bullets fly.
> He shot the wives and children,
> The wives and little children,
> He shot the wives and children,
> And laughed to see them die.
>
> *Chorus*:   So now we're off to Berlin,
> To Berlin, to Berlin,
> So now we're off to Berlin,
> To ask the reason why.

---

[64]   John Brophy and Eric Partridge, *The Long Trail: What the British Soldier Sang and Said in the Great War of 1914–1918* (London: André Deutsch, 1965).

[65]   Joan Littlewood and Theatre Workshop, *Oh What a Lovely War* (London: Methuen Drama, 1967, Première Edition 1963); film version directed by Richard Attenborough in 1969.

[66]   Max Arthur, *When This Bloody War Is Over: Soldiers' Songs of the Firtst World War* (London: Piatkus, 2001).

[67]   John Brophy and Eric Partridge, *Dictionary of Tommies' Songs and Slang 1914–1918* (London: Frontline Books, 2008), 15.

[68]   The money raised was intended for the Belgian Relief Fund.

[69]   A. C. Ainger, *Marching Songs for Soldiers, Adapted to Well-known Tunes* (London, Jarrold & Sons, 1914).

He sacked the shrines of Louvain.
Of Senlis, Reims, and Louvain,
He sacked the shrines of Louvain,
They flamed against the sky.
He swore his heart was bleeding,
His tender heart was bleeding,
He swore his heart was bleeding,
And winked his wicked eye ...

Then he proposed that the soldiers support for their generals be expressed. Thus one of his songs aims at praising Sir John Denton Pinkstone French, the first commander of the British Expeditionary Force. The song is set to the tune of the traditional Scots ditty 'Do you Ken John Peel?'

D'ye ken John French, with his khaki suit,
His belt and his gaiters, and stout brown boot,
Along with his guns, and his horse, and his foot,
On the road to Berlin in the morning?

Chorus: Yes, we ken John French, and old Joffre too,
And all his men to the Tricolour true,
And Belgians and Russians, a jolly good few,
On the road to Berlin in the morning.

The Prussian Kaiser must be made to kneel,
The Prussian Eagle must be made to feel
The force of the bullet and the good cold steel,
On the road to Berlin in the morning!

As a final example, here is Ainger's suggestion in praise of diverse imperial symbols:

Here's to the health of the King and the Queen,
Ever at work for a living,
Morning and evening and all that's between
Cheering and helping and giving, –
Give them a shout,
Lengthen it out,
Tell friends and enemies what we're about!

Here's to Lord Kitchener, brown with the sun,
Sure to be keeping his promise,
Giving his orders, and getting them done,
All that he wants for his Tommies, –
Give him a shout ...

Ainger was not alone. *The New Army Songbook,* published in London in 1917, included a series of songs of similar tone.[70] Soldiers were enjoined to sing of their dreams of heroic martyrdom:

> Yes, let me like a soldier fall
> Upon some open plain
> This breast expanding for the ball
> To blot out every stain
> Brave manly hearts confer my doom
> That gentler ones may tell
> Howe'er forgot, unknown my tomb
> I like a soldier fell
> (*repeat last two lines*)
>
> I only ask of that proud race
> That ends its blaze in me
> To die the last and not disgrace
> Its ancient chivalry
> Tho o'er my clay no banner wave
> Nor trumpet requiem swell
> Enough they murmur
> O'er my grave:
> He like a soldier fell.[71]

And they were to sing of the joy of the military life:

> The smith to his anvil the child to his toy
> A rose for the maiden's adorning
> But there's nothing half so sweet to the soldier boy
> As the roll of the drums in the morning
> Then here's three cheers for the folks on the shore
> And a rose for my love's adorning
> And one cheer more for we're going off to war
> With the roll of the drums in the morning

As the reader may have guessed, these songs had no success at all among the troops. There does not appear to be a single recorded instance of them being sung. They stand mostly as a witness to the chasm between the conceptions of some sections of the elite, and those of ordinary soldiers.

The *New Army Songbook* does, however, include one ironic marching song, in which the soldier narrator explains that life in the army will be an absolute joy

---

[70]   Arthur Grenville (Ed.), *The New Army Songbook* (London: Joseph Williams, 1915).
[71]   This song was written in 1845 by William Vincent Wallace for his opera *Maritana.*

('No more I'll want for anything'). He will, moreover, have 'lots of time to find a girl'. In the chorus the narrator explains that he knows all this is true, 'because the sergeant told me so'.

These attempts to propose songs for soldiers were not the work of isolated or marginal people. On *The Times'* letters page at the beginning of 1915, one saw expressed the hope that the elite would be able to choose what was appropriate for soldiers to sing:

> Since, two months ago, we published a letter from Sir Charles Villiers Stanford urging the necessity of some form of military music to inspire the men of the new armies, on their route marches, the movement has gradually gathered strength and shape, and there is good hope of seeing practical steps taken in this direction very soon. The Lord Mayor has undertaken to convene a meeting at the Mansion house in support of the movement. and other influential people are taking part.
>
> A central committee has been formed, of which Sir. Douglas Sladen and Sir Charles Stanford are leading spirits, to promote the object in view. ... 'What we want to do,' said Sir Charles, 'is to get the soldiers to get to know the great old folk-songs, which were as popular in former days as 'Tipperary' is now. As, for example, 'Lillibullero', which was sung all through the Marlborough wars. There is the famous 'Song of Agincourt,' which dates from the time of Henry V, and the original manuscript of which is in the library of Trinity College Cambridge, and many others. If these songs were played by instrumental bands until the Tommies got them into their bones, they would pick them up more quickly than some of the modern music-hall ditties, and sing them with as much gusto ... if Mr. Rudyard Kipling could be induced to adapt suitable words, there would be no doubt about their popularity.[72]

In the pages of the *Musical Times*, the complaint was aired that the soldiers on the Western Front loved mostly to sing 'the most wretched of music hall songs', whereas first-class English composers such as Elgar and Bantock would be more suitable, in the author's view.[73] Another group, the defenders of folk music, added their twopence-worth, organizing musical evenings for troops in training camps, hoping to persuade them that folk song would be what they needed at the Front, and that they should abandon their support of the music-hall idiom. 'The art of a nation is the expression of its people. The people's songs are what the people enjoy,' insisted the lecturer on one of these occasions. His lecture was accompanied by the singing of traditional songs such as 'Lord Randall', a ballad in which a young man is poisoned by his fiancée.[74]

---

[72]   *The Times*, 13 January 1915.

[73]   Quoted in Glenn Watkins, *Proof Through the Night: Music and the Great War* (Berkeley: University of California Press, 2003), 34.

[74]   Francmanis, *National Music*, 21. An explanation and singing of the ballad can be heard on Youtube at https://www.youtube.com/watch?v=UCN4BQlXOR4 (accessed 27

All these attempts by sections of the elite to impose songs on the troops had little practical effect, and are mainly notable in that they represent a continuation of a powerful current of Victorian Britain, the giving of elite advice to ordinary people about the values and leisure that would be best for them. The Tommies, however, wanted music which they felt to be their own. This was partly music-hall, and partly their own newly invented songs to fit their new lives.

Favourite themes

Black humour and mocking the army were central aspects of soldier songs.[75] One should not, however, forget that the army was far from being homogeneous, as officer discourses about 'reliable' and 'weak' battalions clearly show. In some regiments, songs which were defeatist in tone could be widely sung, in others almost only silly and playful songs, and so on.[76]

The corpus this chapter is based on is made up of 168 soldier songs. Of these, 49 come from the two books which Nettleingham published in 1917 and 1918, 62 from the collection by Brophy and Partridge in the 1930s, and 59 from the collection edited in 2000 by Max Arthur. The others were found in soldiers' memoirs or autobiographies. Twenty-three of the songs appear in more than one collection.

The collections are not all of the same nature. Nettleingham's were published while the war was still going on, by an officer whose priority was encouraging the war drive. Brophy and Partridge collected songs some years after the war had been won, in the hope of preserving oral culture which they felt valuable. Max Arthur is a historian responding to the tremendous public demand, a century later, to have a close-up view of the lives and culture of ordinary soldiers. Thus, each collector has his selection criteria, but the general tone of the soldiers' songs does not change. There are however, two categories of song which are more common in the collections published during the war than those published much later. Firstly, there are the songs which depend very much on technical jargon (of the soldier or airman). These pieces were no doubt omitted in post-war collections because they were difficult for audiences to understand. Secondly, in the wartime collections, there are three or four (but only three or four) anti-German songs, whereas later collections contain none at all.

To analyse is to categorize, so the songs have been divided by main theme, even though a given song may deal with more than one theme. Here is the result:

July 2014).

[75]   The lyrics of a dozen or so songs can be found at: http://www.oucs.ox.ac.uk/ww1lit/education/tutorials/intro/trench/songs.html (accessed 3 July 2014).

[76]   Robert Graves, *Goodbye to All That* (Harmondsworth: Penguin, 2000), 125.

Category	No. of songs	Percentage of corpus (base 168 songs)	No. of songs appearing in more than one collection
Satire on war and on life as a soldier	56	33 %	6
Attacks on the military system	19	11.3 %	3
Nonsense songs and other playful songs	17	10 %	2
Bawdy songs	13	7.8 %	2
Attacks on superior officers	11	6.5 %	4
Songs on the paradise which is civilian life	11	6.5 %	4
Songs of pride in the regiment	8	4.8 %	0
Patriotic songs	5	3 %	0
Recruitment songs	4	2.4 %	0
Anti-German songs	4	2.4 %	0
Drinking songs	4	2.4 %	1
Attacks on civilians	1	0.6 %	1

The absence of patriotic songs

All commentators seemed to agree that British soldiers did not sing patriotic songs. 'What is markedly missing in the genuine soldiers songs is "patriotism" in the sense it was understood and promoted at home,' Palmer explains.[77] On the contrary, 'soldiers especially appreciated the deflation of home front propaganda'.[78] A music-hall star who organized show tours for troops stationed in France is of a similar opinion: 'nothing bores the British soldier so much as high flown martial sentiments, references to his own nobility and so on'.[79] A number of British observers expressed surprise at hearing French soldiers singing the Marseillaise whereas the British Tommies were singing 'We want to go home'. 'We had not got the thing right it seemed; we had no word about the Patrie or Glory or the Fun of Dying for the War Office',[80] commented one wry soldier. These reflections are fully confirmed by the corpus. It should be noted, moreover, that the few patriotic songs which do occur are all in the Nettleingham collection; none are in those

---

[77] Roy Palmer, *What A Lovely War! British Soldiers' Songs from the Boer War to the Present Day* (London: Michael Joseph, 1990), 3.

[78] George Robb, *British Culture and the First World War* (New York: Palgrave, 2002), 182.

[79] George Graves, *Gaieties and Gravities – The Autobiography of a Comedian* (London: Hutchinson, 1931), 66.

[80] Quoted by Fuller, *Troop Morale*, 35.

collected after the war. It may be that Nettleingham, as an officer, felt the need to include a sprinkling of patriotism, or that the patriotic songs were less often used and therefore less present in later memories.

A number of pieces attack jingoism directly. The music-hall song 'We Don't Want to Lose You, But We Think You Ought to Go' was parodied as:

> We don't want your loving
> And we think you're awfully slow
> To see we don't want you
> So please won't you go
> We don't like your sing-songs
> And we hate your refrain
> So don't you dare sing it near us again.
> Now we don't want to hurry you
> But it's time you ought to go
> For your songs and your speeches
> They bore us so.
> Your coaxings and pettings
> Drive us insane
> Oh we hate you, and we'll boo you
> And hiss you
> If you sing it again.

Another piece which criticizes civilian jingoism and recruitment fever is a parody of the music-hall piece 'A Broken Doll':

> A lady came to me a year ago
> She said that she should very much like to know
> Why aren't you in khaki or navy blue?
> Why don't you serve your country as your country serves you?
>
> I looked at her quite startled and replied
> 'Don't think that I'm a shirker after all
> I think I've had my chance
> For my right arm's in France
> I'm one of England's broken dolls

While a music-hall song 'The Conscientious Objector's Lament', which had as its primary objective to mock British pacifist dissenters, was transformed into a humorous protest at the condition of soldiers: 'Send out my brother, my sister or my mother, but for Gawd's sake, don't send me!'[81]

---

[81]   Online at www.firstworldwar.com/audio/1915.htm (accessed 22 August 2014). A more complete account of the reception of this song can be found in John Mullen,

The expression of hatred for Germans does not exist in the corpus, and anti-German songs of any sort are very rare. There is, however, one song about the Kaiser in Nettleingham's collection:

> To the Kaiser: curse his sons!
> Curse Von Tirpitz and the Huns!
> Curse his blinkety blankety[82] guns!
> Curse him!
>
> May his blood be sucked by chats,
> Ticks and other vampires, bats
> And his earhole gnawed by rats!
> Curse him!
> Freeze his nose and give him piles!
> Stretch his lousy eyelids miles!
> Rasp his legs with rusty files!
> Curse him!

It is to be noted that the Kaiser and his family are the main target, not Germans in general, and also that the humorous hyperbole does not seem to transmit a true sentiment of hatred. This song is a sarcastic response to a poem by Ernst Lissauer, a hymn of hate against England, which was used during the war by German propagandists:

> Come, let us stand at the Judgment Place,
> An oath to swear to, face to face,
> An oath of bronze no wind can shake,
> An oath for our sons and their sons to take.
> Come, hear the word, repeat the word,
> Throughout the Fatherland make it heard.
> We will never forego our hate,
> We have all but a single hate,
> We love as one, we hate as one,
> We have one foe and one alone –
> – ENGLAND! – [83]

'"You can't help laughing, can you?"': Humour and Symbolic Empowerment in British Popular Song during the Great War', in *Humour, Entertainment and Popular Culture during World War One*, ed. K. A. Ritzenhoff and C. Tholas-Disset (Basingstoke, Palgrave Macmillan, 2014).

[82] One imagines that Nettleingham has suppressed here more colourful adjectives.

[83] Translation by Barbara Henderson, as it appeared in the *New York Times*, 15 October, 1914.

In the soldier-song repertoire one can even find pieces where sympathy with the enemy soldier is perceptible, such as this one:[84]

> Keep your head down Alleyman![85]
> Keep your head down Alleyman!
> Last night in the pale moon light
> We saw you – we saw you
> You were mending your broken wire
> When we opened rapid fire
> If you want to see your father in the fatherland
> Keep your head down Alleyman.

Another variant of this song gives 'when we almost opened fire' rather than 'When we opened rapid fire', a further indication of the 'live and let live' attitudes common in the front line. Yet another version speaks about 'the Alleyman' in the first verse, and of the British 'fusilier' in the second: the parallel positions of the two enemies in the song structure reflect the understanding of the common fate of German and British soldiers. Occasionally 'Fritzy Boy' was sung instead of 'Alleyman', both being humorous and almost affectionate nicknames.

If, as we have seen, soldiers had little desire to sing of the glory of fighting for their homeland, they were somewhat less reticent to sing the praises of their own regiment.[86] Almost 5 per cent of the corpus of soldier songs fit into this category; here is a piece from the 29th division:

> With a roll of drum, the division came
> Hotfoot to the battle's blast
> When the good red sign swings into the line
> Oh there they'll fight to the last!

Similarly, it was possible to sing the exploits of the troops, as long as King and Empire were not mentioned, and the tone was more down-to-earth working-class pride than national heroic poetry:

> We beat 'em on the Marne
> We beat 'em on the Aisne
> They gave us hell at Neuve Chapelle
> But here we are again

---

[84]   The melody is from the music-hall song 'Hold Your Hand Out, Naughty Boy': a version by Florrie Forde can be found at: https://www.youtube.com/watch?v=PtWC5L1sXt8 (accessed 3 July 2014).

[85]   'Alleyman' is soldier slang for 'German', from the French 'Allemand'.

[86]   Fuller, *Troop Morale*, 103.

Mocking the war

Songs of unpatriotic tone or antipatriotic tone are very striking, but make up only a small part of the corpus. One might imagine that such songs could cause an argument among soldiers, whereas the aim of sing-along is generally to bring people together. Let us now look at the larger categories of songs, which were more widespread because their subject matter and tone were more consensual.

Around a third of the songs fit into the category 'satire on war and on life as a soldier'. These are almost all comic songs which complain about the miseries of being a soldier without blaming anyone in particular. Complaints are made against the rain, the food, the bombs, or about death, but a tragic tone is never present. There was so much to hate about the life that it could be a relief to sing a complaint about a trivial difficulty, like the monotony of always receiving the same flavour of jam with the rations:

> Plum and Apple, Apple and Plum …
> The ASC[87] get strawberry jam
> And lashings of rum
> But we poor blokes, we only get
> Apple and Plum

More seriously, the desire was expressed to be allowed home:

> I don't want to be a soldier
> I don't want to go to war!
> I'd rather stay at home
> Around the streets to roam
> And live on the earnings of a lady typist[88]
> I don't want a bayonet up my arsehole
> I don't want my bollocks shot away!
> I'd rather stay in England
> In merry, merry England
> And fornicate my bleeding life away!

One of the songs in Nettleingham's collection is 'I'm Sick of This Blooming War!':

> 'Your king and country need you!
> Be a soldier little man!'
> I thought I'd like to swank a bit

---

[87] Army Service Corps, responsible for food preparation and distribution.
[88] The rhyme gives us to expect another profession.

So I joined and here I am!
What a mug I must have been!

Another piece lamented:

What did you join the army for?
Why did you join the army?
What did you join the army for?
You must have been bloody well barmy!

Or one might express envy at those who have been wounded and sent home, at the same time as laughing about the risk of death by shelling:

We're all waiting for a shell (Send us a whizzbang!)
We're all waiting for a shell (Send us a nine two!)[89]
We don't care whether it's round or square
Whether it bursts on the parapet or in the air!
We're all waiting for a shell (Send us a nine two!)
Please don't keep us waiting long
For we want to go to Blighty
Where the nurses change our nighties
When the right shell comes along!

And this song from the Shropshire Regiment went even further, and sang the praises of fleeing from the enemy.

At La Clytte, at La Clytte
Where the Westshires got well beat
And the bullets blew our buttons all away
And we ran, yes we ran, from that fucking Alleyman
And now we are happy all the day![90]

The songs which 'caught on' and were sung by regiment after regiment included these which expressed an overwhelmingly negative view of joining up and of life in the army. Because they were sung as a group, they reminded each soldier that they were not alone faced with the misery of wartime life. At the same time, the comic tone ensures that they are not too plaintive: expressing self-pity was generally not allowed by the rules of Edwardian masculinity.

---

[89] In slang, two common types of shell.
[90] Quoted by Palmer, *What A Lovely War!*, 16.

Singing about death

We saw in Chapter 5 that music-hall songs which deal with the war avoid singing about death in any way. This is much less the case for soldier songs; death is dealt with with devastating black humour. One example, often sung by soldiers leaving the front line to their replacements,[91] maintains:

> The Bells of Hell go ting-a-ling-a-ling
> For you but not for me:
> The little devils sing-a-ling-a-ling,
> For you but not for me.
> Oh! Death, where is thy sting-a-ling-a-ling?
> Oh! Grave, thy victory?
> The Bells of Hell go ting-a-ling-a-ling
> For you but not for me.

Another piece expresses mock reassurance. Based on the music hall with the rousing stoic chorus 'Never mind!', advice is given to remain calm faced with trivial or tragic wartime destinies:

> If the sergeant steals your rum, never mind
> And your face may lose its smile, never mind
> He's entitled to a tot but not the bleeding lot!
> If the sergeant drinks your rum, never mind!
>
> When old Jerry shells your trench, never mind
> And your face may lose its smile, never mind
> Though the sandbags bust and fly you have only once to die!
> If old Jerry shells the trench, never mind!
>
> If you get stuck on the wire, never mind
> And your face may lose its smile, never mind
> Though the light's as broad as day
> When you die, they stop your pay!
> So if you get stuck on the wire, never mind!

In the Air Force, the music-hall hit 'What Do You Want to Make Those Eyes at Me for, if They Don't Mean What They Say?' gave rise to the following parody, to the same romantic melody:

> What did you want to have a crash like that for?
> It's the sixth you've had today.

---

[91]   Arthur, *Bloody War*, 63.

It makes you sad, it makes me mad
It's lucky it was an Avro not a brand new Spad[92]
What did you want to have a crash like that for?
You'd better clear the wreckage away![93]

Attacks on the military system

The category 'attacks on the military system' is again dominated by caustic humour, but the songs can be more bitter:

My tunic is out at the elbows
My trousers are out at the knee
My puttees are ragged and frazzled
But the Q.M.[94] says nothing for me
My tummy knocks hard on my backbone
My dial is as thin as can be
Still, all we get handed at mealtimes
Is bully and Maconochie![95]

This mocking tone is not necessarily a result of disillusion or so-called 'war fatigue' towards the end of the war, since songs of this type appear from the early months, like this one sung by new recruits in training camps in Britain:

Where are our uniforms?
Far far away!
When will our rifles come?
Perhaps, perhaps some day!

The music-hall hit 'Hello, Hello, Who's Your Lady Friend' provided the music for this song sung by troops in North Africa:

Hullo hullo what's their dirty game?
Working us at ninety in the shade
It wasn't the tale they told us when we enlisted
Now it's all parade parade parade!

---

[92]   Types of aeroplane.
[93]   A 1917 version of 'What Do You Want to Make Those Eyes at Me For?' can be found online at https://www.youtube.com/watch?v=PHA7j9aFOUw (accessed 28 July 2014).
[94]   Quartermaster, in charge of supplies.
[95]   A tinned stew.

While soldiers punished for having eaten their emergency rations ('iron ration') without being authorized by a superior officer composed this ditty to the tune of Harry Champion's hit 'Any Old Iron':[96]

> Where's your iron, where's your iron
> Where's your iron ration?
> It's not for use that's no excuse
> Your iron rations you must produce!
> It's only meant for ornament
> You must be in the fashion
> you'll get it hot if you ain't got
> Your iron iron ration!

It was also possible to mock the whole army, including oneself:

> We are Fred Karno's army, we are the ragtime infantry.
> We cannot fight, we cannot shoot, what bleeding use are we?
> And when we get to Berlin we'll hear the Kaiser say,
> 'Hoch, hoch! Mein Gott, what a bloody rotten lot, are the ragtime infantry'

Against superior officers

A number of songs attack, with some violence, superior officers, and we have already mentioned the rigidity of the military hierarchy. The novelist J. B. Priestley expressed his view in colourful style:

> The British Army never saw itself as the citizens' army. It behaved as if a small gentlemanly officer class still had to make soldiers out of under-gardeners' runaway sons and slum lads known to the police. These fellows had to be kept up to scratch. Let them get slack, they'd soon be a rabble again. … The British command specialised in throwing them away for nothing.[97]

Junior officers died in great numbers during the war, proportionally even more than ordinary soldiers. The most complete inequality between officers and men in everyday life was combined with a grim equality in the face of death: the junior officer often had to lead the attack. Soldiers knew that officers were not all the same; those at the front line enjoyed greater respect than the ones safely behind the lines, and among the junior officers they worked under every day, men could

---

[96] The original can be heard at http://www.archive.org/details/HarryChampion-Any OldIron (accessed 27 July 2014).

[97] J. B. Priestley, *Margin Released: A Writer's Reminiscences and Reflections* (London: Heinemann, 1962), 136.

distinguish between the cruel and the fair, the brave and the cowardly. Nevertheless, officers as a whole are treated as those who not only force a soldier into dangerous situations, but also oblige one to carry out the thousand daily chores, often useless, which make up army life. Forced marches and square-bashing, compulsory church parades and polishing buttons for inspection – there was no shortage of reasons for anger. The sergeant is the officer most insulted in the songs, no doubt because of his presence in everyday life:

> When this lousy war is over no more soldiering for me,
> When I get my civvy clothes on, oh how happy I shall be.
> No more church parades on Sunday, no more begging for a pass.
> You can tell the Sergeant-Major to stick his passes up his arse!
> No more NCOs to curse me, no more rotten army stew.
> You can tell the old cook-sergeant, to stick his stew right up his flue!
> No more sergeants bawling, 'Pick it up' and 'Put it down'
> If I meet the ugly bastard I'll kick his arse all over town!

Whereas this one credited the sergeant with a variety of moral defects:

> We've got a Sergeant-Major who's never seen a gun.
> He's mentioned in dispatches for drinking privates' rum
> And when he sees old Jerry, you should see the bugger run!
> Miles and miles and miles behind the lines!

Senior officers were rarely seen by the ordinary soldiers who were inventing the song repertoire. But this tongue twister mocks directly the staff officers:

> One staff officer jumped right over another staff officer's back.
> And another staff officer jumped right over that other staff officer's back,
> A third staff officer jumped right over two other staff officers' backs,
> And a fourth staff officer jumped right over all the other staff officers' backs.
> They were only playing leapfrog,
> They were only playing leapfrog,
> They were only playing leapfrog,
> When one staff officer jumped right over another staff officer's back.[98]

The mockery is clear, but the words have two possible interpretations. Most commentators suggest that it is about staff officers being obsessed with promotion, but it is also important to remember that, since at least the eighteenth century, 'leapfrog' has been used as a slang expression for sexual activity between two men. The song may well be homophobic mocking of staff officers.

---

[98]   The tune is that of the US folk song 'John Brown's Body'.

Angry at having been sent back up to the front after only a few rest days, one battalion's soldiers sang this song criticizing their commander, to the tune of a very well-known music-hall hit, 'Another Little Drink Wouldn't Do Us Any Harm':

> There was a famous div went to take a certain farm
> They put the wind up Fritz and caused him great alarm
> But the corps commander said, when he heard what they had done
> 'Well another little stunt wouldn't do 'em any harm!'[99]

While one general, Sir Cameron Deane Shute, has the doubtful honour of having a soldiers' song written directly about him:

> The General inspecting the trenches
> Exclaimed with a horrified shout
> 'I refuse to command a division
> Which leaves its excreta about.'
> But nobody took any notice
> No one was prepared to refute,
> That the presence of shit was congenial
> Compared to the presence of Shute.
> And certain responsible critics
> Made haste to reply to his words
> Observing that his staff advisors
> Consisted entirely of turds!
> For shit may be shot at odd corners
> And paper supplied there to suit,
> But a shit would be shot without mourners
> If somebody shot that shit Shute!

Several songs propose killing superior officers. It is almost always a matter of immediate superiors: we do not see songs calling for the murder of Douglas Haig or Lord Kitchener:

> You've got a kind face, you old bastard
> You ought to be bloody well shot!
> You ought to be tied to a gun wheel
> And left there to bloody well rot!

One of the bitterest songs in the corpus, which appears in the two collections put together by ex-soldiers, attacks one by one different figures of authority, before speaking of the fate of the common soldier, hanging, dead, on the barbed wire in no-man's-land. There are of course quite a number of variants.

---

[99] Fuller, *Troop Morale*, 100.

If you want to find the Sergeant, I know where he is (x3)
He's lying on the canteen floor!
I saw him, I saw him
Lying on the canteen floor I saw him,
Lying on the Canteen floor

The quarter master ... Miles and miles and miles behind the lines!
The brass hats ... Drinking claret at Brigade HQ!
The General … Pinning another medal on his chest!
The politicians ... Drinking brandy at the House of Commons bar!

If you want the old battalion, I know where they are (x3)
They're hanging on the old barbed wire.
I saw them, I saw them
Hanging on the old barbed wire I saw them
Hanging on the old barbed wire.[100]

Some versions of the song are more graphic:

If you want to find Joe Driscoll, I know where he is
… Half his bleeding face is blown away.

To end this selection of soldiers' songs, it is worth underlining the fatalism which comes through many of the lyrics. Comic fatalism was common in the music-hall repertoire, and remains so in the soldiers' song. One of the favourite soldiers' songs is simply a long repetition, to the tune of 'Auld Lang Syne' of the refrain:

We're here because we're here because we're here because we're here.
We're here because we're here because we're here because we're here;

A poignant expression of young men caught up in a machine they have no control over.

What is specifically British about the British soldiers' song?

If the experience of the soldiers on the Western Front, whether British, French, German, Canadian, Indian or from elsewhere, was very much similar, the reaction to the experience in soldiers' song was not. Antipatriotic sarcasm and self-deprecation are central characteristics of British (and Australian and Canadian)

---

[100]   Recent versions of this song have been recorded by a number of different groups and artistes, the most well-known being Chumbawumba, online at https://www.youtube. com/watch?v=_K1BdDVvV9Q (accessed 28 July 2014).

songs alone. A rapid overview of French, German and American soldiers' songs show this specificity. Song themes and tones are not the same, but also the production of songs and the organization of singing are distinct.

There is as yet no substantial analytical work on the songs invented or sung by the French soldiers in the Great War, though a few collections have been produced.[101] These contain songs of complaint, put to well-known tunes, about life in the army. Occasionally black humour can be found, but the systematically humorous tone, and the caustic criticism of officers so characteristic of the British songs are not present. It is also to be noted that the French soldiers, fighting on their own nation's soil and in accordance with a bitter national conflict with Germany going back at least as far as 1870, sang many anti-German songs, such as 'La Crève aux Boches' which recounts joyfully the experience of bayoneting, shooting and chasing 'the Hun'.[102]

In the US army, group singing was taken very seriously by the military hierarchy. In each battalion, song leaders were appointed, and compulsory group singing every day became the norm. In the 54 training camps in the United States, an official songbook[103] was used at these sessions. This booklet included the national anthems of most of the allied countries, a few religious hymns, nostalgic Dixie songs and negro spirituals, old English and Scottish folk songs, and recent music-hall hits. A monthly bulletin was published to permit exchanges of views and experiences between song leaders. In US rest camps and training camps in France, it was recommended that collective singing be organized 'at least twice a week'.[104]

A comprehensive study of German soldiers' songs has been undertaken by Reinhardt Olt.[105] He collected a large corpus of the songs from ex-soldiers, and included a careful analysis of the ranks of those sending the songs to him. A full comparison with our own corpus is not possible here, but it is clear that patriotism is much more present in the German corpus, and humour much less.

Understanding the soldier songs: the folk songs of the powerless?

As we have seen, the general tone of soldier songs is one of dissent, and this occasionally led to repression by officers. At one point, there was even an attempt

---

[101]   See, for example, *Le 137e R.I. pendant la Guerre 1914–1918, par 'un soldat'* (Fontenay-le-Comté: Imprimerie Moderne, 1936), or Théodore Botrel, *Les chants du bivouac* and *Les chants de route* (Paris: Payot, 1915).

[102]   Théodore Botrel, *Chansons de route* (Paris: Payot et Cie, 1915), 203.

[103]   *US Army Songbook* (Washington: US Army, 1918).

[104]   Christina Gier, 'Gender, Politics, and the Fighting Soldier's Song in America during World War I', *Music and Politics* 2:1 (Winter 2008), 19.

[105]   Reinhardt Olt, *Krieg und Sprache: Untersuchungen zu deutschen Soldatenliedern des Ersten Weltkrieges* (Giessen: W. Schmitz, 1980–1981).

to ban singing in the trenches, since German newspapers had printed a translation of the extremely popular 'I want to go home' and the generals were concerned about the usefulness of such songs for enemy propagandists.[106] Max Arthur notes that officers would sometimes try to stop soldiers from singing the last verse of 'Hanging on the Old Barbed Wire' in the hope of avoiding harm to fighting spirit.[107] Such attempts generally had little effect, and toleration was the general rule, as songs almost never moved on from dissent to calling for mutiny.

Soldiers' songs have taken a particular place in the national memory of the Great War; the interpretation of these lively expressions of soldiers' attitudes has become a source of polemic. An ideological conflict, often undeclared, divides those who believe these songs contradict or at least relativize the view of Tommies as enthusiastic and patriotic heroes from those who see the dissenting content as little more than ritual grumbling, not to be taken seriously.

The soldiers' songs have been praised as the authentic, dissenting voice of a rebellious popular soul, whereas music-hall songs have been considered mere commercial products, tainted with distasteful jingoism. The 1960s musical comedy *Oh What a Lovely War*, which was mentioned in an earlier chapter, opposed the two genres of song in this way.

In contrast with this emphasis on authentic dissent, the sardonic humour of the soldiers' songs has in some ways been integrated into populist patriotic commemoration of the Great War in Britain. It is the conservative press which has published some of the collections of songs.[108] This has been due to a very widespread desire to communicate the close texture of soldiers' lives and psychology which underlies much of the success of First World War writing. The soldiers have been presented as all the more heroes in that they rejected the title of 'hero', and the songs as expressing 'Tommy's undaunted spirit'. So, for example, Malcolm Brown, author of a dozen titles on the First World War, writes in the introduction to the 2000 edition of Brophy and Partridge's collection

> Oh yes, there's anger and cynicism, and a world-weary longing for the whole damned thing to be over, and couldn't we all go back to dear old Blighty? But there's also a strong sense that by slagging off the war, and finding ways of laughing, even jeering, at it, the men deputed to fight it could find a courage that gave them the determination to win through.[109]

John Brophy, in his own introduction to the 1965 edition, seems to go even further:

---

[106] Arthur, *Bloody War*, xix.

[107] Ibid., p. 68.

[108] It was the conservative newspaper the *Daily Telegraph* which reissued, in 2008, Partridge and Brophy's collection.

[109] Brophy and Partridge, *Dictionary of Tommies' Songs and Slang*, viii.

These songs satirized more than war: they poked fun at the soldier's own desire for peace and rest, and so prevented it from overwhelming his will to go on doing his duty. They were not symptoms of defeatism, but strong bulwarks against it.[110]

Each reader will have his or her own view on this debate which cannot be separated from the general debate about the legitimacy of the British state's policy a century ago. Nevertheless, it seems to us that Brophy's analysis here has two important weaknesses.

Firstly, it does not take into account the fact that the meaning of the songs might be quite different from one soldier to another and from one regiment to another. The reception of a popular song has always contained an element of the personal. These songs, which were spread from one group of soldiers to another by sing-along, represent a sort of ideological compromise which enables them to persuade everyone to join in. This is done by excluding almost all sentiments which are openly jingoistic or openly anti-imperialist. A song which called for Britain to surrender or a song which spoke of the glory of dying for one's country could not succeed, since it would be rapidly shouted down by disgruntled Tommies. All successful soldiers' songs had to pass this initial test: this is why the strongly dissenting tone which is dominant must be taken seriously, in this configuration which only allows the survival of consensual opinions.

Secondly, though it is obviously true that the songs helped the soldiers survive, it by no means follows that their main effect was to increase the determination to fight of the troops in question. As Tony Ashworth's work comprehensively shows, soldiers frequently had other priorities, such as working out how to avoid fighting without being caught by superior officers.

Finally, even if, as ex-soldiers themselves, Brophy and Partridge deserve their voice to be heard, does this discourse not represent a typical case of dominant ideology reinterpreting the voice of the dominated? Through their songs, the soldiers appear to be showing their hatred of their superior officers and their cynicism about official patriotism, but we are told that this only appears to be the case. Popular grassroots expression is reduced by post-hoc cultural revisionism to a simple means of psychological relief aiming at reinforcing fighting spirit.

My analysis does not of course imply that the dissenting tone of the British soldier songs shows a structured pacifist ideology or a reasoned political opposition to Empire war aims. In a situation where practically all the available political leadership – union leaders, feminist leaders and influential intellectuals – campaign in favour of the war, a politicized opposition is simply not available to most rank-and-file soldiers.

Clearly, it is difficult for us a century later to draw excessively firm conclusions about the exact meanings of the soldiers' songs. We may even find, as one historian says of First World War songs in general:

---

[110]   Brophy and Partridge, *The Long Trail*, 18.

It is not just that the traps of writing history loom at every turn – of question-framing, factual verification, generalization and authorial motivation . Rather more simply put, it is the frustrating recognition that, in recounting the stories and making an arrangement, 'first meanings' invariably prove to be irretrievable ...[111]

Nevertheless, the approach taken in this chapter – the analysis of a large corpus of songs, and a reflection based on the conditions in which the songs were sung – allows this study to be based on firm ground.

---

[111]   Watkins, *Proof through the Night*, 8.

Conclusions

When writing the history of entertainment of a period of traumatic and tragic upheaval, one must take care to take full account of the presence in people's minds of the battles, the deaths and the mutilations which were so common; nevertheless, in the war years almost everyone – soldiers and civilians, entrepreneurs and government – took entertainment very seriously, and historians should also do so. The faded, yellowed sheet music which survives from the war years is not only a dusty illustration of history happening elsewhere, in grand prime ministerial offices or muddy trenches. It is a part of history, a keyhole through which we can glimpse the activity of millions of ordinary people who loved popular music and refused to do without it, whether their participation was singing along, performing on stage, playing in the orchestra or dancing in the chorus.

The arrival of the war increased enormously, for ordinary people, traumas and hardships which were not unknown. The families in the wartime music-hall audience trying to forget their dead and wounded were used to tragedy: unemployment and periods of hunger, old relatives taken off to the workhouse and separated from one another after many years of marriage, and the institutionalized disdain which constituted the lot of domestic servants or factory workers. The centenary of the Great War has transformed the experiences of the whole population, for those few years, from private memory to public memory. Innumerable commentators define our Tommy ancestors as all heroes. It is tempting to suggest that they should generally be seen as such before the war too, and their wives no less so, when they struggled to survive and feed their families in a society which was profoundly unequal and cruel, or when they fought back in the name of justice as trade unionists or campaigners for women's suffrage.

What have we discovered, then, on our voyage into the world of wartime music hall? On the stage, the exhibition of disabled people as 'freaks', the sketches about syphilis or the women singing seductive recruitment songs remind us that 'the past is a different country'. It is a world much more varied and changing than it might appear at first sight. We have seen, for example, that the majority of songs do not speak of the war, and of those that do, only a tiny proportion glorify war. This goes against the image which wartime music hall has so far enjoyed, in the absence of studies of a representative corpus of songs.

The repertoire and performances seem to go well beyond being 'a naturalistic mode that both documents and confirms a common way of life' which Peter Bailey identified.[1] The fantasy of Dixieland or Killarney, or the comic tongue twister, for example, are not naturalistic. We see, too, the slow rise of the romantic song, which will so dominate the future of popular music. In looking at what people are singing about, the theme 'How to survive and enjoy oneself despite the war' certainly deserves at least as much attention as 'How to support the war'.

The almost total absence of English folk songs on the stage is striking. The well-meaning campaigns of Cecil Sharp and his establishment backers, aiming at giving folk song back to the people, remained entirely marginal.

Throughout the war, the two key engines of entertainment history of the time rumbled on. The first was a material force: the concentration of capital, which encouraged the rise of the theatre chains and of the revue, and made times hard for the 'good old way' of doing music hall. This concentration is accompanied, despite wartime austerity, by ever more lavish dance numbers and special effects. The second engine, as we have seen, was ideological, the obsessive search for the respectable. We may be surprised to see theatre managers fined for an 'indecency' which would be completely acceptable today, or mainstream editorialists railing against the expression 'Oh my Gawd!'. And what should we think about the front-line soldiers writing to Lena Ashwell to thank her for having brought, with her classical music, some defence against the threat of vulgarity? By the time she read the letter, how many of these respectable soldiers were already dead?

On a number of points, the analysis of the present work contradicts the simpler versions of mass culture theory, and in this way follows the path of most thinkers in the modern discipline of Popular Music Studies. The entertainment industry is not homogeneous and cannot systematically impose its taste on audiences. The content of the songs is the result of a continuous negotiation between differing pressures, through which an ambiguous consensus is built and rebuilt. The same industry makes money in 1914 from recruitment songs and in 1920 from songs about wanting to assassinate, after the war, one's superior officer.

For the singers, entertainers and sometimes the composers, this was perhaps above all a way of making a living without the daily domination of the foreman or the mistress of the house; but they were also people who believed there was 'no business like show business', who were caught up in the usefulness and the magic of getting masses of people to enjoy themselves.

My aim has been to portray as much context as possible, without losing sight of the main object of study, the song. Collective merry-making takes its meaning from its link with other activities. The man or the woman of the war years goes to the music hall instead of other activities and because of other parts of his or her life. Popular song of the war years constitutes a part of the final chapter of the music-hall era. In the 1920s, the new technologies of radio and talking cinema, US domination of the entertainment industry and the more sophisticated song repertoire born from these different transformations will marginalize the music hall.

---

[1]   Peter Bailey, 'Conspiracies of Meaning: Music-Hall and the Knowingness of Popular Culture', *Past and Present* 144 (1994), 138–170.

Wartime music hall was a way of escaping temporarily the terror of the conflict, but also a tool which could reinforce support for the Empire's cause or, on the contrary, insist on other priorities. It was a way of exploring collectively the hardships and confusions of its audiences' lives. Frequently the song lyrics are neither openly ideological nor moralistic but express socio psychological tensions. The tension between pride in the new achievements of women in wartime conditions was theatricalized, along with the fear that changes in women's role provoked; the tension between enjoying life and sexuality, which seemed ever more precious in wartime, and the fear of losing treasured respectability was another tension portrayed and played with on stage. In any case, the music hall was never a genre of protest song; that wide consensus which would keep the whole audience singing along and keep the artistes' name on the manager's books remained the singer's absolute priority.

As we have said, music hall was in some ways the prehistory of pop music. The themes of love, play and everyday life were well in place, the surreal, the modernist, the intimate, the rebel and the sarcastic were to come considerably later. It was also an entertainment which existed by its opposition to high culture, despite the extracts of high culture which were sometimes staged. Gaining little by little respectability as a business activity (the music-hall managers were gradually joining local elites), it kept in the mind of the elite an image of an imbecilic if excusable waste of time. This image of pop music was to last a long time, and has not completely disappeared even today.

The soldiers' songs studied in this book show something of popular consensual attitudes among the lower ranks of the army in the war years. The need for consensus excluded many types of songs – songs on the glory of war or songs calling for surrender could not be successes. The consensus in this case, though, was among a specific social group, since officers almost never take part in the composition nor the singing of the songs. The enormous gap between the repertoires proposed by sections of the elite and the songs chosen by the rank and file is striking. The ordinary soldiers rejected entirely glorious and pompous patriotism, and preferred to insult and criticize their superior officers.

There is much room to research other non-commercial repertoires of the time: hymns, and activist songs, for example. The Irish activist song repertoire was particularly rich and merits a study of its own. It would also be valuable to study how the music hall presented itself in the big cities of the Empire outside Britain: in Toronto and Melbourne, in Capetown and Delhi. Comparisons with vaudeville in the USA are also needed. Yet if all this remains to be done, we hope to have, in the present work, made a contribution to the history of the First World War and the men and women who lived through it.

From 1953 to 1983 in Britain, a television series, presenting an imitation of the Edwardian music hall had tremendous success. It was entitled quite simply 'The Good old Days'. Our own voyage in the world of the music hall of a century ago might be more likely to make us reflect on the tremendous social progress made since, even if, on a Saturday night out, we are perhaps not so different from our ancestors of 1914–1918.

Appendix
A Political, Military and Cultural
Timeline of the Great War

1914

January

In the silent cinemas, the latest blockbuster tells the story of the life of Napoleon and his defeat at Waterloo.
In new case law, a judge declares that selling a film made of a music-hall turn, without consent, contravenes the artistes' rights.

February

The Bishop of London preaches a sermon against 'vulgarity' in the music hall and in favour of 'wholesome entertainment'.
The manager of a music hall in Birmingham is fined for allowing 'indecent language' on the stage.
The Moss Empires theatre chain pays 10 per cent dividends to its shareholders. The Empire Palace theatre in London pays 20 per cent.
The Times comments on the increasing numbers of night clubs in London, where the atmosphere is ever more informal: 'nobody is wearing gloves'.

March

In the press, the debate goes on about whether a child who works on the music-hall stage should be excused from compulsory schooling. Sir Oswald Stoll, owner of a large theatre chain, insists that the stage in itself is an education, and that school is not necessary for these children.
Cecil Sharp begins a lecture tour of Britain with the aim of popularizing folk song and folk dance.
Suffragette Mary Richardson damages the Venus painting by Velasquez in the National Gallery in London, as part of the direct action campaign for women's suffrage.

April

The second edition of the revue *Hullo Tango!* is an immense success.

First performance of George Bernard Shaw's play, *Pygmalion*.
The House of Common approves the Irish Home Rule Bill.

May

Announcement of an August programme of extracts from Wagner's operas at a leading London music hall, with artistes invited from Germany.
The House of Lords again votes to reject women's suffrage.

June

The new musical comedy *The Cinema Star* opens.
The Arch-Duke Ferdinand is assassinated in Sarajevo by a Serbian nationalist.

July

The Anglo-Jewish Actors Union calls a strike at the Pavilion theatre in the East End of London.

August

Germany invades Belgium. Britain joins the war. The USA declares neutrality.
The national music-hall trade union, the Variety Artistes Federation, votes that members should refuse all contracts which offer less than one week's work, and decides that members not following this directive should be expelled.
The first war songs appear at the music halls, along with the first short war documentary films.
The Union for Democratic Control, an anti-war organization, is founded.
Kitchener is appointed Secretary of State for War. He calls for the formation of new armies and appeals for 100,000 volunteers.
The British Expeditionary Force arrives in France. The Battle of Mons begins.

September

Fearing that box-office receipts will collapse and theatres will close because of the war, the artistes' trade union signs an agreement to accept reduced salaries. The agreement will be abandoned in January 1915 when it becomes clear that receipts are rising.
The Finsbury Park Empire presents a special show with guest artistes from all the allied countries.
The First Battle of the Marne mobilizes two million soldiers: half a million are killed or wounded.
The French government is moved to Bordeaux.
Winston Churchill takes over as head of the Admiralty.

Thomas Highgate is the first British soldier shot for desertion.
The Battle of the Aisne breaks out.

October

The revue *Irish and Proud of It, Too!* is a great success.
The trade press encourages theatres to only buy greasepaint made in Britain.
Before the war, the most popular brand had been German.
In the Hippodrome in London, an acrobat is killed in an accident on stage.
The editorial in the influential trade paper, *The Encore*, proposes measures to ensure there are no Germans on stage in Britain (even naturalized British citizens). Artistes with German-sounding stage names promptly change them.
Release of the hit song 'Well Done, Little Ones! Bravo Belgian Boys!'
First Battle of Ypres.

November

Star Maude Mortimer announces that she has raised enough money to send 40,000 packets of cigarettes to British soldiers on active duty in France.
Britain annexes Cyprus and declares war on Turkey and on the Ottoman Empire.
First subscriptions to war loans.

December

The first revue entirely written by Irving Berlin opens in New York.
The first silent feature-length film is shown in cinemas: *Tillie's Punctured Romance,* with Charlie Chaplin.
Marie Lloyd and other stars produce a show for British soldiers at Boulogne in France.
The No Conscription Fellowship is founded to campaign against the eventuality of compulsory military service.
The Archbishop of York gives a series of much remarked-upon sermons of enthusiastic support for the war.
All printed copies of the Irish newspaper *Irish Freedom* are seized in response to its opposition to the war.
First German bombings of British coastal towns.
Unofficial truces and fraternizations are organized by front-line troops along most of the Western front.
The number of allied prisoners of war in Germany reaches 575,000.

1915

January

Trade journal *The Encore* declares itself satisfied with the high levels of box-office revenue in the music halls.

In Manchester, the anti-German revue *Kultur* is staged. In the final scene the 'Germans' are all drowned on stage by a spectacular series of special effects involving several tons of water.

The biggest pantomime hits of the year are 'Are We Downhearted – No!', 'Then They All Sang God Save the King', 'Irish, and Proud of It Too!' and 'I Want to Go Back to Michigan'.

At the Alhambra, a special benefit show is staged to raise money for the 'Grand Duke Michael appeal to buy gloves and mittens for soldiers in the trenches'.

The War Office receives a delegation of suffragists who are protesting against the curfew imposed in some towns on soldiers' wives, after a moralist scare about dissolute women.

First use of poison gas in the war, by German troops on the Eastern Front.

February

The Birth of a Nation, a film by D. W. Griffiths on the American Civil War, since considered a classic, is released to great acclaim.

A proposal is made to establish a 'Pals Battalion' only composed of music-hall entertainers.

Harry Lauder begins his tour to encourage recruitment.

Germany decrees a blockade of Britain.

The Dardanelles operation begins.

The local newspaper in Bristol sets up a special collection to buy gramophones for front-line troops.

In Dublin, the Coliseum, a brand-new variety theatre with 3,000 seats, opens.

March

A census of all women is taken as part of a campaign to involve them further in war work.

Britain, France and Russia sign an agreement that Constantinople will be given to Russia in case of victory.

Battle of Neuve Chapelle.

Turkish victory in the Dardanelles.

The government signs an agreement with 35 of the biggest trade unions in order to avoid strikes during the war.

The King announces that he will drink no more alcohol until the war ends.

April

Second Battle of Ypres
The secret Treaty of London is signed by France, Russia, Britain and Italy. Italy
is promised territories in Turkey, in Africa and in Albania in exchange for its
participation in the war. The promises will not be honoured.

May

The Lord Chamberlain, government representative responsible for censorship in
the theatre, writes to all music-hall managers to urge them to reduce the amount of
vulgarity on stage and to insist that female performers should not appear scantily
dressed.
The *Lusitania* is sunk by a German U-boat: 123 are killed, including many US
civilians.
The Times prints sharp criticism of the government concerning the shortage of
shells on the Western Front.
A new coalition government is established, but Asquith remains prime minister.

June

For the fifth consecutive year, an annual charity collection day for artistes in
distress is held. This year, the money collected is to be divided equally between
music-hall charities and funds for wounded soldiers.
The government establishes a control commission to apply stricter rules on the
selling of alcohol.
British troops occupy Cameroon.

July

Launch of the second war loan scheme.
Women's demonstration in London for the 'right to serve'.

August

German troops take Warsaw.
A grand ceremony takes place at Saint Giles' Cathedral in Edinburgh at which
leaders of the Church of Scotland express strong support for the war and for the
Empire.

September

George Robey, addressing a recruitment meeting in Trafalgar Square, complains
that around the country he sees a tendency 'not to take the war seriously'.

A London magistrate decrees that D. H. Lawrence's novel *The Rainbow* is obscene. All copies are seized and destroyed.
The British army tests its first tank prototype.
The Trades Union Congress votes against conscription.
A number of women postmen are recruited in Bradford.
Battle of Loos.

October

First British use of poison gas.
Execution of Edith Cavell.
Women bus and tram conductors begin work in London.

November

His Master's Voice release a record collection of the songs of the revue *Bric à Brac*.
The right of theatres to allow smoking in the auditorium during shows is confirmed by magistrates.

December

A Birmingham theatre manager is fined for having allowed Harry Champion to sing 'a vulgar song' on stage.
The head of the British Army in France, John French, resigns and is replaced by Douglas Haig.
Albert Einstein publishes his theory of general relativity.
British and Empire troops evacuate Gallipoli.
Some Christmas truces are respected, but far fewer than in 1914.

1916

January

Compulsory conscription of all men between 18 and 41 years of age.
In *The Performer* one reads that pantomimes have scarcely changed for 25 years.
This year's hit songs include 'I'm Glad I Raised My Boy to Be a Soldier' and 'Pack Up Your Troubles in Your Old Kit Bag'.
The artistes' trade union decides to re-establish monthly meetings in all the large towns.
In Glasgow, premiere of Granville Bantock's *Hebridean Symphony*.

The letters' page of the *London Evening News* publishes a complaint by a lady that domestic servants can no longer be found, while 2,000 women are working in revues on tour.

February

Beginning of the Battle of Verdun, which was to last ten months.
Sarah Bernhardt performs at the Coliseum music hall in London.
The artistes' union expresses concern that large numbers of American vaudeville artistes might come to Britain and take the jobs of British music-hall performers who have left for the war.
The union decides that any member who has joined the forces will conserve their right to union benefits for their family in case of death. Nevertheless, the organization feels obliged to refuse many new applications for membership by artistes who have been attracted by these benefits.

March

A special music-hall show for wounded soldiers is put on every evening for a week at Buckingham Palace, in the presence of the royal family. A thousand soldiers are invited each evening.

April

In Dublin, the insurgents declare the Irish Republic. The insurrection is defeated by the British Army and the leaders are executed a few days later.
The musical comedy *The Bing Boys Are Here* is an enormous success, in particular because of the hit song 'If You Were the Only Girl in the World' sung by the duo George Robey and Violet Lorraine

May

First performance, in Paris, of Erik Satie's composition 'Three Pieces'.
The Battle of Jutland between the German and British navies, only major naval battle of the war, ends with a victory for neither side.

June

Conscription of married men.
Colonel Norton Griffiths launches an attack on music hall in the national press, claiming it constitutes a 'waste of national resources'.
The Original Dixieland Jass Band (*sic*) gives its first concert in Chicago.
The *Ziegfeld Follies* 1916 revue opens on Broadway.
The popular Minister of War, Lord Kitchener, is killed when his ship is sunk.

The Hippodrome, a new music hall with seats for 3,000, opens in Folkestone.

July

Battle of the Somme. During the first few hours on the first day, 20,000 British soldiers are killed and 40,000 wounded.

August

The musical comedy *Chu Chin Chow* opens in London. It will break box-office records and play for a total of 2,238 shows.
The Anglican Men's Association complains about the caricaturing of Anglican vicars on the music-hall stage. Some of its members would like censorship authorities to intervene.
Rumania declares war on Germany.
A strike breaks out in the music hall at Golders Green. The manager sacks all stage hands who are union members.
The minimum wage for stage hands in London is raised.
Falkenhyn is dismissed as head of the German armed forces. He is replaced by Hindenburg and Ludendorff.

September

Two young men are prosecuted for having thrown bags of flour at artistes during a show. 'A common event' in some variety theatres, according to *The Performer.*
Tanks are deployed for the first time, by the British Army.
Germany begins the construction of the Hindenburg line, planning a retreat to better fortified positions.
The musical comedy *Theo and Company* opens in London, before undertaking a national tour.

October

Coal rationing is introduced.
The Catholic press denounces 'vulgarity' and 'scantily dressed women' on the music-hall stage.

November

A new law compels all shops to close at 8 pm.
The Battle of the Somme finally draws to a close.

December

David Lloyd George becomes Prime Minister.
Robert Nivelle replaces Joffre as Commander in Chief of the French armies.
German troops take Bucharest.
The US president attempts to set up peace talks. The Allies refuse unless Germany promises to pay reparations.

1917

January

The number of days' leave available for British soldiers is raised.
An accidental explosion in a munitions factory in London kills 73 people and injures 400.
According to *The Encore*, this year's pantomimes avoid referring to the war. The two most popular hits of the season are 'Take Me Back to Dear Old Blighty!' and 'What a Night! What a Waltz! What a Girl!'
Germany re-establishes a total blockade in war zones.
The music halls present giant working models of airships which, it is claimed, will make a decisive difference in winning the war.
The government decides to fix unilaterally prices paid to farmers for their crops.

February

The USA breaks off diplomatic relations with Germany.
The revue *As Irish as Ever* is on tour around Britain.
Sharp rises in the price of fish lead to the closure of large numbers of fish and chip shops.
In Lancashire and elsewhere, temperance organizations set up anti-alcohol meetings at factory gates.

March

The 'February Revolution' overthrows the Russian tsar.
British troops take Baghdad.
An exhibition of battlefield souvenirs is organized to raise money for blinded soldiers.
The Women's Army Auxiliary Corps (the WAAC) is founded.
According to the trade magazine *Phono Record*, 'all over the far flung battle line the gramophone is ubiquitous'.
'Take Me Back to Dear Old Blighty' sells 38,000 records: an exceptionally high figure for the times.

April

The US senate votes to join the war.
A scandal breaks out in Burnley when it is reported that soldiers coming back from the war with shell shock receive the same harsh treatment as civilian 'lunatics'.
Organization of a boxing tournament for music-hall artistes.
Battle of Arras.
In London, the manager of the Coliseum music hall is invited to give a talk at Saint Martin's church on the subject 'The Church, entertainment and the War'.
In the USA, the vaudeville artistes are on strike. Their British counterparts organize a solidarity fund.
Scott Joplin, the great ragtime composer, dies in the USA.
In Madrid, Manuel de Falla's ballet *The Three-cornered Hat*, with set designs and costumes by Pablo Picasso, has its first performance.

May

The US government decides on conscription.
Mutinies affect fifty or so regiments of the French army.
Adverts in the local press declare: 'YOU CANNOT stop the war but you can stop the German bayonet by sending a soldier a Chemico body shield that will save him from half the dangers of active service. 35 shillings.'
The revue *The Bing Girls Are Here* is a great success. The plot concerns a competition between all the young ladies of a small town, who must try to pass an entire year without being kissed.
The rationing campaign 'Eat Less Bread' organizes a week of talks in primary schools.

June

The first US troops arrive in France.

July

The poet Siegfried Sassoon publishes his radical anti-war declaration.
A special show is given at the Royal Albert Hall for an audience of 10,000 wounded soldiers.
King George V decrees that his family will abandon their name of 'Saxe-Cobourg' and take the name of 'Windsor' instead.
The Battle of Passchendaele begins.
A new 'All-Black' revue goes on tour round Britain under the title *Coloured Society*.

August

The musical comedy *A Better 'Ole*, a farce about life in the trenches, opens in London. It will last for more than 800 showings.
The artistes' trade union wins a landmark court case which obliges theatres to pay salaries for extra matinee shows. Previously they had often been added without additional pay.

September

There is a court case between the Moss theatre chain and a dancer seriously injured during a rehearsal. Since rehearsals are not paid, the Moss chain claimed not to be responsible for compensation to the injured performer.
The 'Harry Lauder Million Pound Fund for Maimed Men' is launched.
The song 'The Military Representative', which mocks the conscription procedure, is a tremendous success.
Death in Paris of Edgar Degas.

October

First British bombing of Germany.
Charlie Chaplin signs a cinema contract for over a million dollars.
According to the trade magazine *Phono Record*, 'The war has occasioned widespread prosperity among the working classes, and certainly the gramophone trade has shared the prosperity to the full'.

November

The 'October revolution' in Russia brings the Bolshevik party to power.
The Music Hall Ladies Guild, a charitable organization, aims at giving a Christmas hamper to all artistes' families in distress.
Hetty King presents on stage 'Songs the Soldiers' Sing'.
The Balfour Declaration affirms British support for Jewish settlement of Palestine.
British troops occupy Tel Aviv.
Battle of Cambrai. The British make large-scale use of tanks for the first time.
Death of Auguste Rodin.
Fred Astaire appears for the first time on Broadway.

December

The new Russian government publishes all the secret treaties and partition plans signed by the different powers.
New law on state schooling: all fees for state schools are abolished. Education is now compulsory up to the age of 14.

1918

January

The Germans move 75,000 troops from the Eastern Front to the Western Front.

Various pantomimes include the mocking song 'The Conscientious Objector's Lament'.

Allegations are aired that dancers hired in some military training camps are paid only one pound a week. Military authorities deny this.

Government attempts to restrict the more 'extravagant' shows and special effects seem to have little effect.

The artistes' trade union, now with 3,250 members, celebrates the twelfth anniversary of its founding.

February

The artistes' trade union complains that wages were stopped when air raids caused the temporary closure of some halls.

More than 50 different revues are on tour in Britain.

A music hall in Lincoln sees its licence challenged after accusations of 'vulgarity' on stage.

The last exemptions to conscription are abolished, despite union protests.

The right to vote is enacted for women over 30 in the United Kingdom.

March

Soviet Russia signs the Treaty of Brest-Litovsk.

The German armies launch a major offensive on the Somme.

Music halls are compelled to close at 10.30 pm every evening, in order to save fuel for the war economy.

Lord Derby congratulates the artistes' and actors' profession for what he says is their indispensable role in the war.

The great music-hall magician Chung Ling Soo, dies after his 'bullet catch trick' goes terribly wrong in a theatre in Wood Green.

Death in Paris of the composer Claude Debussy.

April

The stage hands at theatres in Cardiff and in Blackpool go on strike. They demand that the working week be reduced, to 48 hours for men and 36 hours for women.

Meat rationing is established.

May

Conscription is extended to all men under the age of 51.

The Scottish socialist and anti-war activist John Maclean is tried for sedition. He is sentenced to five years of forced labour, but will be released as soon as the war is over.

English artistes travelling to Ireland are advised by the trade press not to use the British flag in their acts.

The Encore launches another campaign against 'vulgarity' in the music hall.

The government forms a new commission for theatre propaganda.

Dr Brodie tours British music halls with his 'miracle cures' for serious diseases.

June

The song 'Oh, What a Lovely War!' is a great success, confirming the entry of a new, black humour into the wartime music halls.

The German advance is blocked at Chateau-Thierry.

Stage hands go on strike for several weeks in Newcastle when theatre managers announce they will not recognize the trade union.

July

Second Battle of the Marne.

Enrico Caruso records the US patriotic war song 'Over There'.

An accidental explosion in a munitions factory in Nottinghamshire kills 134 people.

August

The governmental message marking the fourth anniversary of the start of the war is read out at the same hour in music halls, theatres, cinemas and concert halls throughout the country. It is estimated that 2.5 million people heard it at this hour, in 4,000 venues.

Battle of Amiens.

A strike in English police forces mobilizes 12,000 striking officers.

September

The German armies are pushed back further than their positions the previous year.

Death of Eugene Stratton, the best-known of the 'blackface' performers.

October

A new law allows women to be candidates at parliamentary elections.

A touring show scheme is set up specifically to entertain women workers in munitions factories, sometimes lodged in barracks far from home.

November

An armistice is signed between the Allies and the Austro-Hungarian Empire.
The Kaiser is overthrown and a German republic declared.
The armistice is signed between the Allies and Germany.

Bibliography

The literature of the history of entertainment, and that of the First World War, is immense; I have listed here only the works I have quoted from or referred to directly.

Abbott, John. *The Story of Francis Day & Hunter.* London: Francis Day & Hunter, 1952.

Adorno, Theodor Wiesengrund. *Essays on Music.* Berkeley: University of California Press, 2002.

Adorno, Theodor Wiesengrund. *The Culture Industry: Selected Essays on Mass Culture.* London: Routledge, 1991.

Arthur, Max. *Forgotten Voices of the Great War.* London: Ebury, 2002.

Arthur, Max. *Last Post: The Final Word from Our First World War Soldiers.* London: Phoenix, 2005.

Arthur, Max. *Lost Voices of the Edwardians.* London: Harper Perennial, 2006.

Arthur, Max. *The Road Home: The Aftermath of the Great War Told by the Men and Women Who Survived It.* London: Phoenix, 2009.

Ashwell, Lena. *Modern Troubadours.* Copenhagen: Gyldenal, 1922.

Ashwell, Lena. *Myself a Player.* London: Michael Joseph, 1936.

Ashworth, Tony. *Trench Warfare 1914–1918: The Live and Let Live System.* London: Pan, 1980.

Askwith, George Ranken. *Industrial Problems and Disputes.* London: John Murray, 1920.

August, Andrew. 'A Culture of Consolation? Rethinking Politics in Working-class London, 1870–1914'. *Historical Research* 74:184 (2001).

Bailey, Peter. 'Conspiracies of Meaning: Music Hall and the Knowingness of Popular Culture.' *Past and Present* 144:1 (1994).

Bailey, Peter. *Leisure and Class in Victorian England: Rational Recreation and the Contest for Control, 1830–1885.* London: Routledge & Kegan Paul, 1978.

Bailey, Peter (Ed.). *Music-hall: The Business of Pleasure.* Milton Keynes: Open University Press, 1986.

Bailey, Peter. 'Naughty but Nice: Musical Comedy and the Rhetoric of the Girl.' In *The Edwardian Theatre: Essays on Performance and the Stage*, edited by Michael R. Booth and Joel H. Kaplan. Cambridge: Cambridge University Press, 1996.

Bailey, Peter. *Popular Culture and Performance in the Victorian City.* Cambridge: Cambridge University Press, 1998.

Bailey, Peter. 'Will the Real Bill Banks Please Stand Up? Towards a Role Analysis of Mid-Victorian Working Class Respectability.' *The Journal of Social History* 12:3 (1979).

Baker, Richard Anthony. Marie Lloyd: Queen of the Music-halls. London: Robert Hale, 1990.

Barker, Felix. *The House that Stoll Built.* London: Frederick Muller, 1957.

Barret-Ducroq, Françoise. *Le mouvement féministe anglais d'hier à aujourd'hui.* Paris: Ellipses, 2000.

Barret-Ducrocq, Françoise. *Love in the Time of Victoria: Sexuality and Desire Among Working-Class Men and Women in Nineteenth-Century London.* Harmondsworth: Penguin, 1991.

Baxendale, John. '"... into another kind of life in which anything might happen ...": Popular Music and Late Modernity, 1910–1930.' *Popular Music* 14:2 (1995).

Beaud, Paul, 'Et si l'on reparlait d'Adorno.' In *Popular Music Perspectives,* edited by David Horn and Philip Tagg. Exeter: International Association for the Study of Popular Music, 1982.

Beckett, Ian. *Home Front 1914–1918: How Britain Survived the Great War.* London: National Archives, 2006.

Bet-El, Ilana. *Conscripts: Forgotten Men of the Great War.* Stroud: The History Press, 2009.

Bevan, Ian. *Top of the Bill: The Story of the London Palladium.* London: Frederick Muller, 1952.

Booth, J. B. *The Days We Knew.* London: T. Werner Laurie, 1943.

Booth, Michael R. Booth and Kaplan, Joel H. (Eds). *The Edwardian Theatre: Essays on Performance and the Stage.* Cambridge: Cambridge University Press, 1996.

Bowers, Judith. *Stan Laurel and Other Stars of the Panopticon.* Edinburgh: Birlinn, 2007.

Bratton, J. S. 'Beating the Bounds: Gender Play and Role Reversal in the Edwardian Music Hall.' In *The Edwardian Theatre: Essays on Performance and the Stage,* edited by Michael R. Booth and Joel H. Kaplan. Cambridge: Cambridge University Press, 1996.

Bratton, J. S. 'King of the Boys: Music Hall Male Impersonators.' *Women's Review* 20 (1987).

Bratton, J. S. (Ed.). *Music Hall: Performance and Style.* Milton Keynes: Open University Press, 1986.

Braybon, Gail. *Women Workers in the First World War.* London: Croom Helm, 1981.

Brown, A. J. *The Taxmen's Tale – the History of the IRSF.* London: Inland Revenue Staff Federation, 1983.Brown, Malcolm (Ed.). *Suffering from Cheerfulness. The Best Bits from The Wipers Times.* London: Little Books, 2007.

Brown, Malcolm and Seaton, Shirley. *Christmas Truce.* Basingstoke: Pan Books, 2001.

Campbell, Olive and Sharp, Cecil. *English Folk Songs from the Southern Appalachians*. London: G. P. Putnam's Sons, 1917.

Carter, Alexandra. *Dance and Dancers in the Victorian and Edwardian Music Hall Ballet*. Aldershot: Ashgate, 2005.

Chastagner, Claude (Ed.). *La musique des iles britanniques (1835–1915), Cahiers victoriens et edouardiens* (special themed issue) 50 (1999).

Cheshire, D. F. *Music Hall in Britain*. Newton Abbot: David & Charles, 1974.

Cloonan, Martin. *Banned! The Censorship of Popular Music in Britain*. Aldershot: Arena, 1996.

Corns, Catherine and Hughes-Wilson, John. *Blindfold and Alone: British Military Executions in the Great War*. London: Cassell, 2005.

Corvisy, Catherine-Émilie and Molinari, Véronique. *Les femmes dans l'Angleterre victorienne et édouardienne: entre sphère privée et sphère publique*. Paris: L'Harmattan, 2008.

Crowhurst, A. J. 'The Music Hall 1885–1922.' PhD Thesis, University of Cambridge, 1991.

Crump, Jeremy. 'Provincial Music Hall: Promoters and Public in Leicester, 1863–1929.' In *Music-hall: The Business of Pleasure*, edited by Peter Bailey. Milton Keynes: Open University Press, 1986.

Daniels, Henry and Collé-Bak, Nathalie (Eds). *1916, La Grande-Bretagne en guerre*. Nancy: Presses Universitaires de Nancy, 2007.

David-Guillou, Angèle. 'Early Musicians' Unions in Britain, France, and the United States: On the Possibilities and Impossibilities of Transnational Militant Transfers in an International Industry.' *Labour History Review* 74:3 (2009).

David-Guillou, Angèle. 'Premiers syndicats d'artistes musiciens, sociabilités musicales et art en France et en Angleterre.' Seminar paper given at Paris 13 University, 2005.

De Frece, Matilda. *Recollections of Vesta Tilley*. London: Hutchinson, 1934.

Department of Employment and Productivity. *British Labour Statistics: Historical Abstracts, 1886–1968*. London, HMSO, 1971.

Disher, Maurice Willson. *Winkles and Champagne: Comedies and Tragedies of the Music Hall*. Bath: Chivers Press, 1974.

Eby, Cecil D. *The Road to Armageddon: The Martial Spirit in English Popular Literature 1870–1914*. Durham, NC: Duke University Press, 1988.

Ehrlich, Cyril. *Harmonious Alliance: A History of the Performing Rights Society*. Oxford: Oxford University Press, 1989.

Ehrlich, Cyril. *The Music Profession in Britain since the Eighteenth Century: A Social History*. Oxford: Clarendon Press, 1985.

Ehrlich, Cyril. *The Piano: A History*. London: J. M. Dent, 1976.

Ellsworth-Jones, Will. *We Will Not Fight...: The Untold Story of World War One's Conscientious Objectors*. London: Aurum Press, 2008.

Farson, Daniel. *Marie Lloyd and Music Hall*. London: Tom Stacey, 1972.

Faulkner, Neil. 'La Somme, une bataille pour l'empire et le profit.' In *1916, La Grande-Bretagne en guerre*, edited by Henry Daniels and Nathalie Collé-Bak. Nancy: Presses Universitaires de Nancy, 2007.

Francmanis, J. 'National Music to National Redeemer: the Consolidation of a "Folk-song" Construct in Edwardian England', *Popular Music* 21 (2002).

Fuller, J. F. G. *Troop Morale and Popular Culture in the British and Dominion Armies 1914–1918*. Oxford: Clarendon, 1990.

Gier, Christina. 'Gender, Politics, and the Fighting Soldier's Song in America during World War I.' *Music and Politics* 2:1 (2008).

Gillies, Midge. *Marie Lloyd: The One and Only*. London: Gollancz, 1999.

Gold, John R. and Revill, George. 'Gathering the Voices of the People? Cecil Sharp, Cultural Hybridity, and the Folk Music of Appalachia.' *Geojournal* 65 (2006).

Goodall, Felicity. *We Will Not Go to War Conscientious Objection during the World Wars*. Stroud: The History Press, 2010.

Graves, George. *Gaeties and Gravities – the Autobiography of a Comedian*. London: Hutchinson, 1931.

Graves, Robert. *Goodbye to All That*. London: Penguin, 2000 (1957).

Gregory, Adrian. *The Last Great War: British Society and the First World War*. Cambridge: Cambridge University Press, 2008.

Guéno; Jean-Pierre and Laplume, Yves (Eds). *Paroles de poilus: Lettres et carnets du front*. Paris: Librio, 2003.

Gwynne, Bishop L. (Ed.). *Religion and Morale, the Story of the National Mission on the Western Front*. London: Society for Promoting Christian Knowledge, 1917.

Hallett, Terry. *Bristol's Forgotten Empire: The History of the Empire Theatre, Bristol*. Westbury: Badger Press, 2000.

Hannavy, John. *The English Seaside in Victorian and Edwardian Times*. Princes Risborough: Shire, 2003.

Harding, James. *George Robey and the Music-Hall*. London: Hodder & Stoughton, 1990.

Harker, David. *Fakesong: The Manufacture of British 'Folksong', 1700 to the Present Day*. Milton Keynes: Open University Press, 1985.

Hardy, Rev. E. J. *The British Soldier, His Courage and Humour*. London: T. Fisher Unwin, 1915.

Hennion, Antoine and Vignolle J. P. *Artisans et industriels du disque – essai sur le mode de production de la musique*. Paris: CSI-Cordes 1978.

Herbert, Trevor. 'Volunteers, Salvationists and Committees: Consensus versus Regulation in Amateur Victorian Brass Bands.' *Cahiers victoriens et édouardiens* 50 (1999).

Hermon, E. W. and Nason, Anne. *For Love and Courage, Letters Home from the Western Front 1914–1917*. London: Preface, 2009.

Hobson, John Atkinson. *The Psychology of Jingoism*. London: Richards, 1901.

Hoggart, Richard. *The Uses of Literacy: Aspects of Working-class Life*. London: Chatto & Windus, 1957.

Holmes, Richard. *Tommy: The British Soldier on the Western Front 1914–1918*. London: Harper Perennial, 2005.

Honri, Peter. *Music Hall Warriors: A History of the Variety Artistes Federation 1906–1967*. London: Greenwich Exchange, 1997.

Honri, Peter. *Working the Halls*. Farnborough: Saxon House, 1973.

Horrall, A. *Popular Culture in London c.1890–1918: The Transformation of Entertainment*. Manchester: Manchester University Press, 2001.

Kennedy, Thomas Cummins. *The Hound of Conscience: a History of the No-conscription Fellowship, 1914–1919*. Fayetteville: University of Arkansas Press, 1981.

Kidson, F. and Neal, M. *English Folk-Song and Dance*. Cambridge: Cambridge University Press, 1915.

Kilgarriff, Michael. *Sing Us One of the Old Songs: A Guide to Popular Song 1860–1920*. Oxford: Oxford University Press, 1999.

King, Laura. '"Matrons, Maidens and Magdalenes": Women's Patronage of 19th Century Music Halls.' Master's diss. Simon Fraser University, 1993.

Lauder, Harry. *A Minstrel in France*. New York: Hearsts, 1918.

Lauder, Harry. *Between You and Me*. New York: James A. McCann, 1919.

Lauder, Harry. *Roamin' in the Gloamin'*. London: Hutchinson, 1928.

Leask, Margaret. 'Lena Ashwell 1869–1957: Actress, Patriot, Pioneer.' PhD thesis, University of Sydney, 2000.

Lee, Arthur Gould. *No Parachute: A Fighter Pilot in World War I*. London: Jarrolds, 1968.

Liddington, Jill and Norris, Jill. *One Hand Tied Behind Us: Rise of the Women's Suffrage Movement*. London: Virago, 1978.

Littlewood, Joan. *Oh What a Lovely War*. London: Methuen, 1967.

Livingstone, Thomas. *Tommy's War: The Diary of a Wartime Nobody*. London: Harper Press, 2008.

Lynch, E. F. P. *Somme Mud*. London: Bantam, 2008.

Macdonald, Lyn. *The Roses of No Man's Land*. London: Penguin, 1993 (1980).

Macinnes, Colin. *Sweet Saturday Night: Pop Song 1840–1920*. London: Panther Arts, 1967.

Macqueen-Pope, W. *Marie Lloyd, Queen of the Music-halls*. Norwich: Oldbourne, 1957.

Macqueen-Pope, W. *The Melodies Linger On: The Story of Music-Hall*. London: W. H. Allen, 1950.

Mcshane, Harry. *No Mean Fighter*. London: Pluto Press, 1978.

Maitland, Sara. *Vesta Tilley*. London: Virago, 1986.

Makepeace, Clare. 'Punters and their Prostitutes: British Soldiers, Masculinity, and maisons tolerées in the First World War.' In *What Is Masculinity? Historical Dynamics from Antiquity to the Contemporary World*, edited by John H. Arnold and Sean Brady. London: Palgrave Macmillan, 2011.

Malcolmson, Robert W. *Popular Recreations in English Society, 1700–1850.* Cambridge: Cambridge University Press, 1973.

Maloney, Paul. *Scotland and the Music Hall, 1850–1914.* Manchester: Manchester University Press, 2003.

Mander, Raymond and Mitchenson, Joe. *British Music Hall: A Story in Pictures.* London: Studio Vista, 1965.

Marlow, Joyce (Ed.). *The Virago Book of Women and the Great War.* London: Virago, 1999.

Marwick, Arthur. *The Deluge: British Society and the First World War.* London: Macmillan, 2006 (1965).

Middleton, Richard (Ed.). *Studying Popular Music.* Milton Keynes: Open University Press, 1990.

Mullen, John. 'Anti-Black Racism in British Popular Music 1880–1920.' *Revue française de civilisation britannique* special issue (2012).

Mullen, John. 'Stéréotypes et identités: Irlande et les Irlandais dans le music-hall britannique 1900–1920.' In *Racialisations dans l'aire anglophone*, edited by Michel Prum. Paris: L'Harmattan, 2012.

Mullen, John. 'The Campaign for "Respectability" in late Victorian and Edwardian Music Hall 1880–1920: A Campaign against Antisocial Behaviour?' In *Antisocial Behaviour in Britain: Victorian and Contemporary Perspectives*, edited by Sarah Pickard. Basingstoke: Palgrave Macmillan, 2014.

Mullen, John. 'The Popular Music Industry in Britain in 1900.' *Civilisations* 13 (2014).

Mullen, John. 'Velours rouge et piquets de grève – la grève du music-hall à Londres en 1907.' *Cahiers victoriens et édouardiens* 67 (2008).

Mullen, John. '"You can't help laughing, can you?": Humour and Symbolic Empowerment in British Popular Song during the Great War.' In *Humour, Entertainment and Popular Culture during World War One*, edited by Karen A. Ritzenhoff and Clémentine Tholas-Disset. Basingstoke: Palgrave Macmillan, 2014.

Nott, James. *Music for the People: Popular Music and Dance in Interwar Britain.* Oxford: Oxford University Press, 2002.

Omissi, David E. *Indian Voices of the Great War: Soldiers' Letters, 1914–18.* Basingstoke: Macmillan, 1999.

Owen, Wilfred,. *The Poems of Wilfred Owen.* Ware: Wordsworth, 1994.

Pankhurst, Sylvia. *The Home Front: A Mirror to Life in England during the First World War.* London: The Cresset Library, 1987 (1932).

Parsonage, Catherine. 'A Critical Reassessment of the Reception of Early Jazz in Britain.' *Popular Music* 22:3 (2003).

Pearsall, Ronald. *Edwardian Life and Leisure.* Melbourne: Wren, 1973.

Pearsall, Ronald. *Edwardian Popular Music.* Newton Abbot: David & Charles, 1975.

Peddle, Ian. 'Playing at Poverty: the Music Hall and the Staging of the Working Class.' In *The Working-Class Intellectual in Eighteenth- and Nineteenth-Century Britain*, edited by Aruna Krishnamurthy. Aldershot: Ashgate, 2009.

Perry Curtis, Lewis. *Anglo-Saxons and Celts: A Study of Anti-Irish Prejudice in Victorian England*. New York: New York University Press, 1968.

Pickering, Michael. '"A Happy Instinct for Sentiment": A Profile of Harry Hunter.' *Cahiers victoriens et édouardiens* 50 (1999).

Pickering, Michael. *Blackface Minstrelsy in Britain*. Aldershot: Ashgate, 2008.

Priestley, J. B. *Margin Released: A Writer's Reminiscences and Reflections*. London: Heinemann, 1962.

Prost, Antoine and Winter, Jay. *The Great War in History: Debates and Controversies, 1914 to the Present*. Cambridge: Cambridge University Press, 2005.

Purvis, June. *Emmeline Pankhurst: A Biography*. London: Routledge, 2002.

Purvis, June. 'The Prison Experiences of the Suffragettes in Edwardian Britain.' *Women's History Review* 4:1 (1995).

Quigley, Private J. *The Slogan – Sidelights on Recruiting with Harry Lauder's Band*. London: Simpkin, 1916.

Ribouillault, Claude. *La Musique au fusil avec les poilus de la Grande Guerre*. Rodez: Éditions du Rouergue, 1996.

Richards, Private Frank. *Old Soldiers Never Die*. Uckfield: Naval & Military Press, no date.

Richardson, William. *A Union of Many Trades: The History of the Union of Shop, Distributive and Allied Workers*. Manchester: USDAW, 1979.

Rioux, Jean-Pierre and Sirinelli, Jean-François. *La Culture de masse en France de la Belle Epoque à aujourd'hui*. Paris: Fayard, 2002.

Robb, George. *British Culture and the First World War*. Basingstoke: Palgrave, 2002.

Roberts, Elizabeth. *A Woman's Place: An Oral History of Working Class Women, 1890–1940*. Oxford: Blackwell, 1984.

Roberts, Robert. *A Ragged Schooling: Growing Up in the Classic Slum*. London: Fontana, 1978.

Roberts, Robert. *The Classic Slum: Salford Life in the First Quarter of the Century*. Harmondsworth: Pelican, 1973.

Rose, June. *Marie Stopes and the Sexual Revolution*. Stroud: Tempus, 2007.

Rosenberg, Chanie. *1919: Britain on the Brink of Revolution*. London: Bookmarks, 1995.

Royle, Trevor. *The Flowers of the Forest: Scotland and the First World War*. Edinburgh: Birlinn, 2007.

Roynon, Gavin (Ed.). *Home Fires Burning: The Great War Diaries of Georgina Lee*. Stroud: Alan Sutton, 2006.

Russell, Dave. *Popular Music in England, 1840–1914: A Social History*. Manchester: Manchester University Press, 1988.

Russell, Dave. 'Varieties of life: the making of the Edwardian Music Hall', In *The Edwardian Theatre: Essays on Performance and the Stage*, edited by Michael R. Booth and Joel H. Kaplan. Cambridge: Cambridge University Press, 1996.

Ryser, Tracy. 'A White Man's Inadequate Portrait of a Slave: Minstrel Shows and Huckleberry Finn.' Master's diss., University of Youngstown, OH, 2004.

Sartre, Jean-Paul. *Un théâtre de situations*. Paris: Gallimard, 1992.

Schneer, Jonathan. *Ben Tillett: Portrait of a Labour Leader*. London: Croom Helm, 1982.

Scott, Derek, B. 'The Music Hall Cockney: Flesh and Blood, or Replicant?' *Music and Letters* 83:2 (May 2002).

Sczelkun, S. A. *The Conspiracy of Good Taste: William Morris, Cecil Sharp, Clough Williams-Ellis and the Repression of Working Class Culture in the Twentieth Century*. London: Working Press, 1993.

Self, Geoffrey. *Light Music in Britain since 1870: a Survey*. Aldershot: Ashgate, 2000.

Senelick, Laurence, Cheshire, David F. and Schneider, Ulrich. *British Music-Hall 1840–1923: A Bibliography and Guide to Sources with a Supplement on European Music-Hall*. Hamden CT: Archon Books, 1981.

Shaw, George Bernard. *Annajanska, the Bolshevik Empress*. London: Kessinger, 2004 (1918).

Silbey, David. *The British Working Class and Enthusiasm for War, 1914–1916*. London: Frank Cass, 2005.

Stedman Jones, Gareth. *Languages of Class: Studies in English Working-Class History 1832–1982*. Cambridge: Cambridge University Press, 1983.

Stedman Jones, Gareth. 'Working-Class Culture and Working-Class Politics in London, 1870–1900: Notes on the Remaking of a Working Class.' In *Languages of Class: Studies in English Working-Class History, 1832–1892*, edited by Gareth Stedman Jones. Cambridge: Cambridge University Press, 1983.

Strinati, Dominic. *An Introduction to Theories of Popular Culture*. London: Routledge, 1995.

Summerfield, Penny. 'The Effingham Arms and the Empire: Deliberate Selection in the Evolution of Music Hall in London.' In *Popular Culture and Class Conflict 1590–1914*, edited by S. Yeo and E. Yeo. Brighton: Harvester, 1981.

Tagg, Philip (Ed.). *Popular Music Perspectives*. Exeter: IASPM, 1982.

Taylor, J. *From Self-Help to Glamour: The Working Man's Club 1860–1972*. Oxford: History Workshop, 1972.

The Lost World of Mitchell and Kenyon (DVD). London: Bfi Video, 2005.

Thompson, Andrew. *The Empire Strikes Back?: The Impact of Imperialism on Britain from the Mid-Nineteenth Century*. London: Pearson, 2005.

Thompson, Flora. *Lark Rise to Candleford*. Harmondsworth: Penguin, 2000 (1945).

Tillett, Ben. *Who Was Responsible for the War and Why?* London: Whitwell Press, 1917.

Tournès, Ludovic. 'Reproduire l'œuvre: la nouvelle économie musicale.' In *La culture de masse en France*, edited by Jean-Pierre Rioux and Jean-François Sirinelli. Paris: Fayard, 2002.

Tressell, Robert. *The Ragged-trousered Philanthropists*. London: Flamingo, 1993 (1914).

Van Emden, Richard. *Boy Soldiers of the Great War*. London: Headline, 2005.

Van Emden, Richard. *Prisoners of the Kaiser*. Barnsley: Pen & Sword, 2000.

Van Emden, Richard. *The Soldier's War*. London: Bloomsbury, 2008.

Van Emden, Richard and Humphries, Steve. *All Quiet on the Home Front: An Oral History of Life in Britain during the First World War*. London: Headline, 2003.

Waites, Bernard. *A Class Society at War: England 1914–18*. Leamington Spa: Berg, 1987.

Waters, Chris. *British Socialists and the Politics of Popular Culture 1884–1914*. Manchester: Manchester University Press, 1990.

Watkins, Glenn. *Proof through the Night: Music and the Great War*. Berkeley: University of California Press, 2003.

Wearing, J. P. *The London Stage, 1910–1919: A Calendar of Plays and Players*. London: Scarecrow, 1982.

Wigham, Eric. *From Humble Petition to Militant Action: A History of the Civil and Public Services Association 1903–1978*. London: CPSA, 1980.

Wilkinson, Alan. *The Church of England and the First World War*. London: SCM Press, 1996.

Williams, Bransby. *Bransby Williams by Himself*. London: Hutchinson, 1954.

Williams, Michael, Hammond, Michael and Williams, Angela (Eds). *British Silent Cinema and the Great War*. London: Palgrave, 2011.

Wilson, A. E. *Edwardian Theatre*. London: Arthur Baker, 1951.

Wilson, Keith. 'Music Hall London: the Topography of Class Sentiment.' *Victorian Literature and Culture* 23 (1995).

Winter, Jay Murray. *The Great War and the British People*. Cambridge, MA: Harvard University Press, 1986.

Wisenthal, J. L. and O'Leary, Daniel. *What Shaw Really Wrote about the War*. Gainsville: University Press of Florida, 2006.

Wodehouse, P. G. *The Swoop! Or How Clarence Saved England*, London: Alston Rivers, 1909.

Collections of songs

Ainger, Arthur Campbell. *Marching Songs for Soldiers Adapted to Well-known Tunes*. London: Jarrold and sons, 1914.

Collective. *An Appendix to Hymns Ancient and Modern for Use in Time of War*. London: William Clowes and Sons, 1914.

Anderson, Tom. *Class War Songs*. Glasgow: Proletarian Bookstall, 1923.

Arthur, Max. *When This Bloody War Is Over: Soldiers' Songs of the First World War*. London: Piatkus, 2001.

Bayford, Dudley Escott. *A Selection of Great Songs from the Great War*. London: Francis, Day and Hunter, 1965.

Book of Hymns. 30 hymns. Words and music. Manchester: Daisy Bank Publishing, 1915.

Botrel, Théodore. *Chansons de route*. Paris: Payot, 1915.

Botrel, Théodore. *Les chants de route*. Paris: Payot, 1915.

Botrel, Théodore. *Les chants du bivouac*. Paris: Payot, 1915.

Boyer, Lucien. *La chanson des poilus*. Paris: F. Salabert, 1918.

Brophy, J. and Partridge, E. *Dictionary of Tommies' Songs and Slang 1914–1918*. London: Frontline, 2008.

Brophy, J. and Partridge, E. *The Long Trail: What the British Soldier Sang and Said in the Great War of 1914–1918*. London: André Deutsch, 1965.

Butler, Harold Edgeworth. *War Songs of Britain*. London: A. Constable & Co., 1903.

Church Army for the National Mission. *Hymns of Repentance, Hope and Witness*. London: Church Army Bookroom, 1916.

Coronation Song-Book. London, Novello & Co., 1911.

Davison, Peter. *Songs of the British Music Hall*. New York: Oak, 1971.

Downes, John Neill (Ed.). *The Soldiers' and Sailors' Hymn Book*. London: J. M. Dent and Sons, 1914.

Draper, William H. and Bairstow, Edward C. *Twenty Hymns for National Use in Time of War from Old and New Sources*. London: Stainer and Bell, 1914.

Feldman's Annual Comic Annuals, London: B. Feldman & Co. 1896–1920.

Feldman's Marie Lloyd Song Album, London: B. Feldman & Co., 1954.

Francis and Day Annuals. London: Francis & Day, 1914–1922.

Francis and Day's Album of Vesta Tilley's Popular Songs. London: Francis, Day & Hunter, 1910.

Francis and Day's British War Songs for the Melodeon, London: Francis, Day & Hunter, 1900.

Galvin, Patrick. *Irish Songs of Resistance 1169–1923*. New York: Oak Publications, 1962.

Glasier, J. Bruce. *Socialism in Song*. Manchester: National Labour Press, 1919.

Greaves, C. Desmond. *The Easter Rising in Song and Ballad*. London: Workers' Music Association, 1980.

Grenville, Arthur. *The New Army Song-Book*. London: J. Williams, 1915.

Harkness, Robert (Ed.). *Hymns for Use in Time of War*. London: R. Harkness, 1915.

The Bishop of Durham, The Bishop of Ripon, et al. *Hymns for Empire Day also the National Anthem with a new and special verse*. London: Skeffington & Son, 1910.

Independent Labour Party. *ILP Song Book*. Huddersfield: Socialist Newspaper Society, no date [1925].

Le 137e R.I. pendant la Guerre 1914–1918, par 'un soldat'. Fontenay-le-Comté: Imprimerie Moderne, 1936.

Leask, George A. (Ed.). *Hymns in Time of War.* London: Jarrold & Sons, 1916.

Leatham, James. *Songs for Socialists.* Turriff: Deveron Press, 1910.

Lunn, Hubert. *Hymns and Litanies for Use during the War.* London: Novello & Co., 1915.

Neat, John (Ed.). *Wonderland Selection of Popular Successes.* London: B. Feldman & Co, 1913.

Nettleingham, F. T. *More Tommy's Tunes.* London: Erskine Macdonald, 1918.

Nettleingham, F. T. *Tommy's Tunes.* London: Erskine Macdonald, 1917.

Newnes, G. *British Army War-Song Album.* London, Francis and Day, 1914.

Olt, Reinhard. *Krieg und Sprache: Untersuchungen zu deutschen Soldatenliedern des Ersten Weltkrieges.* Giessen: W. Schmitz, 1980–1981.

Palmer, Roy. *A Touch on the Times: Songs of Social Change, 1770–1914.* Harmondsworth: Penguin, 1974.

Palmer, Roy. *'What A Lovely War!' British Soldiers' Songs from the Boer War to the Present Day.* London: Michael Joseph, 1990.

Pierce, T. A. (Ed.). *The Labour Church Hymn and Tune Book.* Nottingham: Labour Church Hymn and Tune Book Committee, 1912.

Powell, Francis Edward. *The National Mission of Repentance and Hope: Supplementary Hymns, with a Litany of Penitence and Hope, and a Short Dissertation on Love as the Supreme Aim and Object of the Christian Church.* Leominster: Orphans' Printing Press, 1916.

Schmidt, Madeleine. *Chansons de la revanche et de la Grande Guerre.* Nancy: Presses Universitaires de Nancy, 1985.

Social Democratic Federation. *The SDF Songbook.* London: SDF, 1910.

Speaight, George. *Bawdy Songs of the Early Music Hall.* London: David & Charles, 1975.

Collective. *Special Hymns for Use during the War, on Christmas Day and the Day of Intercession*, London, Skeffington & Son, 1914.

Star Music Publishing Company's Song Annual. London: Star Music, 1913–1921.

Stoddon, Reg. S. *Empireland ... Selection of Popular Successes*, London: B. Feldman & Co., 1916.

Stoddon, Reg. S. *Feldman's Big Bombardment of Song Successes for 1917 and 1918.* London: B. Feldman & Co., 1917.

Stoddon, Reginald S. *Libertyland ... Selection of Popular Successes*, London: B. Feldman, 1918.

The Clarion Song Book. London: Clarion Press, 1906.

The National Mission Hymn Book. London: Society for Promoting Christian Knowledge, 1916.

The People's Song Book. No. 2. Containing 32 favourite Scottish songs, 33 favourite English songs. 35 favourite Irish songs, 34 favourite Welsh songs (words in Welsh and English), 32 Nigger minstrel songs. London: John Leng & Co., 1915.

The Socialist Sunday Schools Song Book. Glasgow: S.L. Press, 1919.

Turner, Michael R. and Miall, Antony. *The Edwardian Song Book: Drawing-Room Ballads 1900–1914.* London: Methuen, 1982.

US Army Songbook. Washington: US Army, 1918.

Victory, Peace and Remembrance, Hymns of Thanksgiving with two Memorial Hymns, London: Skeffington & Son, 1919.

Ward-Jackson C. H. and Leighton, Lucas. *Airman's Song Book*, Edinburgh: William Blackwood & Sons, 1967.

Wesleyan Methodist Church. *A Brief Litany and Hymns for Time of War.* London: C. H. Kelly, 1914.

Wesleyan Methodist Church: *On Active Service. (Prayers and Hymns, Texts, etc.).* London: Methodist Publishing House, 1914.

Williams, Ralph Vaughan and Lloyd, A. L. *English Folk Songs.* London: Penguin, 1959.

Periodicals

British Citizen and Empire Worker
Burnley Catholic News
Burnley Express
Burnley Gazette
Common Cause, suffragist newspaper
Daily Telegraph
Dreadnought
Gramophone Music and Record
Hitchin Conservative Gazette
Marlborough Express
Rhondda Socialist
Social Gazette - Official Organ of the Salvation Army's Social Operations
The Age
The Encore, trade magazine of music hall and theatre
The Era, trade magazine of the theatre
The Guardian,
The Herald, anti-war paper which appeared throughout the war
The Irish Volunteer
The Liberator
The Marlborough Express
The Performer, variety artistes' trade union journal
The Phono Record
The Pioneer
The Scotsman
The Times
The Toiler

CDs, reissues of recordings from the war years.

Billy Merson, *The Spaniard Who Blighted My Life*, Windyridge, 2004.
Charles Austin, *Parker P.C.*, Windyridge, 2011.
Chœur Montjoie, *Chants de poilus et autres refrains de la Grande Guerre 1914–1918*, Saint-Denis, SD-CMSD, 2007.
Ella Shields, *Burlington Bertie from Bow*, Windyridge, 2002.
Frank Leo, *We're All Equal in the Sea*, Windyridge, 2011.
G. H. Elliott, *Plain Chocolate,* Windyridge, 2003.
George Formby Senior, *Standing at the Corner of the Street*, Windyridge, 2002.
George Robey, *The Prime Minister of Mirth*, Windyridge, 2003.
Gertie Gitana, *Sweet Nellie Dean*, Windyridge, 2004.
Harry Champion, *Down Came the Blind*, Windyridge, 2005.
Harry Lauder, *Foo the Noo*, Windyridge 2005.
Harry Wheldon, *The White Hope*, Windyridge, 2008.
Jack Lorimer, *The Hielan' Laddie*, Windyridge, 2011.
John McCormack, *Come Back to Erin vol 2*, Naxos Nostalgia, 2004.
Little Tich, *In Other People's Shoes*, Windyridge, 2002.
Marie Lloyd, *Wink the Other Eye*, Windyridge, 2002.
Sam Mayo, *I'm going to Sing a Song*, Windyridge, 2006.
The Two Bobs, *Paddy McGinty's Goat*, Windyridge, 2007.
Tom Clare, *The Fine Old English Gentleman*, Windyridge, 2006.
Various Artistes, *A Little of What You Fancy – the Golden Age of the British Music Hall*, Living Era, 2001.
Various Artistes, *A Night at the Music Hall* (4 CDs), JSP Records, 2006.
Various Artistes, *Cockney Kings of the Music Hall*, Saydisc 1995.
Various Artistes, *From the Footlights*, Windyridge, 2006.
Various Artistes, *Laughter on the Home Front*, Pavilion Records, 1994.
Various Artistes, *Oh It's a Lovely War: Songs and Sketches of the Great War 1914–1918*, vol 1, vol 2, vol 3 (4 CDs), Editions CD 41, 2001, 2002, 2003.
Various Artistes, *Oh, What a Lovely War!* (musical comedy), Original London Cast Recording, Editions CD Must Close Saturday, 2004.
Various Artistes, *Royal Command Performance 1912*, Windyridge, 2012.
Various Artistes, *Songs of the Old Plantation*, Windyridge, 2007.
Various Artistes, *The Great War*, Windyridge 2009.
Various Artistes, *Your Own, your Very Own …*, Academy Sound, 1992.
Vesta Tilley and Vesta Victoria, *The Vesta Box*, Windyridge, 2003.
Whit Cunliffe, *Tight Skirts Have Got to Go*, Windyridge, 2004.
Will Fyffe, *I Belong to Glasgow*, Windyridge, 2004.
Zona Vevey, *I Recall the Days*, Windyridge, 2005.

Index